The Diplomacy of Nationalism

The Diplomacy of Nationalism

• • • • • •

The Six Companies and China's Policy toward Exclusion

Yucheng Qin

University of Hawai'i Press

Honolulu

Printed in the United States of America

14 13 12 11 10 09 6 5 4 3 2 1

Library of Congress Cataloging-in-Publication Data
Qin, Yucheng.
The diplomacy of nationalism : the Six Companies and China's policy toward exclusion / Yucheng Qin.
p. cm.
Includes bibliographical references and index.
ISBN 978-0-8248-3274-2 (hardcover : acid-free paper)
1. Chinese Consolidated Benevolent Association (San Francisco, Calif.)—History. 2. Chinese Americans—California—San Francisco—Social conditions—19th century. 3. Chinese Americans—California—San Francisco—Economic conditions—19th century. 4. Chinese Americans—Societies, etc. 5. China—Emigration and immigration—History. 6. United States—Emigration and immigration—History. 7. China—Foreign relations—United States. 8. United States—Foreign relations—China. 9. China—History—Qing dynasty, 1644–1912. I. Title.
F869.S39C566 2006
305.895'1079461—dc22
2009018532

University of Hawai'i Press books are printed on acid-free paper and meet the guidelines for permanence and durability of the Council on Library Resources.

Designed by University of Hawai'i Press production staff

Printed by The Maple-Vail Book Manufacturing Group

To my parents, Honglin Qin and Tongluo Liu,
my wife, Limian Jin,
and my children, Linda Qin and Elijah Qin

Contents

Preface

The original spark of this study came from a sentence in William Speer's "Democracy of the Chinese," an article published by *Harper's New Monthly Magazine* in 1868, which read: "The Six Companies have been a continual puzzle to Americans." My curiosity was aroused, and I began to pay more attention to this overseas Chinese organization. Had the puzzle been solved? Then on rereading Shih-shan Henry Tsai's *China and the Overseas Chinese in the United States,* published in 1983, I was flabbergasted to find the same sentence: "The Six Companies have been a continual puzzle to Americans." This puzzle had lasted more than a century! Perhaps I could be the one to solve it. But first I needed to discover whether the organization was important enough. The Six Companies had been established in San Francisco, so I began to read California newspapers from the period. And in the *San Francisco Chronicle* of August 10, 1878, I was shocked to read that Chen Lanbin, the first Chinese minister to the United States, confirmed to a *Chronicle* reporter that the Chinese Legation would "supersede the authority and influence of the Six Companies." Clearly the Six Companies was important—never in Chinese history, it seemed to me, had an important policy statement been so widely neglected by academia. I then traveled around the Pacific Rim, visiting especially San Francisco, Hong Kong, Guangdong province, and Beijing, collecting information. The result did more than solve the century-long puzzle; it led to a whole new perception about the growth of modern Chinese nationalism at the end of the nineteenth century.

Chinese terms in this book are romanized according to the Pinyin system, which is most commonly used in scholarship and journalism. Wade-Giles romanization is also given for well-known names and terms and also for those for which the original Chinese characters are unknown.

I want to express my deepest appreciation to Shelton Stromquist for his invaluable guidance and wisdom. I also owe a great debt of gratitude to the editors of the University of Hawai`i Press, especially Masako Ikeda, Keith Leber, and Margaret Black for their efforts, which have nurtured this project and finally brought it to publication. I am grateful to David Arkush, Colin Gordon, and Gary Hess for their respectful criticism, sound advice, and encouraging comments. I am appreciative, too, of the invaluable guidance provided by Charles Hayford, who read an early draft. I further benefitted intellectually from the scholars to whom the publisher sent the manuscript for review; many of their thoughtful suggestions refined the material and substantially enriched the quality of this book. My thanks go also to Mary Spencer and James Sellmann for awarding me a research grant in 2007 that helped me complete the final draft of the book. I also wish to thank Marissa Brown for her editorial work, which has helped me to avoid infelicities of English throughout the book.

Introduction

This is the transnational story of how the Chinese Six Companies in California responded to racist challenges by organizing its own community, developing modern nationalism, and teaching the Qing dynasty how modern nationalism should be pursued diplomatically. The Six Companies, or the Chinese Consolidated Benevolent Association, was the most important popular Chinese organization in the United States in the nineteenth century. It began as *huiguan*, or native-place associations, long-standing institutions found everywhere the Chinese migrated both inside China and abroad. During the anti-Chinese movement in the United States, the Six Companies stepped into the void created by the slow and ineffective responses from the Qing government. In the process of adopting new policies and strategies to counter racism, the Six Companies' native-place sentiments evolved into modern nationalism. Unprepared for the practice of modern national diplomacy, the Qing legation turned to the Six Companies for help, and then took over their techniques and arguments. Thus the Six Companies was a major influence in generating the nationalist turn of China's approach to foreign relation in the nineteenth century. This study therefore will show how the early history of Sino-American relations looks if examined in the framework of Six Companies diplomacy, and how, in such a framework, modern Chinese nationalism may be better understood.

I focus on the period before the 1906 San Francisco earthquake for three reasons. First, this was when the Six Companies handled all problems affecting all the Chinese in America, and so it was the time when the organization flourished. Second, it was in the 1870s that the United States began to limit Chinese laborers, a process that reached its zenith in 1904 when Congress made Chinese exclusion indefinite. Only after forty more years, during World War II, would Congress reconsider this issue. Third, this was the most important transition period in the history of China's foreign relations. Before the Opium Wars (the Opium War from 1839–1842 and the Arrow War from 1856–1860),

China's foreign affairs had been conducted through its tributary system, and the ruling dynasty recognized no state as its equal. The establishment of the Zongli Yamen (Office for the Management of the Business of All Foreign Countries) in 1861, and the legations sent to the capitals of the Treaty Powers in the 1870s and 1880s, created a new situation. The transnational experience of the Six Companies in the nineteenth century, when it was the defender of all Chinese in the United States against exclusion, actually provides an opportunity to examine the influence of the *huiguan* on China's policy toward the United States and on China's transition from the tribute system to modern diplomacy.

Transnationalism and the Chinese Six Companies

The past few decades have witnessed an upsurge of transnational history, with more and more historians trying to explain historical phenomena in greater than single national frameworks. In such cross-national and interregional studies, national and regional borders become less essential, as do the boundaries between foreign and domestic affairs. This growing awareness of the linkages between the central and the margin as well as foreign and domestic affairs has encouraged historians to produce many groundbreaking works. Transnational history, which will "be pursued by historians of all nations," is now ascendant.[1]

Political scientists played a vanguard role in this dramatic change in American scholarship.[2] Lyman White, for example, emphasized in 1951 that the field of international relations needed to appreciate the role of international nongovernmental organizations (INGOs) in pursuing cross-national agendas.[3] His initiative concerning the new forces that were shaping the world met with enthusiastic approval from such important political scientists and historians as J. J. Lederer, James Field, Kjell Skjelsbaek, Johan Galtung, Harold Jacobson, Robert Keohane, Joseph Nye, Paul Diehl, Margaret Keck, Kathryn Sikkink, Jeremei Suri, and Akira Iriye.[4]

The surge of transnationalism also spread to the fields of Chinese history and Chinese-American studies. The publication of Prasenjit Duara's "Transnationalism and the Predicament of Sovereignty: China, 1900–1945," Aihwa Ong and Donald Nonni's *Ungrounded Empires*, and *Flexible Citizenship* (1999), of which Chinese transnationality is the primary subject, mark a breakthrough in the historiography of the fields.[5] Following their footsteps, a number of historians have painted a historical picture of how Chinese transnationalism developed across the Pacific Rim. Titles such as *Dreaming of Gold, Dreaming of Home: Transnationalism and Migration between the United States and South China, 1882–1943*, *Chinese San Francisco 1850–1943: A Trans-Pacific Community*, and *Chinese American Transnationalism: The Flow of People, Resources, and*

Ideas between China and America during the Exclusion Era suggest that Chinese American history may be understood in the framework of transnational connections—Chinese immigrants maintained various kinds of ties to China at the same time that they were incorporated into the United States.[6]

Good as these works are in understanding Chinese immigration and China, they are also problematic when we consider the Six Companies, one of the oldest and most important Chinese INGOs. I was struck by the sporadic and unsystematic scholarly attention this important organization received. Even such a standard history of modern China as Jonathan Spence's *The Search for Modern China* includes only two sentences on the Six Companies.[7] Michael Hunt's *The Making of a Special Relationship,* a foundational work in the field of Sino-American relations, devotes only two paragraphs to it, and David Anderson's standard monograph, *Imperialism and Idealism,* does not mention it at all.[8] General syntheses on Asian Americans, such as *Asian America* by Roger Daniels, *Strangers from a Different Shore* by Ronald Takaki, and *Asian Americans* by Sucheng Chan, present just odd scraps of information about the Six Companies.[9] Authors of single-subject monographs on Chinese American history have also been very slow to realize the importance of the Six Companies, let alone make it a focus in their studies.[10]

The only exception is Him Mark Lai, a pioneer of Chinese American historical studies, who published "Historical Development of the Chinese Consolidated Benevolent Association/Huiguan System" in 1987, later republished in his *Becoming Chinese American.*[11] Sucheng Chan regards this as "the best study of the Six Companies,"[12] and its substantially advanced research provides a more scholarly picture of the organization. Nevertheless, the nature, activities, and influence of the "Chinese American spokesman" in the anti-Chinese movement are so rich and colorful that a single chapter is simply not enough.

Despite its importance as the representative for all the Chinese in the United States in the late nineteenth century, the Six Companies has been a rarity for about 150 years in the narrative that chronicles modern China, as well as in the narrative that chronicles Chinese Americans.[13] Although the influence and leadership of the Six Companies declined in the twentieth century, it did not disappear; nor did it become unimportant in Chinese politics and foreign relations, as the following evidence clearly demonstrates.

The Six Companies sent a petition to Prince Tao and the Qing court at the beginning of the twentieth century, a petition published in *Xinning* magazine.[14] The central argument of the petition was that it was essential to have a national assembly and a constitution to meet the challenges of the national crisis. The historical facts indicated that any country with a constitution was likely to develop vigorously, while those without one were ruined. With a constitution,

China would not be subjugated, and overseas Chinese would not be reduced to being the people of a conquered nation. The petition called attention to the fact that in the nineteenth century the imperialist powers had repeatedly forced China to cede territory and pay indemnities, and it demanded immediate action. Otherwise, the petition said, in less than ten years China might be conquered and divided up.[15]

In 1909, after learning of the border talks between China and Portugal, the Six Companies cabled both Governor Yuan of Guangdong and the Qing Ministry of Foreign Affairs: "Never make a concession; fight for every inch of land."[16] On February 22, 1915, after Japan presented the twenty-one demands that would have turned China into a virtual Japanese colony, the Six Companies declared a boycott on Japanese-American services.[17] Also in September 1915, the Six Companies, on behalf of all Chinese in the United States, wrote to President Woodrow Wilson asking him to advise Chinese President Yuan Shikai not to restore monarchism in China.[18] When in 1919 the Paris Peace Conference decided to transfer Germany's sphere of influence to Japan, the Six Companies cabled the conference and the Chinese legation in Paris, rejecting the decision.[19] And on September 29, 1972, the Six Companies, together with other Chinese associations all over the world, demanded that the United Nations restore the lawful rights of the Republic of China.[20]

Nevertheless, as always the Six Companies remained almost invisible to writers in both the Chinese-speaking and the English-speaking worlds. In the words of William Speer in 1868 and Shih-shan Henry Tsai in 1983, the Six Companies "have been a continual puzzle to Americans."[21] As Tony Platt commented in 2007 concerning Jean Pfaelzer's *Driven Out: The Forgotten War against Chinese Americans*: "The core of the book is thoroughly and convincingly documented. Its subjects are fully realized, with the exception of the Six Companies, which remain something of a cipher."[22] While the political significance of the Six Companies in the anti-Chinese movement has not been properly appreciated, its function in the development of modern China has been so thoroughly neglected and its influence on China's policy toward the United States in the nineteenth century so ignored that I have no hesitation in saying that to disregard the Six Companies is to misread the histories of China, Sino-American relations, and Chinese Americans in the nineteenth century.

One problem contributing to the invisibility of the Six Companies is the unavailability of documents for the nineteenth century in its archives. They may have been all lost in the great earthquake of 1906 and the subsequent fires, which lasted in Chinatown for "three or four days and nights"; all buildings in Chinatown were burnt to "flying ashes and scorched earth."[23] Yet documents about the Six Companies' resistance to the anti-Chinese movement in this period do exist elsewhere. The Six Companies sought to challenge the discrimination they faced by publishing articles in American newspapers and journals, by sending letters and petitions to the American and Chinese governments, by filing lawsuits in the American courts, and by reforming their own society. A substantial record of this resistance may be found in American newspapers, periodicals, federal records, the Chinese press, and Chinese governmental records. By making an exhaustive search for these materials, this study has rescued an important part of the Six Companies' history from permanent oblivion and has "rebuilt" its nineteenth-century archives.

Therefore this study is a criticism of much of the literature on Chinese transnationalism which I believe neglects and underestimates the significance of the Six Companies. Indeed we need to re-envision Chinese and Chinese-American history to include and highlight the role of the Six Companies, and to do so in a broad and transnational way. To borrow the words of Madeline Hsu, in order to bridge "historically related but as yet critically unlinked fields of Asian American and Asian Studies,"[24] I argue that the transnational experience of the Six Companies provides a good framework for linking one of the most impressive developments of Chinese history and Chinese-American history.

Culturalism-to-Nationalism, Native Place, and the Six Companies

In addition to inserting the Six Companies into the master narratives of Chinese and Chinese-American history, this study offers a focused critique of the culturalism-to-nationalism thesis and betters our understanding of Chinese nationalism and Sino-American relations in the nineteenth century. Because the current culturalism-to-nationalism thesis is generally accepted as the authoritative interpretation for China's approach to foreign relations, a brief introduction is necessary. In *Liang Chi-ch'ao and the Mind of Modern China*, Joseph Levenson put forward the thesis and immediately won widespread acclaim.[25] Prior to the twentieth century, James Harrison affirmed that the "traditional Chinese self-image" was generally "defined as 'culturalism,' based on a common historical heritage and acceptance of shared beliefs," namely, Confucianism, rather than "nationalism, based on the modern concept of the nation-state."[26] Because of their overwhelming sense of cultural superiority, the Chinese felt it beneath their dignity to adopt foreign ways of thinking or to recognize any country as their equal. "In the eyes of most of the emperor's subjects the empire was not a country but the country, not a culture but culture itself."[27] Therefore, "imperial China was not a nation-state" and was "totally devoid of national consciousness."[28] Though "barbarians," such as Mongols and Manchus, had invaded

China several times before the Opium War, and taken the reins of power, they were all "conquered" by Chinese culture. In the nineteenth century, however, the Western powers and Japan not only defeated China militarily but also posed a real threat to Chinese culture. China suddenly realized that it became "a semi-colonized land in a Eurocentric world" rather than the center of the world any more.[29] In order to save China, Chinese intellectuals rejected culturalism and summoned the Western concept of nationalism "as a new basis for China's defense and regeneration," so China might achieve equality with the other great powers that denied it this status. This great change happened in the late Qing and early Republican period, principally the years between 1895 and 1919, as "the first emergence of modern Chinese nationalism" and a transition from the China-centric universalism to nationalism.[30] This transition, Levenson tells us, was the "biggest change in the Chinese three thousand years' history."[31] And Zhao asserts that "Zhonghua minzu (the Chinese nation) as a modern concept was adopted from the writings of Meiji Japan and was associated with nationalistic writings warning the Chinese people of the danger of annihilation under Western invasion at the turn of the twentieth century."[32]

The institutional expression of Chinese culturalism, the tribute system that dominated the Chinese world order for over two thousand years, is the subject that requires focus here. An expression of Chinese cultural self-focus intended to regulate Chinese foreign relations, it originated in the Shang dynasty (fifteenth- to eleventh-century BCE). It took shape in the Han dynasty (206 BCE–220 CE), after which it was exercised successfully at times when China was strong and "flexibly" when China was weak, reaching its peak during the Ming and Qing dynasties (1368–1911); it declined after the Opium War. In the hierarchical tribute system, China was the "Middle Kingdom," meaning the center of the earth. The Chinese emperor, as the "Son of Heaven," was legitimized by the Mandate of Heaven to rule all-under-heaven. Never seeing other entities as equals and never exchanging any permanent diplomatic envoys with other countries, all Chinese emperors demanded submission under the tribute system from foreigners whom they regarded as "barbarians." Other countries, needing trade with Chinese, sent missions to China to submit to the sovereignty of the Son of Heaven.[33] Before the Chinese emperor, members of foreign missions had to perform ceremonies of "surrender." Known as *kowtow,* this surrender took the ritual form of three separate kneelings, each kneeling followed by three separate knockings of the head on the floor. The whole process was organized by the verbal commands of a lowly ceremonial usher: "Kneel!" "Fall prostrate!" "Rise to your knees!" "Fall prostrate!"[34] The ceremony of the full kowtow was generally administered by the Reception Department of the

Board of Ceremonies, but during the Qing dynasty a new agency, Li Fan Yuan (the Court of Colonial Affairs), was also established to deal with tributary states from the north and west.[35]

All tributary states were dependent states of China. After the rite of kowtow, a certificate that recognized the tributary ruler's status, along with a noble rank and an imperial seal, were granted to him; all documents and other communications between these dependents and the emperor's court were dated by the Chinese dynastic reign-title and calendar.[36] In addition, the authority and superiority of China was perpetuated by China's appointment of new kings in tributary countries. Whenever a new king of a tributary state was to be enthroned, he was required to send a tributary mission to obtain the imperial patent of appointment.[37]

Many people have suggested that tribute was a cloak for trade because for "barbarians" the profits were worth the annoyances. They are doubtless right in part, but some of the tributary kings sincerely acknowledged their inferior status. The following proclamation of a king of Vietnam to his people is just one of many examples I have encountered: "I heard that two heroes cannot appear together, that two sages cannot exist in the same generation. The Han (Chinese) emperor is the sagacious Son of Heaven. Henceforth I shall suppress my own imperial edicts, imperial cart, and the [imperial] banner of the left command."[38]

The extension of authority over foreign entities worked to reinforce "the imperial prestige within China proper." Seeing the rest of mankind acknowledge the rule of the Chinese emperor, Chinese support for the ruler's Mandate of Heaven increased and helped confirm the emperor's claim to rule China.[39] Hence, the nature of the tributary system is not difficult to see. China developed what may be called premodern diplomatic imperialism—a foreign policy of extending authority over foreign entities as a means of maintaining the Chinese empire itself.

As good as the culturalism-to-nationalism thesis is for understanding China, it has one important problem. So much emphasis placed on China-centric universalism obscures the fact that loyalty to one's native place also defined the Chinese self-image before the twentieth century. A critical component of personal identity in traditional China, a person's native-place identity, and even that of his descendents, did not change along with their places of residence. Chinese immigrants were by no means uprooted; they would return to their native places regularly on any important occasion and finally upon death. "The concept of native place was a critical component of personal identity in traditional China, and geographic origin was generally the first matter of inquiring among strangers, the first characteristic recorded about a person (after name and pseudonyms), and the first fact to be ascertained regarding individuals coming before the law," explains Bryna Goodman.[40] These patterns of belief and practice stimulated the cultivation of linkages among fellow-countrymen traveling beyond the native place and promoted the establishment of *huiguan* (sometimes called "guilds" in English)—the institutional expression of native-place sentiment—associations of people from the same places who were staying in distant cities.[41]

The Wuhu *huiguan*, the first such organization in China, was a hostelry established in the early sixteenth century in Beijing for students from the Wuhu district who were preparing themselves for the imperial examinations.[42] In the Chinese cities of Ming and Qing (1368–1911), *huiguan* were very popular and the result of migration. In Sichuan province, for example, there were seven Jiangxi *huiguan*, seven Shanxi *huiguan*, eight Huguang *huiguan*, one Fujian *huiguan*, and eight Guangdong *huiguan*.[43] The constitution of the Ningbo *huiguan* at Wenzhou confirms this view: "*huiguan* were first established at the metropolis by mandarins among compatriots or fellow provincials for mutual aid and protection. . . . Later merchants formed guilds like those of the mandarinate, and now they exist in every province."[44] Like the first *huiguan*, those established by merchants usually erected their own buildings, which were "truly palatial, representing the highest specimens of Chinese architecture."[45]

To deal with matters of common concern, some *huiguan* worked together and formed confederacies. As a case in point, for much of the nineteenth century the eight most important *huiguan* at Chongqing acted in a confederation known as the "Eight Provinces *huiguan*."[46] The example is not isolated. In a medium-sized commercial city near the Hunan-Guizhou border, an umbrella organization of ten major *huiguan* was formed and became the principal vehicle of public-welfare activism after the 1860s.[47]

Huiguan had already been fused into Qing administration system for maintaining public order in the eighteenth century.[48] Officials and merchants who were from the same native places and staying in distant cities cooperated in *huiguan* affairs—some *huiguan* adopted a "[co-district] official management with merchant capital" makeup; some reported to the local government and asked to be put under its protection; and others were established by co-district officials' financial or material assistance. *Huiguan* confederations especially had a close relationship with the government. In the 1840s, for example, the Chongqing Eight Provinces *huiguan*'s arbitration and decision-making power was recognized by the local authorities, and eventually it came to exercise a wide range of governing powers over the city as a whole. When Shi Dakai's Taiping forces attacked the city, the Eight Provinces *huiguan* assumed the authority of central government. After the immediate threat receded, even though its influence was not as great as before, the Eight Provinces *huiguan* continued for the rest of the century to play a primary role in providing local leadership.[49] By this time the *huiguan* in China were not simply organizations of merchant interests, but they also exercised political power.

During the Ming and Qing periods, Chinese emigrants brought this custom to racially and culturally different lands.[50] Malaysia and Singapore are filled with examples. Jiaying *huiguan*, founded in 1801, was one of the earliest native-place associations in Singapore, comprising Hakkas from Mei county, Jiaoling, Xinning, Wuhua, and Pingyuan of Guangdong province. In addition, Singapore's Hakkas from ten counties under Huizhou—namely, Huiyang, Boluo, Longchuan, Heyuan, Zijin, Haifeng, Lufeng, Heping, Lianping, and Xinfeng—were embraced by the Huizhou *huiguan* established in 1805.[51] Indeed, it was a Chinese custom that in every big commercial city the merchants and other temporary residents from other provinces banded together in the form of *huiguan*. Once established, this custom developed a momentum of its own and was carried abroad in the hearts and minds of Chinese emigrants.

The functions of these popular organizations were diverse. *Huiguan* emphasized the solidarity of homeland ties. For example, the objective of the Shanshan *huiguan* in Hankou of China was "to promote friendly relations, to talk about the happiness of the native place, and to create homeland atmosphere in an alien land." In addition, an inscription on a stele records, "We established *huiguan* to promote the solidarity of homeland ties because it is easy for merchants and officials in an alien city to dissolve and become estranged."[52]

Magnanimous acts for the benefit of individual members was another feature. Hosea Morse remarks that one of the most important duties of the *huiguan* was to provide for "the suitable burial of the dead . . . in order that their bones may lie in ground which is substitute for their native soil." It also took their poor members' difficulties into account and provided coffins, "either free or at reduced cost," and had a mortuary for the coffined bodies of the wealthier members so that their bones might be someday taken back for burial in their ancestral homeland.[53]

Huiguan generally provided its members a place for worship in its own *huiguan*-house; there they could offer sacrifices to the gods or the spirits of the dead. Chinese merchants were anxious to take advantage of this service in case misfortune struck them.[54] The *huiguan* building usually had "an open courtyard for the generality, galleries on both sides for privileged spectators, the stage at one end and the altar at the other." The altars were dedicated to minor gods, to the Goddess of Mercy, to canonized emperors, to canonized worthies, or to other famous natives of the home province.[55]

Huiguan also had judicial power over its members. For instance, the constitution of the Huguang *huiguan* at Wuzhou indicated that if conflicts arose between members, the president would act as mediator. Any members who ventured to appeal first to a court of law without authorization would be fined. The constitution of the Canton *huiguan* at Wuzhou further provided that before disputes were laid in front of the *huiguan*, the complainants should first pay the committee 200 coppers for the expenses of a meeting. If the decision of the advisory committee was not acceptable, the complainants then could make an appeal to the courts.[56]

Huiguan were especially important for mediating debt disputes. One *huiguan* constitution stipulated that if members had disputes about money matters with each other, they should submit their cases to arbitration at a *huiguan* meeting for a satisfactory settlement of the dispute. Appeal might be made to official courts if it proved impossible to arrive at an understanding within the *huiguan*. If the complainant went to the official judiciary directly, without first referring to the *huiguan*, he would be subject to a public reprimand, and any future case he might present for the opinion of the *huiguan* would be dismissed without a hearing.[57]

Huiguan usually supported their members' interests against nonmembers and against outside prejudices. The Ningbo *huiguan* at Wenzhou stated in its preamble that Ningboese who could not find employment as local agriculturists usually resorted to other places for trade. "Here at Wenzhou we find ourselves isolated; mountains and sea separate us from Ningbo, and when in trade we excite envy on the part of Wenzhouese and suffer insult and injury, we have no adequate redress." It continued: "It is this which imposes on us the duty of establishing a *huiguan*."[58] Similarly, the Beihai *huiguan*, a district organization of Cantonese established at Beihai, stated in its charter: The Beihai people are "very covetous" and "licentious." Showing little respect for the laws, they rob and steal from "our merchants." When disputes occur "between our trades and local merchants," there is "no way of dealing with the latter." It is hoped, the charter stated, that the establishment of *huiguan* would "lead to uniformity of action and unanimity of feeling among our members" to "secure ourselves against gradual degeneration" and "to oppose wrong, unscrupulous merchants and bad characters."[59]

Another important feature of the *huiguan* is that they were all-inclusive and due-collecting associations. Their structures were similar. All natives of the home district were eligible for membership and were required to register if they wished to get help in the alien place.[60] In order to maintain the organization and promote its interests, its members needed to contribute funds. In the rules of the Hanyang *huiguan* at Yichang, for example, the members were asked to contribute 0.3 percent on their trade, and temporary visitors from the home district were to be assessed 3 percent on the value of their trade.[61]

Leaders of *huiguan* were elected. There were usually a general manager and an assistant manager, elected annually, who received salaries, ranging from as little as $6 to as much as $1,000. Under the managers was an advisory committee, from three to twelve in number, also elected annually. "The most important officer of the club [*huiguan*] is the permanent secretary, a salaried scholar of literary rank."[62]

Scholars in the field of Chinese history are becoming aware of the importance of the *huiguan* for understanding late imperial China. Some studies include: Ho Ping-ti's study, *Zhongguo huiguan shilun* (On Chinese *huiguan*) (1966); William Rowe's *Hankow: Commerce and Society in a Chinese City, 1796–1889* (1984) and *Hankow: Conflict and Community in a Chinese City, 1796–1895* (1989); Bryna Goodman's *Native Place, City, and Nation: Regional Networks and Identities in Shanghai, 1853–1937* (1995); and Wang Rigen's *Xiangtu zhilian: Mingqing huiguan yu shehui bianqian* (The chain of native places: *Huiguan* and social development in *Ming* and *Qing*) (1996). These studies have brought out an important fact that there was an expanding sphere of collective but extragovernmental activism among *huiguan* throughout nineteenth-century China and that *huiguan* played an important role in the social and political development in late imperial China. Goodman further suggests that *huiguan* in Shanghai were actively involved in nationalist social mobilization and "may modify our general understanding of nationalism and more precisely describe the ways in which nationalism developed and worked in a Chinese context."[63]

Although I wholeheartedly agree with these arguments, the scholarship as a whole appears incomplete when the Six Companies in the United States is taken into account. Since current *huiguan* scholarship focuses on *huiguan* within China's territory and takes no note of the Six Companies, this obviously obscures the facts that *huiguan* experience is transnational and the Six Companies may have been the biggest and most important *huiguan* in all *huiguan* history.[64]

The Six Companies' activism in diplomacy is perhaps one of the most spectacular developments in modern Chinese history, although it has received little attention. By moving our historical gaze beyond China to the Six Companies in the United States and back again, this study may redefine and enlarge the significance of the *huiguan* in the making of modern China. By tracing how the two traditional Chinese identities, Chinese culturalism and attachment to native place, were transformed into modern nationalism in nineteenth-century America, this study will argue that however influential the transition from culturalism to nationalism, the transition from attachment to native place to nationalism was equally important. In addition, this study argues that the first emergence of modern Chinese nationalism occurred in the nineteenth century in the United States.

CHAPTER 1

A Meeting of Market Economies

The Arrival of the Gold Mountain Guests

> In this region lies the province of Canton. In this portion of China foreign nations have traded since near the commencement of the Christian era. Its inhabitants are better acquainted with other countries than any other portion of the Chinese. They, and the people of Fuh-kien, the next province on the east, trade in great numbers to all the lands westward of them, to Cochinchina, Siam, Cambodia, Burmah, to all the islands of vast Indian Archipelago, and even to India; and they stretch away northward in their unwieldly junks to Formosa, Loo-choo, Corea, and Tartary. They are the boldest, rudest, and richest people of the Empire. When the news of the discovery of gold on the opposite shores of the "Great Eastern Ocean" reached them, it was natural that they, above all other Chinese, should rush to California. And they find that, with the exception of a few hundred scattering individuals, the entire body of Chinese emigrants to California has been obtained from the one province of Canton, and merely from the districts along its coast. They are the same people who for two hundred years past have trafficked along the Asiatic shores, and been thus fitted for this final and longer flight across the ocean.
>
> —"The Chinese Companies: Their External Organization"

When the Chinese arrived on the west coast of the United States in the nineteenth century, these men, who came without bringing their families,[1] called themselves *"jinshan ke"* (gold mountain [San Francisco] guests). Despite their residence in the United States, they did not alter their Chinese identity. So what was the cause of the exodus from China? It used to be understood as one aspect of a larger historical process—capitalist expansion. The encroachment of capitalism and growing impoverishment were believed to have forced peasants to leave their villages for an industrialized environment. Now scholars in growing numbers are coming to recognize that this interpretation is not satisfactory. Yong Chen emphasizes the economic and cultural vitality of the Canton region as well as the attraction of foreign gold.[2] Benson Tong also points out that some Chinese merchants and artisans, "who were already engaged in a premigration network of business connections in China," emigrated to America "as early as 1849 in a context of prior exposure to capitalism."[3] Indeed, it is no easy task to find the single cause of this complicated phenomenon, which in fact involved several factors.

The Old Cantonese Market Economy

Almost all the Chinese in late nineteenth-century America came from one small region stretching over some two dozen counties in the Pearl River delta near Guanzhou [Canton] in Guangdong province. These included the Sanyi (three districts), which consists of Nanhai, Panyu, and Shunde counties; Xiangshan county (now known as Zhongshan); the Siyi (four districts), which consists of Xinhui, Taishan (known as Xinning prior to 1914), Kaiping, Enping, and certain other counties.[4] Because almost all the immigrants came from a highly concentrated area, it is obvious that we should look at what local conditions may have served as a stimulus.

Long before their emigration to the United States, the inhabitants of Guangdong province, especially those in the area of the Pearl River delta, had belonged to one of the oldest and most advanced marketplaces in China.[5] Panyu county, for example, had, beginning in the Qin and Han dynasties (221 BCE–220 CE), been a busy center attracting merchants from far and near to trade rhinoceros horn, ivory, pearl, silver, copper, cloth, and so on.[6] In the Song dynasty (960–1279), busy commercial networks were also established in Guanghai (a town of Taishan county) and in Nanhai county.[7] During the Ming dynasty (1368–1644), the trade routes in Guangdong were crowded with "clouds of merchants carrying torrents of goods."[8] Nanhai maintained its commercial position in the Qing dynasty (1644–1911), and some of the wealthiest merchants in Guangdong, such as Cui Tongguang and Tang Jingtai, were natives of this county.[9] Even the Emperor Yongzheng noted, in 1730: "Surrounded by sea on three sides, where merchants from other provinces and foreign barbarians purchase commodities, the east Guangdong market is brisk."[10] The Nanhai county gazetteer from 1836 reported that due to "the small territory and dense population...60 to 70 percent of the people deal with commerce, which is most profitable of all."[11] Similarly, it is estimated that less than half of the population of Shunde county at this time was engaged solely in farming.[12] Indeed, until the first Opium War, the delta area of the Pearl River had been one of the wealthiest and most populous regions in China.

Not surprisingly, Cantonese merchants and laborers were already engaged in a network of business connections in China—they migrated wherever in China the profits led them. Many records show that Cantonese merchants were more national in orientation than regional.[13] In 1710, for example, Cantonese merchants established a *huiguan* (native-place association) in Shanghai.[14] During the Jiaqing reign (1796–1820), Cantonese merchants "went all places under heaven"—they "migrated from place to place in Yanjing [Peking or Beijing], traveled to and from between Shunde and Wuyue [Suzhou and Hangzhou], and did business in Chushu [Sichuan] and Qiandian [Guizhou and Yunnan]."[15] As the major merchants for the domestic distribution of foreign imports, tropical food, and ironware, they had become one of the most predominant groups in Hankow and the Middle Yangzi region by the Yongzheng reign (1723–1736).[16]

Like the Cantonese merchants, Cantonese laborers also migrated within China. In the mid-nineteenth century, inhabitants from Xinning and Enping counties, for example, often traveled to the Sanyi counties, such as Panyu, Nanhai, and Shunde, to pursue employment as artisans and in other types of labor. This movement occurred especially during slack agricultural seasons and times of poor harvest.[17] The development of industry in Shanghai after the first Opium War also attracted many Cantonese laborers "swelling the population by tens of thousands." By the 1850s about 3,500 coastal junks had brought over 80,000 Cantonese workers to Shanghai.[18] As a consequence, for example, Cantonese workers became the majority group employed by the Kiangnan Dock and Engineering Works in this period.[19]

The Overseas Expansion of the Cantonese Market Economy

Overlapping with their domestic commercial activities, the Cantonese had also developed overseas networks long before the migration to California.[20] Indeed, the Chinese who migrated to California in the nineteenth century were just one stream, only part of a much broader Chinese emigration movement. Long before the California gold rush, the Chinese had been establishing settlements along the Pacific Rim.

From the thirteenth to the fifteenth century Chinese trade and migration were mainly directed toward Southeast Asia. In the thirteenth century, for example, Chinese merchants constantly came to Cambodia for trade.[21] Chinese traders also traveled between China and India with the northeast and southwest monsoon in this period.[22] In the fifteenth century Chinese businessmen busily exploited the tin mines in southern Thailand and spearheaded a large independent Chinese settlement in Pattani, an important Thai port. The Cantonese merchants there not only gained decisive economic influence, but significant political influence. Perceiving the Chinese to be the most experienced seamen and merchants, the royal court of Thailand employed them at levels as high as trade minister. "In time the Chinese came to manage all the Kings' maritime and mercantile affairs, both in Thailand and abroad."[23]

In the late sixteenth century the Chinese began to expand their commercial activities to the Philippines. After a first group of about forty merchants arrived in Manila in 1570, about thirty ships traveled between China and Manila each year, increasing the numbers of Chinese in Manila greatly.[24] In 1586, for example, about 10,000 Chinese were engaged in various jobs on the island of Luzon. The number reached 30,000 in 1636 and 40,000 in 1749. The heavy influx of Chinese merchants and laborers soon led them to dominate the economy of the Philippines.[25]

As soon as the Chinese consolidated their economic position in the Philippines, they tried to expand their trade with other Spanish colonies. In 1585 three Chinese merchants arrived in Mexico City, and they soon were followed by more Chinese merchants and also laborers,[26] who settled in both Mexico and Peru. Facing competition from the Chinese, some Spaniards in Manila petitioned the Spanish government to prohibit Chinese immigration to the two regions. Although the royal court never curbed Chinese immigration, the local governments of Mexico City, Lima, and Manila did try to limit or prohibit the immigration. However, the number of Chinese in both regions increased rapidly and by 1650 had reached about 6,000. In Mexico City a small Chinatown even appeared. Although they had few political rights, the Chinese competed economically with the native people as weavers, tailors, carpenters, masons, blacksmiths, servants, and bakers.[27]

The Chinese also migrated to other Pacific islands. In the late eighteenth century, Xie Qinggao, a Chinese tourist, recorded the following numbers in his *Hailu (Sea record):* there were about 10,000 Cantonese merchants in Malaysia; about 10,000 Fujianese and Cantonese cultivating pepper in Benang; numerous Fujianese and Cantonese traders and tin miners in Malaysia and Borneo; a few hundred Cantonese exploiting gold mines in Kuala Lumpur, Malaysia; numerous Cantonese tin miners in Bangka; and in Java no less than 10,000 Chinese merchants and more than 2,000 Cantonese and Fujianese gold miners, diamond miners, traders, and farmers.[28] By renting the mines from native rajas and paying a poll tax of $3.00 on their laborers, about 30,000 Chinese were exploiting the gold in Borneo by 1800. A German lady who visited the island during a journey round the world marveled that the Chinese merchants controlled all trades: "The Chinese play in Borneo very much the part of the Jews in Poland and Hungary."[29]

Certain general patterns began to appear in these commercial activities and settlements. First, those who came from Xingning and other less-developed counties were likely to be laborers, while merchants tended to be from the Sanyi counties.[30] Second, it was the Chinese merchants who inaugurated the migration and transported their poorer countrymen to the plantations, mines, and warehouses of other countries.[31] Third, most of the emigrants were indentured and contract laborers who bound themselves into servitude until they had "repaid their passage money and accrued interest."[32] Fourth, because both the merchants and the laborers sought to earn money rather than to settle in the new location, a sojourning strategy characterized both groups, whether free or indentured.[33] Fifth, because they competed successfully with the local people, they sometimes came to dominate the local economy. Finally, in Guangdong one or more sons of less prosperous families, or the sons of every family in a certain clan, would go abroad each generation. Because the migrants usually chose to go to the same place where their kin worked, whole regions chose specific settlements for their emigrants.[34] These patterns are very important, and as we will see, almost all these features strongly shaped Chinese migration to the United States.

All evidence points to the fact that emigration to California was a continuation of prior commercial activities. But however sound this Cantonese market-economy argument may be, it only partly explains the emigration. The greatest Chinese emigration occurred in the years between 1840 and 1900,[35] and this sudden upsurge must also have been stimulated by something else.

An Imposed Meeting of Market Economies and Its Aftermath

The Opium Wars had a profound and lasting impact on China. Guangdong was the first location to be affected, and this occurred just prior to the upsurge in emigration. During the eighteenth century, while some Western nations already in the early stages of the Industrial Revolution sought markets all over the world for the products of their factories, the Chinese government, by contrast, adhered stubbornly to a closed-door trade policy. Led by Britain, the Western powers determined to open China, and they succeeded. The Opium War with England and the Arrow War (or second Opium War) with England and France from 1856–1860, during which Guangdong province was devastated militarily, ended in the Chinese paying an indemnity of $21 million. In addition, China was forced to open a growing number of ports to foreign trade and to cede Hong Kong to the British. Tariffs were fixed by treaty, which prevented China from using them as a way to protect its own industries. Although the United States had not participated in the Opium War, it shared the results by concluding the Treaty of Wangxia (1844), which opened China to American traders on a large scale. The French also signed the Treaty of Whampoa (1844).

These treaties created a serious problem for China, especially Guangdong province. China had to pay an indemnity, 70 percent of which was to come from Guangdong province alone. This indemnity and the military costs of the war were equal to eighteen years' worth of state revenues from land taxes.[36] The Qing government, of course, shifted the burden to the peasants. Unable to pay the high taxes, many lost their lands and had to find employment elsewhere. Moreover, inexpensive mass-produced goods from the industrialized capitalist powers began to flood into China along with opium. Naturally, China's manual industries could not compete with the power-driven mills of Europe and America. The increasing sales of opium led to an outflow of silver from China, which caused inflation and worked even greater hardships on the ordinary people who paid taxes. The treaties were a particularly heavy blow to merchants and others in the Canton area because they opened ports elsewhere in China to foreign trade, which diverted business away from Canton.[37] Until the Opium War, Guangdong had always been one of the richest provinces of China; because of its productivity, although densely populated, the Pearl River delta had never experienced a famine. Even though China had regularly suffered natural disasters since the fourteenth century, Guangdong had remained prosperous or suffered only minor damage.[38] However, the Opium War changed everything.

To make matters worse, the Opium War was a major contributor to uprisings, including the Taiping Rebellion, one of the most destructive in all history, which left the richest region of China devastated.[39] The Canton area did not escape; it also experienced social unrest and political chaos, which may have been directly or indirectly encouraged by the early victories of the Taipings. Beginning in 1854, Triad societies such as the Red Heads (or Red Turbans), launched a series of uprisings in the Pearl River delta region that lasted for nearly a decade. In addition, low-grade conflicts between the Cantonese (the local indigenous Han) and the Hakkas (a subgroup of the Han ancestors who had migrated from central China centuries ago) living in the Siyi districts developed into open warfare in 1856. This soon spilled over into neighboring districts and lasted twelve years.[40]

Indeed, the domestic turmoil caused by great economic dislocation and political chaos was an important factor forcing many people to emigrate from the Pearl River delta region. As an old account noted, owing to "the disturbances caused by the Red Turban bandits and the Hakka bandits," the "able-bodied" went abroad, and the fields were allowed to lie fallow.[41]

Another important stimulus for Chinese emigration to the United States was the cession of Hong Kong after the Opium War and the British occupation of Canton in the Arrow War, which made it impossible for the Qing government to control emigration leaving from Hong Kong and Canton. Despite China's centuries of overseas emigration and trade, the Qing government strictly forbid the Chinese from emigrating until 1868. Section 225 of *Ta Tsing Leu Lee* (the legal code of the Qing dynasty) stipulated, "All government officials, soldiers, and ordinary citizens who emigrate to foreign countries and islands for the purpose of inhabiting and cultivating the same, shall be punished according to the law against communicating with rebels and enemies and consequently suffer death by being beheaded."[42] While the law had proved difficult to enforce—the stream of Cantonese to Southeast Asia and the Philippines never stopped despite the threat of severe punishment—Hong Kong in the hands of Great Britain no doubt facilitated the emigration.[43] In fact, "Hong Kong was the general rendezvous for departure to California."[44] The occupation of Canton from 1858 to 1861 made it even easier for the Cantonese to emigrate. As Sucheng Chan says, during the occupation, "both local Chinese officials and the Allied occupation commanders—for different reasons—took the opportunity to chip away at the Qing government's prohibition against emigration, thereby greatly increasing the number of Chinese who went overseas."[45]

The Chinese Join the Forty-niners

In addition to the push from China, there was the pull of California. For the Chinese, the siren song of the new California market economy began before the gold rush. Soon after the annexation of California from Mexico, Congressman Aaron H. Palmer put forward an ambitious plan to import Chinese labor to California. According to Palmer, San Francisco would be the "great emporium of our commerce on the Pacific," connected by railroad to the Atlantic states and by steam transportation to China. Because "no people in all the East are so well adapted for clearing wild lands and raising every species of agricultural product...as the Chinese," Chinese laborers, Palmer concluded, should be imported not only to build the transcontinental railroad but also to cultivate the land of California.[46]

Cantonese merchants with their considerable experience in overseas travel, work, and residence, were readily lured by the capitalist development in California. As in the past, merchants initiated Chinese immigration. Because of their experience, the distance across the Pacific posed no barrier for the Cantonese. Some of the most recent studies of the American Chinese identify the first Chinese person in San Francisco as a merchant who arrived in the

United States before the news of gold.[47] According to an article in the *San Francisco Chronicle,* Chen Ming [Chum Ming], a young Chinese merchant, arrived in California in 1847 and began living on what is now Stockton Street, near Sacramento. After hearing of the gold strike in 1848, he joined the rush and wrote a friend of his, Cheong Yum, about it. Cheong Yum immediately sailed to California but sent word to his friends and relatives in the Sanyi district before leaving.[48] News of the gold rush circulated throughout that part of the province and generated excitement. That same year another young Cantonese wrote to his brother, a tea merchant in Boston: "Good many Americans speak of California. Oh! Very rich country! I hear good many Americans and Europeans go there. Oh! They find gold very quickly, so I hear. . . . I feel as if I should like to go there very much. I think I shall go to California next summer."[49] Guangdong was filled with more examples of the excitement caused by the news of the gold rush: "Letters from Chinese in San Francisco and further in the country have been circulated through all this part of the province. The accounts of the successful adventurers who have returned would, had the inhabitants possessed the means of paying their way across, have gone far to depopulate considerable towns."[50] Validating the local pattern in Guangdong that the Sanyi districts were famous for their merchants, the Chinese merchants who came to the United States almost all came from Sanyi districts.[51]

The demand for labor in the fast-growing economy of California was also an important motivation for Chinese emigration. Like all frontier areas, California had a scarcity of labor, which was aggravated by the rush to the goldfields. After the discovery of gold, American and European merchants also helped spread the message about the need for labor. As William Speer said, "The early rush of Chinese immigration to California was largely the result of the efforts of our own [American] people."[52] A. C. V. Gillespie, in his letter to Thomas Larkin dated March 6, 1848, said one of his favorite things was "to introduce Chinese emigrants," who sold "their services for a certain period to pay their passage across the Pacific."[53] Like the Chinese merchants, Chinese laborers answered the call of the new California marketplace with great enthusiasm. There is a contract in California dated 1849 between Chinese laborers and an English company called Tseang Sing Hong. According to the contract, the Chinese laborers will borrow "one hundred and twenty-five dollars passage money" and their wages will "be reduced monthly until the debt is absorbed."[54] A. R. Coloquhoun points out that early in 1849 thousands of Chinese poured into Hong Kong to procure, through an English intermediary, employment in the gold mines in America.[55] Wells Williams provided further examples of Chinese "who were eager to accept the offers of the brokers to depart from the country" in the early period of Chinese immigration.[56] As Gunther Barth observes, "A trickle of Chinese merchants prepared the way for the arrival of large groups of laborers."[57]

It is unquestionable that some emigrants paid their own passage or had their passages paid by relatives and friends already in the United States.[58] However, the majority faced fares that were too high for them to pay themselves. The cost of passage from Hong Kong to San Francisco was $40 or $50, while the annual per capita Chinese income was under $10.[59] Thus in the early period some Chinese came to the United States through a contract labor system. A record in Chinese indicated, for example, that having been invited by American capitalists who went directly to China for laborers, "We therefore made contracts to answer the call."[60] Toward the end of 1848 and in the spring and summer of 1849, William Redmond Ryan observed, "numerous Chinese ... [were] consigned, with houses and merchandise, to certain Americans in San Francisco, to whom they were bound by contract as laborers."[61] This pattern of migration was subsequently adjusted because of the different conditions that obtained in California. Labor contracts proved difficult to enforce in the United States, as one Englishman recounted: "The fifteen coolies I brought from China, and who were under a bond for two years with the party who engaged them, were no sooner ashore than they resisted their contract, and each earned his separate way."[62]

As a consequence, the majority of Chinese immigrants came to California during the nineteenth century by means of the credit-ticket system. Under this system, various persons—such as returned emigrants, Chinese companies, Western labor recruiters, and ship captains—provided emigrants with tickets on credit for the voyage abroad. The indebted migrants were obligated to repay the fares out of their future earnings. Interest on this loan was extremely high, ranging from 4 to 8 percent a month.[63] The majority of Chinese immigrants who came under the credit-ticket system were thus subject to a form of debt bondage, not contract labor.

Research on capitalist development has profoundly revised immigration studies. It has placed immigration within the broader framework of the emerging industrial regions, which formed a world market for cheap labor at the same time it distorted traditional feudal relations in nearby rural regions. This theoretical house, however, is not big enough to accommodate the Chinese emigration. To account for the nineteenth-century Chinese emigration to the United States, we need to emphasize the role of three market economies, those of Guangdong, Britain, and California.

Guangdong was one of China's oldest, best-developed, and most aggressive market economies. The Chinese who came to California in the second half of the nineteenth century were continuing an old practice promoted by Cantonese commercial activities. The collision of two market economies that was imposed by Britain on China, but specifically on Guangdong further explains why large-scale Chinese emigration occurred in the mid-nineteenth century and why an overwhelming majority of emigrants came from Guangdong province. Britain's actions not only caused push factors such as economic dislocation and political chaos in southern China, but they also created a pull factor, a safe portal for the exodus. Hong Kong was so near, and a British administrative and commercial structure designed to promote free trade and access to the world economy was of course the ideal springboard for California. The development of California's marketplace meant the opening of bigger and better opportunities for Chinese merchants and laborers. The relations between the California market economy and the Cantonese market economy were call and response. The Chinese emigration to the United States resulted from the combined impact when three market economies met—the historical continuum of Canton's own commercial activities, British imperialism, and California's developing capitalism. Both the old and new market economies left deep imprints on Chinese emigration.

CHAPTER 2

• • • • • •

Continuity and Change

The Chinese *Huiguan* Tradition Crosses the Pacific, 1850s

> When the Chinese visit any other province of their country in considerable numbers, it is their custom to have a common quarters, or rendezvous, which they style an ui-kun, that is, a gathering-place or company's house. It is like a club-house, in being supported wholly by voluntary contributions, and in the provision of food and lodging at their cost. And so when they voluntarily emigrate to any foreign country, in Asia or America, they at once contribute to erect a house. Agents or superintendents are elected, who register the members and manage its concerns. Servants are employed to take care of the building, cook the food, and attend the sick. Provision is made for the interment of the dead, repairs of tombs, and the semi-annual worship of the spirits. And, beyond all this, rules are agreed upon for the government of this club, or company; and these are adopted or repealed at pleasure in the most democratic manner.
>
> —"The Chinese Companies: Their External Organization"

These strangers from a different shore met a reception that ranged from warm to cold. In an address in 1852 Governor John McDougal of California declared that more Chinese migrants would be needed to help drain the state's swamps. As "one of the most worthy of our newly adopted citizens," he found them "peculiarly suited" to California's conditions.[1] In just four months, however, the next governor, John Bigler, sent a message to the California Assembly urging that "to enhance the prosperity of this State," the tide of degraded and inferior "coolie" immigration "under contract to work in our mines for a term" must be checked with heavy taxes.[2] What fluctuations in California's market economy produced this change in attitude? And how, as a race of strangers, did the Chinese survive this changing political and economic climate?

The Early Market Economy in California

In the early 1850s California's new capitalist economy had a crying need for labor. The main characteristics of the Golden State were an abundance of capital and a near total absence of labor. It is not surprising, therefore, that a common laborer in San Francisco received $1 an hour; a carpenter got $14 a day.[3] Also, according to a widely circulated but exaggerated report, "early San Francisco dandies sent their shirts as far as Hong Kong to be washed and ironed. They paid $12 a dozen, and it took four months to get them back."[4] The Chinese were especially welcome in farming, because "for centuries they have been celebrated as skillful and successful, if not scientific cultivators of the soil, and at the present day are probably second only to the English in all that pertains to practical farming."[5]

As before, some Americans played an important role in importing Chinese laborers in the 1850s. As a case in point, Wan-nae-shun (Bryson), an American ship captain, and Chin Suy, a Chinese laborer, signed a contract in 1852 in which Bryson agreed to pay Chin Suy's passage and would get his money back "by means of four equal quarterly installments, to be deduced from [Chin's] wages."[6] Of special importance among American labor brokers was Cornelius Koopmanschap. Arriving in San Francisco from Holland in 1850, Koopmanschap shrewdly realized California's need for labor. Koopmanschap's business organization in Hong Kong employed many brokers in China to gather laborers together. His organization in San Francisco operated its own fleet of vessels and when it received its thousands of laborers, it then assigned them their masters, purchased their food, and secured for them their wages.[7]

Although there is an element of truth in the commonly accepted belief that most of the Chinese in the early 1850s were gold miners,[8] we should not let this fact obscure other aspects of the immigration. In California the old Chinese and new capitalist market economies converged, for like the American labor brokers, Chinese merchants were also impresarios in meeting the demand for labor. One circular distributed by Chinese merchants proclaimed that Chinese laborers were "wanted and welcomed" and that "high wages, large houses, plenty of food and clothing of the finest description" were waiting for them. The United States was a "civilized country" and where "all men are equal; there is no difference between elite and ordinary people."[9] As many migrants were too impatient to wait, at first Chinese merchants hired American vessels to convey their countrymen.[10] The project was of a grand scale. The August 17, 1852, *San Francisco Herald* reported that in the first six months of 1852 the enterprising Chinese merchants gave "profitable employment to 82 vessels," with American clippers profitably carrying laborers to and from California. In October 1853 a Chinese merchant chartered the clipper ship *Gazelle* to transport 350 Chinese from San Francisco to Hong Kong for $8,000.[11] In the same year some Chinese merchants began to utilize ships of their own. When the *Hamilton* arrived in San Francisco from Hong Kong on June 1, 1853, it was reported as the "first vessel owned by a Chinaman which has ever entered this port under their flag."[12] The *Potomac* was a striking illustration of their success. It was purchased in San Francisco for about $5,000 and resold in Hong Kong for some $25,000. Subsequently the ship earned $37,000 for a single voyage from Hong Kong to San Francisco and back. "The *Potomac* brought a large number of emigrants and a small cargo of rice and assorted Chinese goods."[13] On May 14, 1859, the Stockton *Argus* reported the arrival of Chinese miners who were "under contract" to Chinese merchants, who "brought them from China for the purpose of speculating in their labor."[14] Indeed, in the early period, either through operating their own vessels or chartering ships, Chinese merchants controlled the flow of their countrymen to California as efficiently as they did to Malaysia.[15]

Chinese merchants also developed other large import-export businesses and built up an extensive wholesale and retail trade along the Pacific Coast. For these men, it was not difficult to succeed in the new market economy.[16] According to the San Francisco Customs House, in the early 1850s Chinese merchants imported rice, noodles, beans, yams, sugar, tea, vinegar, peanut oil, dried vegetables, salted fish, dried shrimp and oysters, dried bean curd, and dried as well as fresh fruits.[17] Chinese merchants did business not only in their own community but also with Americans. Almost all of J. L. Riddle and Co.'s furniture was of "China importation," and it was declared to be "very commodious, stylish and comfortable."[18] Amos Di Sang, a Chinese merchant, regularly ordered rubber boots from the Goodyear Rubber Company and ladies' clothes from the Montgomery Ward Company. He also conducted "extensive business relations" with other American companies.[19] Chinese merchants were highly thought of and praised for their business acumen and honesty by some Americans in the early period. "As a nation, they are certainly behind the age in many important matters, but those who are brought in contact commercially with the Chinese merchants and traders, generally find them keenly alive to a bargain."[20] It was also reported, in 1854, that several "pretty wealthy" merchants in the Chinese community established a "handsome building" to serve as a merchants' exchange.[21]

Providing valuable goods and services, Chinese merchants were welcomed by the white elite of San Francisco. In 1850 John W. Geary, the mayor of San Francisco, invited them to join with Americans in a memorial for the late President Zachary Taylor. At that time numbering about fifty and commanded by Norman Assing, they proudly held a banner of crimson satin that displayed the

Chinese characters for "China boys."[22] The *San Francisco Alta California* stated that the "China boys" would "vote at the same polls, study at the same schools, and bow at the same altar, as our own countrymen."[23] To promote good will, in 1853 the Chinese merchants made a donation of $1,000 to the San Francisco Fire Department Fund, which was the third largest single amount recorded.[24] The splendid future prospects must have made the Chinese merchants happy.

But this form of immigration did not grow in greater proportions in the 1850s. Labor contracts proved difficult to enforce in the United States. The *San Francisco Alta California* offered an example: In March 1851, six Chinese workers, "who were under contract, in consideration of a free-passage," ran away to the mines. The contractor failed to obtain a warrant for their arrest and as a consequence lost his entire investment.[25] In a country where public outrage against slavery and servile labor was abundant, it was not possible to enforce all contracts made in China. Furthermore, as the physically and culturally different immigrants began arriving in increasing numbers in the early 1850s, Americans quickly, almost inevitably, developed an intense irrational dislike of them, especially as the Chinese began to create economic competition.[26] The problems arising from foreign immigration have occurred from the earliest periods of history. In the early nineteenth-century United States, for example, agitation and anger were excited by the great influx of Irish and Germans. Given this background, it is easy to imagine what the Chinese experienced. Crying "California for Americans," white miners sought state legislation to curb Chinese immigration. A legislative committee of the State of California responded with a report that asserted: "The concentration, within our State limits, of vast number of the Asiatic races . . . [who are] dissimilar from ourselves in customs, language and education, . . . [and simply] servile contract laborers" not seeking to become American citizens, would degrade the white workers and were harmful to the state. To discourage Chinese immigration, the committee suggested the enactment of a foreign miners' license tax. In addition, in 1852 Governor John Bigler sent a message to the California Assembly to check the "tide of Asiatic immigration."[27]

It was inevitable that the Chinese merchants and business class, not merely Chinese laborers, would be swamped by the xenophobia. Early in February 1853, a group of Chinese miners was attacked, and $6,000 in gold dust robbed. A few days later, $30,000 was taken from another Chinese camp by a group of bandits.[28] But even the courts were plainly prejudiced against the Chinese, as the 1854 case of *People v. Hall* demonstrates. On the basis of the testimony of one Caucasian and three Chinese witnesses, the judge at first sentenced George W. Hall to be hanged for murdering Ling Sing. Hall's lawyer, however, lodged an appeal that the Chinese witnesses should not be accepted, since "no black or mulatto person, or Indian, shall be permitted to give evidence in favor of, or against, any white person." Ultimately the California Supreme Court reversed the conviction and set a precedent that Chinese, like all nonwhite peoples, could not testify against whites.[29]

The press also discussed the Chinese unfavorably.[30] The *San Francisco Alta California* complained about the filth and stench of the Chinese settlement. Fear of disease spreading from the Chinese community generated a great anti-Chinese outcry.[31] In 1854 the Chinese were criticized for being "without proper medical attendance, removed entirely from the chance of the friendly care of their fellow countrymen . . . [so that they] sickened and died like dogs."[32] *Graham's Magazine* likewise charged that Chinese were "a semi-barbarous and sickly people."[33] The *New York Tribune* asserted that "the Chinese are uncivilized, unclear, and filthy beyond all conception without any of the higher domestic social relations; lustful and sensual in their dispositions; every female is a prostitute of the basest order."[34] Bayard Taylor's book was even more hostile to the Chinese vice: "It is my deliberate opinion that the Chinese are, morally, the most debased people on the face of the earth."[35]

In 1855 the California legislature passed "An Act to Discourage the Immigration to this State of Persons Who Cannot Become Citizens Thereof," which levied a landing tax of $50 on each passenger ineligible for naturalized citizenship. This fee was to be paid by the owner of the ship carrying the immigrants.[36] Inspired by this state of affairs, some white miners even expressed interest in wiping out all the Chinese.[37]

Transfer of the *Huiguan* Tradition to America

It is not surprising that when Cantonese merchants immigrated to California, they brought their *huiguan* tradition and formed many native-place associations for self-defense and mutual aid. Scholars differ as to when the first American *huiguan* was established. Liu Boji has argued the oldest *huiguan* was established in 1849,[38] while A. W. Loomis regards the earliest possibility to be 1851.[39] According to Him Mark Lai, the first two *huiguan* were established by 1851.[40] William Hoy and Shih-shan Henry Tsai assert that an influential Siyi (four districts) leader named Yu Laoji founded the first *huiguan* in 1851.[41] The case for 1849 is likely to be right since evidence suggests that Chinese merchants in the city were organized by the end of 1849. The *San Francisco Alta California* of December 10, 1849, records a public meeting of the Chinese held on November 19 at the Canton Restaurant. At that meeting "the committee of four" drafted some resolutions concerning the Chinese in the United States.[42]

The first *huiguan* was the Gangzhou (Kong Chow) *huiguan*, because the majority of Chinese in California at that time came from the six districts collectively called Gangzhou.[43]

The second *huiguan*, in English the Canton Company, was formed in 1851.[44] It supported a frame house in San Francisco on Clay Street, another in Sacramento, and a third in Stockton. Its Chinese name Sanyi (Sam Yap) *huiguan*, or three-district *huiguan*, derives from that fact that it included the three districts of Nanhai, Panyu, and Shunde. Two other districts, Sanshui and Xingyun, joined later.[45] Then at the end of 1851 the Siyi (Sze Yap) *huiguan*, or four-district *huiguan*, came into being, comprising individuals from Xinhui, Kaiping, Xinning, and Enping.[46] Its house was situated on Pine Street in San Francisco. Even after the Heshan and Sishui districts joined the Siyi *huiguan*, its name did not change.[47]

In 1852, under the leadership of Norman Assing, Cai Libi, and Liu Zuman, the Yanghe (Yeong Wo) *huiguan* was founded.[48] "The three districts of Heung-shan, Tung-kun, and Tsang-shing, [were] embraced in this company." It had branches in Sacramento and Stockton, but no regular agent employed in either city. The houses were used as lodging places.[49] The Xieji (Hip Kat) *huiguan* appeared in the same year and was composed of Hakka immigrants from the "Bow On, Chak Kai, Tung Gwoon, and Chu Mui" districts. Four years later it changed its name to Renhe (Yan Wo) *huiguan;* its house was in Happy Valley, San Francisco.[50]

The following years saw the fragmentation of the Siyi *huiguan*. An internal dispute in 1854 caused people from Taishan (Toysan), then known as Xinning, to withdraw and organize the Ningyang (Ning Yeung) *huiguan*. The new company's house was situated in "San Francisco, No. 47 Broadway, near Kearny Street" and "consisted of the people of San-ning."[51]

Like some individual *huiguan* within China, those in San Francisco often felt an imperative need to cooperate on certain matters of common concern. In 1853, for example, the presidents of the oldest four *huiguan* formed a federal organization called the Four Houses.[52] The Four Houses became the "Five Companies" (five *huiguan*) in the late 1850s, when Gangzhou (Kong Chow) *huiguan*, Ningyang (Ning Yeung) *huiguan*, Sanyi (Sam Yup) *huiguan*, Yanghe (Yeong Wo) *huiguan*, and Renhe (Yan Wo) *huiguan* incorporated.[53]

There were striking similarities in the functions carried out by the San Francisco *huiguan* and those elsewhere. Urban immigration in China, which was perceived as a temporary sojourn, not a permanent relocation, did not involve a fundamental change of identity. Likewise, "Gold Mountain guests" *(jinshan ke)* in California also referred to themselves as "Chinese sojourners in America" *(lumei huaren)*.[54] Just as *huiguan* did in China, members constructed their own buildings in a traditional style in order to create an atmosphere of home.[55]

The *huiguan* in the United States maintained the tradition of mutual aid and homeland ties; they provided assistance with lodging, storage for baggage, finding jobs, caring for the sick and the dead, as well as a headquarters for friends and acquaintances from the same locality.[56] For instance, the constitution of the Yanghe (Yeung-wo) *huiguan* expressed the intention to promote the solidarity of homeland ties for "the common good" in the United States. It further stipulated that invalids who could not work and were without relatives, would be returned to China "at the expense of the company for their passage-money."[57] The *huiguan*'s upper story and attic were lodging places where people from its districts could stay temporarily. The lodgers might be on a visit from the mines or on their way to and from China.[58] The *huiguan* also acted as post offices, receiving letters from China and directing mail anywhere the Chinese recipients were located.[59]

The mutual-aid features made a deep impression on Americans. The *San Francisco Alta California* of March 18, 1850 even marveled: "They are all very happy and very clannish, the only real socialists in existence."[60] Their benevolent work was further said to be an important reason why the needy and the sick among the Chinese never became a burden to San Francisco and the treasury of the state.[61] Not only were these native-place organizations a great saving to the host country, but they also saved Chinese in this strange land much expense and trouble.

Like their counterparts in China and elsewhere, the San Francisco *huiguan* provided for worship in the *huiguan* house for their members. One room of the Ningyang *huiguan*, for example, had "a shrine not very gaudily decorated." Its back was "composed of a series of miniature stairs, covered with white paper, rising up to the top of the room." Several of the stairs were already covered with the names of deceased members of the *huiguan*, and the names of others were added "as fast as their spirits ascend the heavenly stairway here typified." The *San Francisco Alta California* reporter marveled at the building itself: "To give anything like a description of this establishment [the Chinese temple building] in the English language, or even to convey to the uninitiated outsiders the remotest idea of the general appearance of the place and its decorations and furnishing, is utterly out of the question, and we do not attempt it."[62]

Similar to their counterparts in China, they operated as arbiters of their community disputes, and a vehicle for meeting outside challenges which affected their members. The rules of the Yanghe *huiguan* stated: "Quarrels and troubles about claims in the mines should be referred to the company, where they shall be duly considered."[63] For the Chinese *huiguan* arbitration carried more weight than the deliberations of an American court. William Speer says of the Siyi *huiguan*'s judicial power: "Disputes between miners and others are settled at the company house without the expense, delay and trouble of a resort to our courts of law."[64]

The *huiguan* confederacy settled complicated disputes or those among individuals in different *huiguan*. For example, the constitution of the Yanghe *huiguan* stipulated that disputes with members of other companies should be reported to the *huiguan* agents. If necessary, they should "be referred for the judgment of the five companies conjointly."[65] The Siyi *huiguan* had a similar rule: "A friendly arbitration is held before a meeting of their company, or before a joint committee of the five companies, where the case is more difficult, or when persons of different districts are involved."[66] In the early days, encouraged by the example of lynching among Americans in the California wilderness, the *huiguan* "took the law in their own hands so far as to inflict corporal punishment upon offenders in their houses." This practice came to an end in 1855.[67]

As in China, disputes between Chinese could also find their way into the U.S. courts. Wong Fook, a president of the Yung Wo Company, told a *Chronicle* reporter about this process. If two Chinese had a quarrel, "a Council was called of the two companies to which they belonged." The disputants argued before the Council and a decision would be made to settle their differences. If either party, or both, refused to accept the judgment, "they went to law in the American Courts and spent their money in fighting each other."[68]

In addition to enjoying similar functions, the structure of the *huiguan* in the United States resembled their counterparts in other places. Like the *huiguan* in China, all natives of the *huiguan*'s home districts were eligible for membership in the *huiguan* in the United States. One *huiguan* stipulated, for example: "People of the three districts of Heung-shan, Tung-yuen and Tsang-ching are required to report themselves at the company's room; otherwise, the company will exercise no care for them in their concerns."[69]

As elsewhere, the *huiguan* acted as a soliciting and collecting organization to meet their necessary expenses. For example, the Yanghe *huiguan* set its entrance fee at $10. It usually sent collectors to the mines in April and October each year; stipulating that "if not paid within six months, interest will be expected."[70] The Siyi *huiguan* detailed what its entrance fee covered in the 1850s: (1) the purchase of ground and the erection of buildings used by *huiguan*; (2) the salaries of agents and servants; (3) the purchase of fuel, water, candles, and oil; (4) the costs of assisting the return of the sick and invalids; (5) expenses for medicine; (6) coffin and funeral expenses for the poor; (7) repair expenses of tombs; (8) lawsuit expenses and taxes; (9) drayage and other outlays for passengers landing or departing by ship.[71]

Each San Francisco *huiguan* had two or three elected managers and a management committee. One *huiguan* stated: "This company shall elect three managers; one to attend to the internal affairs, one to attend to the business with the Americans, and one to be the treasurer; and they shall mutually assist one another."[72] Another group noted that "at the election all the district must have a voice." The managers must be "men of tried honesty." If men were found able and faithful to their duties, they were eligible for reelection.[73] In a strange land that was growing increasingly unfriendly, it was essential to elect those most capable of protecting the membership. Each *huiguan* also had a committee "elected from among the Chinese merchants of San Francisco." One important power of the heads of the *huiguan* was to "grant passports" and "allow no person to leave the country if it is ascertained that his debts are unpaid."[74]

A final key point is that from the very beginning of the Chinese immigration, the leaders of the Chinese community realized the importance of obtaining American advisers in a new world where they were unacquainted with the language and customs. In one of the its earliest meetings, that held at the Canton Restaurant in Jackson Street on Nov. 19, 1849, approximately 300 *huiguan* representatives unanimously adopted a resolution to hire Selim E. Woodworth, Esq., as their arbitrator and adviser.[75] Soon after that, S. W. Bonney sent a letter to Woodworth in which he wrote: "I was pleased to learn that they had taken this step of choosing a lawyer with whom to advise...I have...copies of the four Gospels for them, and would ask of you the favor to distribute them to the immigrants who can read and will receive them."[76] As we shall see in the following chapters, many Americans, especially lawyers and missionaries, spoke on behalf of the Chinese against the anti-Chinese movement.

The *Huiguan* as Spokesman

Among its many services, the *huiguan* were also self-defensive organizations, and in this function, they were indispensable. *Huiguan* leaders realized that anti-Chinese sentiment and violence were being caused by the fast-growing Chinese immigration. Therefore, the *huiguan* began in 1852 to discourage their countrymen from coming to the United States. After the miners' demand for Chinese exclusion was articulated by Governor Bigler, the *huiguan* published letters in the Hong Kong *China Mail* to discourage more Chinese emigration. Many of the newcomers, one of these letters emphasized, "were in [a] filthy state, and on that account were mocked by foreigners and their countrymen [were] ashamed of them." Americans, it seemed, had lost their earlier respect for the Chinese due to too large immigration during the previous two years.[77] Evidence suggests that their efforts to curb Chinese immigration were effective to a certain extent. According to the San Francisco Customs House, the number of Chinese immigrants dropped from 20,026 in 1852 to 4,027 in 1853.[78]

It was the prevailing notion that the Chinese knew nothing about American politics and institutions, but that was far from true. Because the Chinese had no vote and could not depend on senators or representatives to help them, the *huiguan* leaders employed a form of modern informal diplomacy; they carried out lobbying efforts against exclusion. In American politics, the power of the press in forming public opinion cannot be exaggerated, and making use of this power is one of the bulwarks of liberty. A few days after Bigler's message, Norman Asing (also spelled Assing and Ashing), a founder of the Yanghe *huiguan*,[79] published an open letter refuting Bigler's accusations in the *San Francisco Alta California* of May 4, 1852. He introduced himself as "a republican, and a lover of free institutions" who was "much attached to the principles of the Government of the United States" and who therefore took "the liberty of addressing you as the chief of the Government of this State." He then argued: "The declaration of your independence, and all the acts of your government, your people, and your history, are against you." In addition to the fact that a dispute regarding immigration was one of the principal causes of the war of independence, he argued, population, particularly a population of producers, represented wealth; immigration actually transferred the United States almost instantly from childhood to manhood and made it great and respectable throughout the world. Asing also countered the charge that the Chinese were inferior by reminding Bigler of China's glorious past. When America was a wilderness, China "exercised most of the arts and virtues of civilized life," was "possessed of a language and literature, and men skilled in science and arts," and had "no small share of the commerce of the world." Although the skin color of the Chinese might differ from many of the European races, Asing stressed, he did not "consider that your Excellence, as a Democrat, will make us believe that the framers of your declaration of rights ever suggested the propriety of establishing an aristocracy of skin." He ended this part of his argument by noting that "it is out of your power to say, however, in what way or to whom the doctrines of the Constitution shall apply." Obviously, the *huiguan* leaders had not only brought Chinese traditions with them, but they had come to understand the democratic and republican ideas of California very well. Countering the claim "that none of the Asiatic class has applied for benefits under our naturalization act," Asing argued that he himself was a naturalized citizen and a Christian as well. In conclusion he pleaded for acceptance: "You find us peculiarly peaceable and orderly. It does not cost your State much for our criminal prosecution."[80]

In a "Letter of the Chinamen to His Excellency Gov. Bigler," which was published in *Living Age* in July 1852, Tang Yazhi, president of the Yanghe *hui-*

guan, and Chen Yaqing, secretary of the Sanyi *huiguan*, denied the governor's charges by "pointing out to your Excellency some of the errors you have fallen into about us. . . . None [of us] are 'coolies' if by that word you mean bound men or contract slaves." The Chinese were actually laborers, merchants, mechanics, gentry, and schoolmasters. In addition, there were no Chinese drunkards in the streets, nor any Chinese convicts in the prisons; the Chinese lived orderly lives, worked hard, and took care of themselves. Tang and Chen further stressed the importance of trade between the two countries. In order to highlight Chinese merchants' success and their contributions to the California economy, they stated that in San Francisco alone there were twenty stores kept by Chinese merchants, who erected the buildings themselves. One of the authors of this reply, who was a clerk in an American store, had sometimes sold $10,000 worth of Chinese goods in a day. The two men warned: "If you want to check immigration from Asia, you will have to do it by checking Asiatic commerce, which we suppose, from all that we have ever known of your government, the United States most desires to increase." In conclusion they argued: "Let us stay here—the Americans are doing good to us, and we will do good to them."[81] The Chinese effort was not a total loss. Although the California legislature enacted the Foreign Miners' License Tax in May 1852, it was in theory applied to all foreigners.[82]

In 1853, when the California State Legislature's Committee on Mines and Mining Interests discussed a bill to increase only the Chinese license fees, the presidents of the four *huiguan* contacted the committee through an American lawyer and requested an interview to oppose this unequal treatment.[83] They refuted the charge that they were slaveholders and emphasized the democratic and benevolent character of the Chinese community. Opposing the opinion that the Chinese were harmful to the United States, they tried to prove that the Chinese presence among Americans was a benefit. They further informed the committee that they had sent letters the year before to those parts of China from which the immigration came, informing those localities of the anti-Chinese feeling in California. They emphasized that the letters had been published extensively in China and had caused the emigration to cease almost entirely. The presidents of the *huiguan* assured the committee they would "exert much influence" to "prevent too large an emigration from China" to the United States even though "they had no authority there."[84] They believed that after learning of their efforts, the government would extend protection to the Chinese who were already in the United States.

Like Tang and Chen, the leaders of the *huiguan* promised that they would increase trade between the two countries if protected by just legislation. They estimated the Chinese capital in California, not including mining, at two million dollars. Given the existence of negative feelings toward the Chinese in California, the *huiguan* leaders did not wish to invite their friends in China to invest more capital in the trade and internal improvements of the state. It was futile to legislate for the protection of their capital in trade, while at the same time their countrymen and property were not safe in other occupations. They complained that the testimony of Chinese individuals was not allowed or accepted in American courts. They also protested that the Chinese were taxed "for the privilege of working in the mines" but that California did not protect them. If the Chinese were promised safe and profitable employment, the writers assured the committee, trade and commerce between the two countries would increase and capital that was lying dormant in China would seek investment opportunities in private trade and public improvements in California.[85] This time the effort of the Chinese leaders was successful, for the committee opposed the proposals for any radical change in the license law.[86]

Hostility arose again in 1854. California not only passed a resolution requesting payment of a head tax immediately upon arrival, but also continued to deprive the Chinese of the right to give testimony in court. Governor Bigler again delivered a message to the legislature on the evils of the immigration from Asia. In January 1855, Lai Chun-chuen of the Sanyi *huiguan* wrote a letter to Bigler entitled "Remarks of the Chinese Merchants of San Francisco on Governor Bigler's Message," which was translated into English by William Speer and circulated as a pamphlet in the state capital. Lai suggested that since Chinese merchants had no power to drive Chinese gamblers and prostitutes away even if they had a desire to do so, the American government should "enact vigorous laws" to break up "brothels and gambling places." Thus, he reasoned, "worthless fellows" would be compelled to find "some honest employments"; "gamblers" would "change their calling," and "moreover, your own policemen and petty officials be deprived of many opportunities of trickery and extortion."[87]

Ignoring the Chinese lobbying, on April 20, 1855, Governor Bigler signed a bill entitled "An Act to Discourage the Immigration to This State of Persons Who Cannot Become Citizens Thereof," and the Foreign Miners' License Tax, which was increased from $4 to $6 a month.[88] But their lobbying was not a total failure, for it generated sympathy among some Americans. A few days later, for example, the *San Francisco Herald* supported a bill to establish a steamship line between San Francisco and Shanghai, which would "add substantially to the greatness, wealth and power of the United States."[89]

The Chinese Merchants' Exchange sent Governor Bigler a letter entitled "To His Excellency Gov. Bigler, and to the Legislature, and the People of the State of California," which was also published in the *Oriental*. As before, the leaders of the Chinese community refuted many new charges. Opposing the notion that too many Chinese came alone "without their families," it highlighted: "To this we rejoin, that the manners and customs of China and of foreign countries are not like. This is an ancient principle, and is prevalent now."[90] It also stressed the relationship between Chinese labor and the Chinese merchants: "Suppose you say, 'we will restrain only those who work in the mines. We would not forbid merchants,' it is replied, that the merchandise imported by Chinese merchants chiefly depends on Chinese consumption." Therefore "the occupations are mutually dependent, like tooth and lip; neither can separate [from] the other." The Chinese should not be singled out for discrimination because "the principle of your honorable country [is] to protect the people," and all "nations are really the same."[91] Obviously they were asserting that the whole matter should be considered in the spirit of liberty and unprejudiced deliberation that modern nations value most.

In 1856 William Speer, a friend of the leaders of the *huiguan*,[92] became a lobbyist for the Chinese against the license tax. A former missionary in Canton, he opened the first Christian church in Chinatown in San Francisco in 1853. His knowledge of China and his interest in the Chinese in California made him a spokesman for the Chinese in this early period.[93] In a pamphlet entitled *An Humble Plea, Addressed to the Legislature of California in Behalf of the Immigrants from the Empire of China*, published in 1856, and circulated in Sacramento, Speer denied the charge that Chinese were "coolies" or slaves. By showing that the word "coolie" came from India, where the entire social system was widely different, he emphasized that China had no equivalent of the Hindustani word "coolie" in its language and had no similar caste or class. Chinese laborers were not imported to the United States by the *huiguan;* the "very mistaken notions" arose from "not understanding, as was natural enough, the nature of their 'companies.'"[94] He highlighted the morality of the Chinese as "immeasurably superior to any other unchristianized people." Speer also argued that "the interests of California [forbade] a policy calculated to exclude or debase Chinese immigration." Basing his argument on a wealth of statistical evidence, he emphasized how trade with China benefited West Coast shippers, rents from Chinese tenants benefited California landlords, and taxes from Chinese enriched the state treasury. He pointed out that not California alone, but all the states and territories of the West Coast, were eager to establish "regular and reliable commerce with Asia.... China, our merchants [report], favor the American article, as its importation is likely to gradually increase."[95] The result was quite heartening for the Chinese—on April 19, the legislature returned the Foreign Miners' License Tax to its former level of $4 a month.[96]

In addition to lobbying against American exclusionists and discouraging potential Chinese immigrants from coming to the United States, the *huiguan* leaders also became reformers within the Chinese community. These leaders were obviously troubled by incessant Caucasian criticism, and therefore improving the well-being of the Chinese community and image became one of their priorities. In 1853 the Chinese *huiguan* confederacy called a public meeting, attended by William Speer and some leading Chinese merchants. Three resolutions were passed and signed by Norman Asing, one of the *huiguan* leaders, and C. Carvalho, the interpreter: (1) a fund would be raised and a committee appointed for the purpose of establishing a Chinese hospital; (2) Charles Jane would be appointed to keep the Chinese localities in a clean and proper condition; and (3) a petition, signed by the directors of the Five Great Companies, would be presented to the American government for the effective suppression of the Chinese brothels and gambling houses.[97] After establishing the first Chinese hospital in 1856, the leaders of the Chinese community invited some Americans to see the building, which was described by the *San Francisco Alta California* as being "substantial and commodious, and will compare favorably with any public institution in our midst."[98]

In the 1850s, therefore the native-place organization of the Chinese tradition had taken on in California a momentum of its own. There were many similarities between the Chinese domestic *huiguan* and the *huiguan* of San Francisco. Like their counterparts in China, they operated as arbiters of their community disputes and a vehicle for mutual aid. They offered solace and protection for members facing outside challenges. Like their counterparts in other places, they solicited and collected funds to provide for their necessary expenses. Through the payments of small fees they secured comforts and conveniences. At the *huiguan* house the immigrants received shelter, information from home, and facilities for cooking and washing when they lodged there temporarily. If they died, the *huiguan* ensured that their remains were sent back home. It was exactly what sojourners unaccompanied by their families and living in the changeable California political climate needed most.

To be sure, there were differences. Unlike Chinese domestic *huiguan,* these American *huiguan* can be described as some of the oldest "international" nongovernmental organizations in the world. Although there was no easy solution for the problem of the immigrants' unfamiliarity with the language and customs, they quickly realized the necessity of hiring American advisers. Having to deal with the new ideologies and methods in the United States—not readily available to Chinese living within China and other countries in the nineteenth century—meant the traditional *huiguan* needed to adapt. History is filled with examples of the American *huiguan* acting as the first Chinese lobbyists. Though their lobbying and reform efforts were sporadic and restricted in California in this period, the earliest four *huiguan* achieved their first unified action in 1853. This American-style lobbying was of critical importance. Arguing against anti-Chinese propaganda was the essential first theme, but what is novel about the lobbying effort is that scattered in their rebuttals were Western liberal ideas. Norman Asing even called himself a republican and a lover of free institutions. The second theme, the importance of China trade for California, was also a strong argument. The lobbyists made clear that it was the height of absurdity for California to attempt to attract the trade of Asia, and then attempt to exclude the Chinese. Indeed in the early period, when California was a new state needing to change its own backward condition, the *huiguan* put their finger exactly on the contribution of the Chinese merchants and on the latent potentialities of China trade in the development of the state. Many of the politicians of California were businessmen, and they were naturally apt to give commercial considerations a foremost place. It is certainly likely that the *huiguan* leaders realized that arguments relating to national progress carried much weight in the United States. The early *huiguan* leaders simply could not fail to observe, be impressed by, and make use of modern Western methods, ideologies, and California's concrete conditions as they defended their community in the United States.

CHAPTER 3

Toward a New Chinese Self-image

The Beginning of Modern Chinese Nationalism in California, 1860s

> The young, impulsive, progressive civilization of America comes in direct contact with the ancient, venerable and peculiar civilization of Asia. Events, some of which are, perhaps, not culminated in unlocking the Chinese mind from the fetters in which it has been bound by centuries of exclusion from Caucasian progress; until we see the remarkable spectacle of a citizen of our young republic selected as the bearer of offers of commerce and amity between the Eastern and Western World. I will not attempt, at this time, to picture the grand results which I trust will flow from this auspicious event, not merely to America and to Europe, but to China and mankind.
>
> —"Grand Dinner for the Chinese Embassy"

> Why and for what purpose have the Chinese "Six Companies" been formed, exactly what are their powers and duties, how they conduct their various transactions wherein the welfare and, very often, the lives of their members are at stake, is a matter of wonderment to most people.
>
> —"The Six Companies"

In late April 1868 the Gangzhou *huiguan,* dressed in its holiday best, displayed the following poetic couplets inside its building: "Wandering aimlessly in a strange land, under the canopy of the moon and the stars, we were without the blessing of the throne; Meeting [the Qing officials] in a foreign country, why not present wine with all respect to share the affection for our mother country."[1] The Chinese had special reason to be excited—the year was witnessing the first Qing mission to the United States, a great change in Sino-American relations.

After Anson Burlingame resigned as American minister to China in 1868, he was appointed by the Qing court to serve as the Chinese minister to the

United States. As such, he paid a state visit to his native country. In San Francisco, the Chinese mission's first station in America, the leading citizens of California gave a grand banquet to honor Burlingame and the other members of the Chinese embassy. This took place at the Lick House, "the finest dining-hall in the United States," on April 28, 1868. "All the arrangements were in excellent taste, and the gathering was one of the most strictly representative ones convened in the State." California Gov. H. H. Haight spoke of the mission's arrival in glowing terms: It marked "a step forward in human progress," introducing "an Empire, one of the oldest, if not the oldest, of all that exist on the globe, into the great family of nations." As Burlingame proposed the next toast, the entire company stood up and greeted him with three cheers, "which made the banquet tremble." Zhigang (Chih Tajen) also responded.[2] He read from a Chinese manuscript, while the interpreter of the embassy provided a translation. At the end of his address, he communicated to the Six Companies the Qing emperor's special interest in the welfare of the Chinese in California: "I would, with permission, say a word to my own countrymen resident in California. Gentlemen, Directors of the Six Companies—I address you, and through you all our fellow countrymen in the state."[3]

Why did the Qing government choose an American as the Chinese minister for a mission that looked like the dawn of a new era in China's foreign relations? What was the Six Companies, which seemed to represent all the Chinese in California? Before delving into these questions, we should first look briefly at Chinese immigration in the 1860s.

Chinese Immigration in the 1860s

Strong evidence of the role the new American market economy played in Chinese immigration is that the Chinese migration mirrored the economic development of California. In order to develop a general picture of the occupational distribution of the Chinese in California, Sucheng Chan has drawn on data from the United States Census.[4] In her statistical analysis of these materials, she demonstrates that Chinese immigration and occupation coincided with changes in the California economy, which was based first on mining, followed by railroad construction, and then by agriculture and manufacturing. This suggests not only "that economic factors exerted the most important influence on Chinese settlement patterns in the state," but also that the geographic shifts of the Chinese population also "followed so closely the developments in California's economy."[5]

We need to emphasize especially the building of the transcontinental railroad and the later railroad network in California and other parts of the West. From the beginning the Central Pacific Railroad recognized its role in immigration. Lewis Clement, a member of the Central Pacific's engineering department, testified to the Pacific Railway Commission: "We had a good deal of difficulty getting labor, [which] was not in the country and had to be imported."[6] Railroad-builder Charles Croker receives the credit for "recruiting the Chinese laborers in Canton province and bringing them to California."[7] In the mid-1860s, agents of the Central Pacific recruited Chinese laborers in the Pearl River delta, paid their passage, and received in return from each Chinese laborer a promissory note for $75. The contract stipulated payment of regular installments in order to complete repayment of the debt within seven months from the time the Chinese laborers started working on the railroad.[8]

The *Overland Monthly* enthusiastically supported the use of the Chinese in agriculture because they were "the descendants of the people who drained those almost limitless marshes on either side of their own swiftly-flowing Yellow River, and turned them into luxuriant fields"; the publication asserted that they would be "able to do the same thing on the banks of the Sacramento and the San Joaquin."[9] In 1869 Cornelius Koopmanschap himself pointed out that his company had imported 30,000 Chinese into California who were employed in mining, on railroads, in agriculture, and as domestics.[10] The contracts were made in California for twelve months, with the employers paying the cost of transportation in addition to the laborers' wages. The same arrangements were made with Southern plantation owners for Chinese labor, but the contract length was longer to offset the increased cost of transportation.[11]

Southerners imported Chinese laborers to take the places of freed slaves. During his visit in South Carolina in 1869, "Mr. Joseph," a labor broker from San Francisco, received many letters from planters who were anxious to make arrangement to secure Chinese labor before the beginning of planting season.[12] One agent expected to take his shipload of Chinese laborers by rounding Cape Horn or the Cape of Good Hope, sailing to New Orleans and then up the Red River to the interior of Arkansas.[13] In the same year, after planters from the lower Arkansas River formed the Arkansas River Valley Immigration Company to import Chinese laborers into the state, they dispatched Capt. George W. Gift directly to China with letters of credit and authorized him to bring back 1,000 Chinese laborers.[14] On July 13, 1869, delegates from other Southern states gathered in the opera house of Tennessee's largest city, with Isham G. Harris, governor of the former Confederate state, as permanent president of the Arkansas River Valley Immigration Company, to discuss how to preserve the traditional Southern labor system by substituting Chinese laborers for slaves. The Transportation Committee of the company suggested that the Chinese could be brought from California to Memphis by rail in groups of five hundred for fifty gold dollars each.[15] "Isham G. Harris and his fellow conspirators," the

San Francisco Alta California commented, "bring together their conventions, leave the plough share in the furrow, lay down the shovel and the hoe, and wait for Koopmanschap."[16] American labor brokers were also active in Hawai`i. In 1865 the Hawaiian Board of Immigration asked Dr. William Hillebrand to recruit about 500 Chinese laborers from Hong Kong, indicating that the planters would pay for their passage.[17]

The newly established *huiguan* also facilitated the immigration, as the following story illustrates. In 1864 Win Kang, who had embarked on a steamship for California from an interior town near Canton in China, was the first member of the Kang family who emigrated. He was sick and had no friends on the ship or in California. When the steamship docked at the wharf, about a thousand Chinese came aboard, including the Ningyang *huiguan* secretary, who wanted to see if there were any countrymen from his district of China. The secretary found Win Kang and took him to the company on Broadway, in San Francisco. In the *huiguan* house, Win Kang was fed and nursed for about two weeks, until he regained his health. He then went to the temple on the upper floor of the *huiguan* building and gave offerings of thanks to the gods. The secretary helped him to find a job near Sacramento. His employer there, however, abused him and refused to give him his wages. Win Kang wrote to the secretary about his experience in Sacramento and afterwards received help from a white man who was the secretary's friend. Win Kang got his wages and traveled back to San Francisco. He paid the *huiguan* $5 or $6 for the assistance he had received when he was sick. But on the very next day he was robbed in an alley on the Barbary Coast. The Ningyang *huiguan* located and seized the robber and had him arrested and put into jail with the assistance of evidence given by Americans. Win Kang then found another job, this time in San Jose. He was soon, however, accused of theft. After learning of the matter, the Ningyang *huiguan* sent an agent to San Jose, and it was proved that the guilty person was the employer's own son. Though the employer's son was not punished, Win Kang was released. Later he had a quarrel with another Chinese, but they referred their case to the advisory committee of the *huiguan,* and at last their dispute was settled.[18]

In the 1860s the commercial activities of Chinese merchants were no longer restricted to San Francisco, for interior trade was developing. This can be seen in the development of the Chinese community in Los Angeles in 1861: "About the middle of June of that year Chun Chick arrived from San Francisco, and created a flurry not merely in 'Chinatown,' but throughout our little city, by the announcement that they would open a store here; and by the 13th of July, this pioneer Chinese shop, a veritable curiosity shop, was opened."[19] Pon Yam, a Chinese merchant in Idaho City in the late 1860s, built a brick building for his store on Montgomery Street, which became a landmark in the city.[20] The appearance of a Chinese merchant's jewelry store has been preserved for us by an *Atlantic Monthly* article entitled "Wo Lee, and His Kinsfolk." The Chinese merchant, who was a handsome fellow and spoke English readily, "had his showcases well filled with American and foreign watches, and silver, and notions, and on his work-bench was as complete a set of first-class tools as I ever saw in any jeweler's shop."[21] The *San Francisco Alta California* of 1866 held that Chinese merchants "were acknowledged to be second to none in the world in intelligence, enterprise and business ability."[22] Chinese merchants themselves were very proud of their reputation of being both honorable and commercially successful. Fang Tang, a well-known merchant in San Francisco, told a newspaper reporter that Chinese merchants were "really trusted by them [American bankers]" and could "borrow money on our name alone."[23]

Among the successful Chinese merchants was Chen Le (Chung Lock), who came to San Francisco in 1850 from Nanhai county and immediately founded Chy Lung & Co. jointly with Xie Mingli, Fang Ren, Sheng Wen, and Chen Nu. The *San Francisco Alta California* said that Chen Le was "in every sense of the word, a gentleman, and was widely known and universally respected and esteemed... by all classes, and the mean prejudice of caste and race, never displayed by him, was seldom exhibited towards him by anyone in our community.... [His enterprise] was as great as that of any of our American or European merchants.... The firm had a home in Shanghai, one at Canton, other at Hong Kong, and recently one in Yokohama, in addition to that in San Francisco."[24]

Members of the Chinese business class along with community leaders tried to establish a harmonious relationship with Americans. In 1864 the Ningyang *huiguan* gave a banquet at which a number of Chinese merchants and Americans were present, including the chief of police, the police judge, the police court clerk, the district attorney and his assistant, the chief of the fire department, and newspaper reporters. "The dinner for twenty people," the *San Francisco Alta California* stated, "consisted of over 100 dishes and could hardly have cost less than $1,000, and may have cost double that sum." It would be "long remembered with pleasure by all the guests."[25] In August 1865, the *huiguan* leaders provided another grand dinner for the Hon. Schuyler Colfax and other Americans at the Hang Heong Restaurant in San Francisco. The dinner consisted of 336 dishes and 130 courses and was divided into three separate sittings. At the end of the first sitting, the six presidents of the *huiguan* "paid their formal compliments to Mr. Colfax and party." The dinner was enjoyed "in the highest degree by the distinguished gentlemen in the whole honor it was given." None of them would be "apt to soon forget their first Chinese state dinner."[26]

They also made a donation and expressed their condolences to the American people upon the death of President Abraham Lincoln. The *San Francisco Alta California* noted: "When informed on Wednesday morning that a place was reserved for them in the procession they immediately set about raising funds to meet the necessary expenses and in less than ten minutes $170, more than was required for the purposes, was paid over."[27] In 1868 the *San Francisco Alta California* singled out for specific mention one particularly generous Chinese merchant: Chy Lung "gave liberally towards the Sanitary Relief Fund" during the Civil War and "the great Sacramento flood of 1861" which brought desolation and distress to so many American households, and "no call for a contribution by our Relief Committee passing unheeded by him."[28]

But as in the 1850s, many Americans considered the Chinese presence to be undesirable. It was a Chinese tradition that a migrant usually left behind his wife and children, and as a male society, the Chinese community in California had its own problems. Any visitor to the nineteenth-century Chinese sojourner communities would almost inevitably have been struck by the abundance of vices such as brothels, fighting tongs, and other non-family-oriented establishments.[29] In 1864, for example, about 150 Chinese prostitutes were rounded up by San Francisco police and instructed to "keep their door closed, refrain from exhibiting themselves to the public and making proposals to passers-by."[30] Two years later the *San Francisco Alta California* stated: "It is well known that a system of slavery exists among the Chinese in this State, and that women and children are bought and sold like cattle."[31]

Violence against Chinese immigrants also continued. Because the Foreign Miners' License Law continued to be enforced primarily against the Chinese, the Chinese complained in 1862: "People of all nations have taken advantage of this law to injure us; to take from us our mining claims; to enter our houses and stores destroying our property; to rob us; to beat and abuse us."[32] In 1864 a Chinese merchant living in Camancho "was brutally robbed and murdered," and his body was found about a mile away from his store by the roadside. The *San Francisco Chronicle* commented: "It is a great pity some laws could not be enacted to reach such murderous brutes. They rob these poor devils almost daily, and no one to interfere."[33]

The fears of physical diseases brought in by the Chinese continued, as did the fear of Chinese vice. Some editors in the 1860s began to warn that if Chinese immigration continued, the explosion of vice would destroy morality and the republican spirit of the United States. In an 1865 editorial, the *New York*

Times declared that "if there were to be a flood-tide of Chinese population—a population befouled with all the social vices, with no knowledge or appreciation of free institution or constitutional liberty ... we should be prepared to bid farewell to republicanism and democracy."[34]

Politicians continued to credit all the popular fears and charges. In his inaugural address in 1862, Gov. Leland Stanford called for legislation to check further Chinese immigration. "There can be no doubt," he warned, "that the presence among us of numbers of a degraded and distinct people must exercise a deleterious influence upon the superior race, and to a certain extent repel desirable immigration."[35] Furthermore, unlike in the 1850s, some invectives directed against the Chinese business class began to appear in the late 1860s. An anti-coolie meeting in 1868, for example, was composed of persons who were "opposed to the continuance of commercial and social relations between China and the United States."[36]

The Birth of a National *Huiguan*

In the late 1850s and early 1860s, there was an urgent need for one organization that would oversee the welfare of all Chinese in the United States. First, and most important, anti-Chinese sentiment and discriminatory legislation was aimed at all Chinese in the United States, not just certain groups, which made it imperative to have an inclusive organization. In addition, having one overarching society would provide a better means for solving disputes between members of the different *huiguan*.[37] As William Hoy says, "Naturally, since the courts and majority of the Americans were plainly prejudiced against the Chinese, the latter didn't bring their disputes to the American courts for settlement."[38] The frequent and notorious feuds among the fighting tongs who were trying to control "Chinese vices" heightened the need for an overall organization to help keep peace and order among the Chinese.

As a consequence in the late 1850s the Gangzhou *huiguan*, Ningyang *huiguan*, Sanyi *huiguan*, Yanghe *huiguan*, and Renhe *huiguan* came together and jointly established the Zhonghua Gongshuo (Chung Wah Kung Saw; meaning the Chinese national public place association). This *huiguan* federation then recruited the Hehe (Hop Wo) *huiguan* and so earned its unofficial name, the Chinese Six Companies. We do not know the exact year of its founding because "whatever records of it having been long since destroyed."[39] According to Hoy, "historical evidence" supports "the fact that it was established prior to 1862."[40] But the following story provides evidence that it may have been founded before 1860. On January 3, 1860, "six Chinese," representing the "Chinese district associations," visited the Rev. A. W. Loomis, William Speer's successor as head of the San Francisco mission to the Chinese from the Presbyterian Board of

Foreign Missions in Philadelphia. The leaders of the *huiguan* told him that Speer had championed the Chinese against anti-Chinese sentiment and asked if Loomis would continue to provide assistance. Loomis replied that although he did not want to be overly involved in politics, he would try to help. In less than a month, Loomis found a lawyer, a former city judge, to lobby for the Chinese, and the leaders of the six *huiguan* approved his choice. As Charles McClain points out: "The episode, however, clearly demonstrates the well-developed political consciousness of some Chinese (here the leadership of the most important organizations in the community) at this very early period in the history of immigration and their willingness to make aggressive use of American institutions to protect Chinese interests."[41]

It should be noted that "Six Companies" was "a term bestowed on the organization by the Americans." The Chinese name, which was originally Chung Wah Kung Saw (Zhonghua Gongshuo or Chinese national public place association), was changed to Chung Wah Wui Kwoon (Zhonghua Huiguan or Chinese national native-place association). "This was a change in terminology only, since the characters for both Kung Saw and Wui Kwoon could, in actual use, mean the same thing, that is, a meeting hall or assembly place."[42] Whatever the year of establishment, the formal Chinese name for the combined federations had undoubtedly been accepted and established before 1860. Its appearance in California marked a new epoch in modern Chinese history, for it was the first national federation of native-place associations. Later the Zhaoqing *huiguan* and the Enkai *huiguan* were formed, but they too joined the Six Companies. Although the number of *huiguan* was no longer six, Americans still called the overarching organization the Six Companies.[43]

Clearly the Six Companies was a federation of the *huiguan* in California, with a central headquarters for top-level liaisons and a mandate to deal with problems concerning all the Chinese in the United States. All Chinese, not just groups from separate small districts, were eligible for membership in the Six Companies, which kept a register of names and addresses for all the Chinese in the United States.[44]

The administration of the Six Companies consisted of a board of presidents and a board of directors. The presidents of each individual *huiguan* made up the board of presidents, the chairman of which, was appointed in round-robin process. The chairman became president of the Six Companies. Therefore, each president of a *huiguan* had an opportunity to serve as president of the Six Companies at least once during his term as head of his *huiguan*.[45] The board of directors was elected according to a system of proportional representation: "In apportioning delegates to the Chinese Six Companies to serve as members of its board of directors, each district company is allowed one representative per 500 members in its roster."[46] Usually these officials met one or two times a month to discuss the matters concerning the Chinese as a whole.[47] In the late nineteenth century, it was Chinese merchants who occupied most of the important positions of *huiguan* leadership in the Six Companies. "They dominated the presidencies, vice presidencies, boards of directors, and committee chairs."[48]

Like other *huiguan,* the Six Companies was a combined charitable, mutual-aid, and self-defense society, in addition to serving as a judicial system for dealing with both internal disputes and external assaults. In the late 1860s it collected and remitted to Canton the savings of the migrant Chinese, sending from $20,000 to $100,000 by each steamer. "This amount is made up of thousands of small sums from $2 to $100, which are sent by the poorer class of Chinamen to their parents or friends."[49] William Hoy, who was eventually a secretary of the Six Companies, stated that the association was responsible for the care of deceased Chinese throughout California, "arranging for the shipment of their bones back to China for final burial"; it also "organized general community medical and hospitalization services for sick and indigent Chinese."[50] When discussing the Six Companies in 1864, the *San Francisco Evening Bulletin* also reported: "The bones of every Chinaman who died on the passage to this country are preserved and sent back. No Chinese are ever buried at sea."[51]

The Six Companies settled complicated disputes and those among individuals in different *huiguan.* For example, the constitution of the Yanghe *huiguan* stipulated that disputes with members of other companies should be reported to the *huiguan* agents. If necessary, they should "be referred for the judgment of the five companies [predecessor of the Six Companies] conjointly."[52] Hoy summarized the situation in 1942: "It [the Six Companies] functioned as a general board of arbitration to handle all disputes referred to it by the district associations."[53]

As was true of decisions of the individual *huiguan,* complainants who did not accept decisions of the Six Companies could then make an appeal to the American courts. The Rev. Otis Gibson of San Francisco gave an example in the 1870s that involved two groups of quarreling Chinese. At first, they called upon the Six Companies to help settle their problem. However, one group refused to accept the decision as final and so asked Gibson "to write to the Judge of the Court to tell him that they were right and others wrong."[54]

Also a place for worship, the Six Companies established a temple in 1864 for the Chinese to offer sacrifices to the gods or spirits of the dead; it was an "odd-looking piece of graveyard furniture, in the highest point of the western edge of the hill at Lone Mountain cemetery." Because there was "a fine view of the Pacific Ocean," those worshiping could "kneel at their devotions, out towards the 'Central Flowery Empire.'" It was also reported that idols or idealistic images were placed on the pavement on either side of the marble tablet.[55]

Funding for the Six Companies came from two regular sources—contributions from each subsidiary *huiguan* and regular fees from "all Chinese individuals above eighteen years who are on the point of making a trip to China."[56] "There is some evidence that for a long period no Chinaman could obtain passage home unless he presented a card of demission from some one of the Six Companies."[57] Because the number of trustees assigned to the board of directors varied according to the numerical membership of each of the *huiguan*, the financial contributions by each *huiguan* were also different.[58] Of the Six Companies, the largest and most powerful was the Ningyang *huiguan* (Ning Yong Company), while the smallest was the Renhe *huiguan* (Yan Wo Company).[59]

The Six Companies took the place of the individual *huiguan* in championing all Chinese in the United States against anti-Chinese action. The Six Companies "employed a dozen private policemen and watchmen to watch and guard the Chinese stores and properties of the Chinese inside Chinatown,... [and it] fought through legal counsel, all anti-Chinese legislation enacted by the city, state and Federal governments."[60]

Soon after its establishment the Six Companies began to act as the lobbyist for all Chinese in the United States. Refuting anti-Chinese charges continued. In response to revived charges that the *huiguan* were labor brokers, the Six Companies sent a communication to the Joint Committee of the Legislature on the Chinese Question to deny that the Chinese had imported any slaves: "We deny, most emphatically, that there are any Chinese held to service or labor as slaves in this state." They then asked the committee "to make a thorough examination of this charge of the Chinese being held to service or labor," which was "erroneous in every particular."[61]

It was in this period that the Chinese leaders began to realize that the greatest argument against immigration restriction was the American Constitution. Citing its emphasis on equality, they demanded that the United States live up to its own professed standards. By testing the constitutionality of discrimination, they tried through court cases to obtain an authoritative ruling on the status of all Chinese immigrants. In 1862, for example, California passed legislation imposing a tax of $2.50 per month, called the Chinese Police Tax, on almost all the Chinese living in California. After paying $5 to a tax collector, one Chinese, named Lin Sing, immediately brought suit for a refund.[62] The *Sacramento Record-Union* reported concerning this challenge: "The several Chinese organizations [*huiguan*] in this city and state are making arrangements to test in the Supreme Court the constitutionality of the Police Tax Law. Those of this city are in negotiation with N. Greene Curtis and J. W. Coffroth to represent them in the case."[63] The Chinese failed in the county court but appealed the matter to the California Supreme Court and succeeded. That the Chinese Tax Law singled out the Chinese for taxation, the California Supreme Court concluded, discriminated against foreign trade, an exclusive domain of the national government.[64]

Like the *huiguan* leaders in the 1850s, the Six Companies continued to work on improving the Chinese image, which they hoped would regain the confidence of the American public and authorities in the Chinese, who would thus achieve acceptance and equality. As part of this effort, the Six Companies was especially determined to curb Chinese prostitution in San Francisco's Chinatown.[65] Early in 1864, for example, a shipment of thirty Chinese prostitutes landed in San Francisco before the Six Companies could stop them. The *San Francisco Alta California* afterwards reported: "These [women] have been, so far as possible, gathered together by the agents of the Companies, taken from the haunts of vice on Jackson Street and Bartlett Alley, by force, in some instance, and will be sent home to their parents on the first vessel."[66] In another instance, in July 1964, on the basis of information from the Six Companies that a group of Chinese prostitutes was being brought to California, San Francisco policemen boarded a vessel and took off nineteen Chinese prostitutes.[67] In September 1867, the presidents of the Six Companies sent a letter to P. Crowley, the chief of police, and A. Rix, the judge of the Police Court, informing them that an incoming steamer was arriving with many women intended for prostitution on board. Knowing the practice of having some Chinese men among the passengers claim these women as their wives and thus smuggle them into the United States, the Six Companies officials offered to provide assistance in ascertaining whether the women were actually the wives of the men who wished to bring them ashore. The letter emphasized in conclusion: "By the presence of such women, in the city and state, the good name of our people and the honor of our country has heretofore greatly suffered."[68]

To keep order, the leaders of the Chinese community developed a program of giving the names of law breakers to the police and providing rewards for information leading to the arrest of these criminals.[69] In the 1860s the Six Companies also employed private white policemen to patrol Chinatown, and the group tried to send some Chinese vagrants back to China.[70] On November 17, 1867, for example, the Six Companies informed a police judge that they would provide passage home for three mendicants who were convicted and sentenced in the Police Court.[71]

Such efforts elicited praise from American newspapers. The *San Francisco Alta California* commented in 1864, for example: "The Companies certainly deserve credit for their praiseworthy efforts to put a stop to this accursed traffic in human beings, and we trust that they may be successful."[72] The efforts of the Six Companies "should relieve them from the charge of being in any manner implicated in the importation of female slaves for vile purposes, which demagogues have made against them."[73] Again in 1868 the *San Francisco Alta California* stated: "In this concern for the morals and well-being of their countrymen and countrywomen, they set us an example we might well follow."[74]

Qing China Enters the Family of Nations

Before continuing the discussion of the Six Companies in 1868 and 1869, however, we need to turn our attention to the Qing government, which was under no less pressure for a fundamental change in its approach to foreign relations in the early 1860s than the *huiguan* in the United States. It was the British who first expressed a hope that China would send envoys to England immediately after the Beijing treaties in 1860, and. according to the Zongli Yamen (Office for the Management of the Business of All Foreign Countries), the foreign ministers in Beijing also repeatedly requested from that time on that Chinese diplomatic representatives be appointed to go abroad.[75] Without modern diplomatic experience, China was unprepared for Western contact;[76] and this was clearly indicated in the "secret" memorials and "secret" letters of the Qing officials. In its memorial asking the emperor's permission to send Bin Chun and his entourage to Europe in 1866, for example, the Zongli Yamen stated that the Qing government, since it had no knowledge of the West, had nothing upon which to base a wise foreign policy, and mistakes would be hard to avoid. The Zongli Yamen considered it an excellent opportunity to send Bin Chun abroad on a short-term mission, since he would bring back much needed information.[77]

After the Bin Chun mission, the Zongli Yamen became increasingly aware of its own unpreparedness and submitted another secret memorial to the court in 1867. After stressing the advantages of sending missions abroad, it acknowledged that suitable men for a permanent mission were hard to find. An unsuitable envoy, it said, would invite contempt from the foreigners and would be easy prey to Western duplicity.[78]

Similar opinions were expressed in other "secret" letters. On October 12, 1867, in a secret imperial decree to all the leading provincial officials soliciting more opinions, the Yamen once again expressed its unpreparedness: in addition to language difficulties, it could not find persons who had the ability to handle situations "independently" and who were "good at initiating and maintaining things."[79]

The opinions of the Zongli Yamen were echoed and expanded in the secret replies of various high officials. Concerning the language and cultural difficulties, for example, Ying Gui, the governor-general of Henan, stated that the language barrier would make it difficult for Chinese ministers to avoid strife and insult. Even if they were suitably conversant with foreign languages, he argued further, it would be impossible to secure a profound knowledge of the cultural fundamentals immediately.[80]

In discussing the possible establishment of Qing legations abroad in the late 1860s, Qing officials did, however, demonstrate their knowledge of how foreigners used their merchants in diplomatic affairs. Shen Baozhen, the director-general of the Fuzhou Naval Dockyard, answered to the Zongli Yaman's secret letter on December 16, 1867, pointing out that foreign ministers relied on their merchants and missionaries for spying out China's actual conditions because they were scattered over the interior of China and had daily contact with Chinese officials and people.[81] If foreign merchants worked well in for these purposes, perhaps Chinese merchants could help establish Chinese legations in other countries.[82] In his reply to the secret letter, Cong Hou, the superintendent of trade for the Northern Ports and Left Palace Attendant of the Ministry of War, suggested that the problem of expenses in foreign countries might be solved by cooperation between the overseas Chinese merchants and the Chinese envoys.[83]

Similar attitudes can also be found in another secret letter in 1867. Only after "careful consideration," Zuo Zongtang, the governor-general of Shanxi and Gansu, stated, could Chinese merchants be used in future Chinese missions abroad. Even though there must be many scholars and merchants from the seaports of Jiangsu, Zhenjiang, Fujian, and Guangdong who were thoroughly versed in foreign languages, it was not wise to make use of them without careful consideration, because some of them were "unsteady, deceptive" and made "trouble." He suggested that the governor-general, provincial governors, and the imperial commissioner in charge of the Fuzhou shipyard be given the responsibility for carefully seeking out and choosing appropriate men to fulfill the duties of Chinese ministers.[84] The suspicions Qing officials had of merchants stemmed partially from their traditional disdain for merchants. As almost all Qing officials had been trained in the Confucian classics, without exception they were influenced by the Confucian bias against commercial activity.

Even before all the replies to the secret letter had been received, the Zongli Yamen decided to send another short-term mission to the United States and Europe to persuade the Western powers not to be too severe toward China. The unpreparedness of the Qing government was further highlighted by the Zongli Yamen in its recommendation in October 1867 to the court: "The lack of [suitable] men to go abroad indeed baffles us. Now that Burlingame [Anson

Burlingame] intends to make a name for himself, readily taking the task upon himself, we believe his sentiments to be sincere."[85]

In addition to acknowledging their unpreparedness among themselves, Qing officials also confessed this weakness to their foreign friends. In the autumn of 1870, Wen-xiang, a minister in the Zongli Yamen, paid a visit to William H. Seward, who was in Beijing in the course of a round-the-world tour after being the secretary of the state. In their conversation Seward expressed "the hope of sending consuls to other countries, who could look after the interests of Chinese emigrants there, and represent their condition and wishes to Qing government." In reply to this kindness Wen-xiang highlighted the "only difficulty"—the lack of qualified persons—"that the Emperor had this in view and the only difficulty in the way had been the want of qualified men to perform diplomatic duties."[86]

The Diplomatic Activism of the Six Companies

The Chinese in California felt great excitement when they heard the astounding news that Anson Burlingame had been accredited Chinese plenipotentiary to the United States and Europe. Soon after his arrival to San Francisco in April 1868, the presidents of the Six Companies paid a formal visit to Zhigang and Sun Jiagu, two Chinese envoys of the Burlingame mission, in order to draw attention to the issues of Chinese equality and rights. To illustrate that they were victims of discrimination, the presidents stressed that the Foreign Miners' License Tax was aimed exclusively at Chinese miners and that evidence offered by Chinese individuals was never accepted in American courts; Chinese plaintiffs had to produce white men as witnesses. They asked the two Qing officials to complain to the American government about this injustice and discrimination. Zhigang and Sun Jiagu replied that Burlingame would discuss with the American government ways to redress their grievances.[87]

The news that Daniel Cleveland was preparing a report on the Chinese in California in preparation for treaty negotiations between the United States and China led the Six Companies to ask Cleveland for a meeting. Airing their grievances again before Cleveland, the presidents hoped the Chinese would gain equality and be protected by just legislation. They promised Cleveland that better protection would certainly result in more Chinese investment in the permanent improvement of California. In return, Cleveland suggested that the presidents should prepare a paper detailing the misery they had experienced and protection they considered essential to their security.[88] It is obvious that the meeting was a success for the Chinese. Their influence on Cleveland was clearly shown in his letter dated July 27 to J. Ross Browne, the U.S. minister to China. The letter concerned an evaluation of the Chinese in California "to be laid before the United States Government," which emphasized the advantages of Chinese immigration to the development of California.[89] Cleveland wrote again on February 10, 1869, to Browne that the Chinese were "a very valuable part of the permanent population" in life, business, employment, and contribution to revenues.[90]

Evidence shows that the negotiations were a success for the Six Companies. The Burlingame Treaty of 1868 gave the Chinese the same footing as other nationalities. Of the eight articles of treaty, three were directly related to the protection of Chinese rights in the United States. Article 4 granted entire liberty of conscience to the Chinese in the United States, exempted them from all persecution on account of religious faith or worship, and provided that cemeteries for the dead should be held in respect and free from disturbance. In Article 6, the Chinese were guaranteed the same privileges, immunities, and exemptions to travel or residence as were enjoyed by nationals of the most favored nations. Although it did not confer on the Chinese the right to be naturalized, the article secured for them coverage under the equal protection clause of the Fourteenth Amendment. Article 7 ensured the Chinese equal access to the educational institutions of the United States and their right to establish and maintain schools.[91] In addition to these protection items, the Burlingame Treaty granted Chinese the "inalienable right" of free immigration.

In fact, Burlingame had overstepped his authority because he had not obtained prior permission from the Zongli Yamen before signing the treaty. The Qing government nevertheless accepted the treaty due to the understanding that Zhigang, Sun Jiagu, and the other officials had of the Six Companies' petition and their sympathy for the Chinese in the United States. When submitting the text of the treaty to the Qing government, Zhigang and Sun Jiagu not only repeated the Six Companies' arguments emphasizing that the Chinese were not allowed to act as witnesses in American courts and were singled out to pay a special tax, but also pointed out that the Qing government needed to send officials there to prevent the Chinese from becoming a lower social stratum in America.[92] The Qing government accepted this interpretation of the treaty. In a letter to Burlingame, Prince Gong and the Zongli Yamen expressed their sympathy for the Chinese: "We trust and hope that after the treaty has been put into force, the Chinese in California will cease to be subjected to the ill-treatment they have hitherto met with."[93] Without making any modification in its terms, the Qing government ratified the treaty in 1869.

The Six Companies continued to work on the issue of Chinese prostitution, which it saw as a shame and one of the major reasons for the anti-Chinese movement.[94] They not only cooperated with the San Francisco chief of police to send recently arrived prostitutes back to China,[95] they also requested that the governor of California use his influence with the steamship companies to curb the prostitute traffic by requiring new women immigrants to show certificates of good character signed and sealed by an agent in Hong Kong.[96]

In 1868 the Six Companies sent a comprehensive petition to the United States Congress for the purpose of suppressing vice among the Chinese. In it three items discussed prostitution, gambling, and the management of criminal cases. Article 9, entitled "A request for the adjustment of the difficulties in regard to abandoned women," asked that the American Congress enact laws "for the correction of this grievance" so that the Chinese would be rid of "this spreading poison" and be relieved of "this disgrace." Under the heading "A petition that gambling may be severely punished," Article 10 appealed to Congress to pass a law against this practice. "If people knew that they must rigidly obey it, and if from this time forth there shall be no secret granting of licenses, then we might hope that those who had learned this vice might return to honest occupations."[97] Article 11, "A request in regard to the management of criminal cases," demanded extraterritorial rights to manage Chinese criminals: "Among our Chinese there are some bad people," they reasoned, and "only the Chinese can know who they are." If American government granted Chinese merchants extraterritorial rights, they would "prepare private statements as to such persons, vouching for them by the signature of their names." Thus criminals would be "justly punished" and "deterred from the commission of crimes."[98] Certainly, although its own intentions were honorable, the Six Companies' ability to control others was limited. Those engaged in illegal pursuits were desperate, lawless characters who sought revenge when interfered with. Under such circumstances it was not strange that the Six Companies asked for extraterritorial rights.

Soon after the Burlingame Treaty was signed, the Six Companies tried to use the very principle of the nation-state system—the sanctity of treaties—to justify its protests. In 1869, at the Six Companies' banquet for the Congressional Subcommittee on Ways and Means, which including Senator Benjamin Wade of Ohio and Senator Roscoe Conkling of New York,[99] Fung Tang, a spokesman of the Six Companies, gave a formal address in which he complained that the miners' tax was "not according to our treaty with your government" and that it was not only unfair for the Chinese to be singled out for taxation—"We are willing to pay taxes cheerfully, when taxed equally with others"—but also such discrimination also contradicted America's claim to be "a free country." Finally he protested the ban on Chinese testimony in court: "Most of all, we feel the want of protection to life and property when Courts of Justice refuse our testimony, and thus leave us defenseless, and unable to obtain justice for ourselves."[100] After pointing out that "China is a very old nation, but our people have learned many new things from Americans," he highlighted the importance of the China trade for the enhancement of collective development—a typical goal of any nation-state. Tang assured his audience that if the United States enacted just laws to protect Chinese, the trade would be very "intimate." If the Chinese felt sure they had full and proper protection, much gold and silver hoarded in China could be used profitably in the United States. He further emphasized Chinese merchants were very honest and fair in their dealing with American merchants. At last, and consistent with the development of agriculture in California in this period, he called attention to the fact that "we have introduced your grain and other American produce into China, and labored to establish a trade, which, properly encouraged, must prove of great value to this country." He concluded with a plea for them to "speak favorably of us to the United States Government."[101]

The criticisms of the Chinese Six Companies were effective. On December 6, 1869, Senator William Stewart of Nevada urged Congress to make an investigation if any states denied any class of persons the equal protection of the law, violated treaty obligations with foreign countries, or violated the Fourteenth Amendment to the Constitution. He raised the question again on the floor of Congress on December 22, 1869, and May 20, 1870.[102] In addition, the Civil Rights Act of 1870, although applying specifically to the civil rights of blacks, also contained a friendly tone for the protection of the Chinese: All persons in the United States, it emphasized, have the same right to "sue, . . . give evidence, and to the full and equal benefit of all laws and proceedings for the security of person and property as is enjoyed by white citizens . . . any law, statute . . . to the contrary notwithstanding." In addition, "no tax" should be imposed "by any State upon any person immigrating thereto from a foreign country which is not equally imposed and enforced upon every person immigrating to such State from any other foreign country."[103]

The appearance of the Six Companies around 1860 was a profound event, for it indicated a radical departure from the traditional pattern of narrow local-place identity. What previous students of the *huiguan* have failed to perceive is the importance of the Six Companies' formal Chinese name: Zhonghua *huiguan* meaning Chinese national native-place association. Never prior to this in Chinese history had any domestic *huiguan* or *huiguan* confederacy engraved "China" on its badge. Nor had Chinese identity transformed itself from "cultural" to "national" "in the past one or two centuries," as Townsend argues.[104] It was the overseas Chinese in the United States who had to confront the issue of identity because of the differences between the Chinese and the indigenous American population and the hostility the Chinese faced because of these differences. The Six Companies, the Zhonghua *huiguan*, the Chinese national native-place association is a crucial institution in the development of nationalism in the changing self-perception of Chinese.[105]

What is impressive about the Six Companies is not simply the national consciousness the organization represented, but also the fact that it immediately began acting in a manner congruent with the system of modern nation-states. Clearly the traditional Chinese world order could not protect the overseas Chinese from anti-Chinese activities because there was no Chinese diplomatic representation in the United States or in other countries either. In any case the tributary system was already clearly doomed. The only unified Chinese action against anti-Chinese sentiment in the United States came from the leaders of the Six Companies, who not only brought Chinese *huiguan* traditions with them to California but also quickly adopted democratic ideas when they arrived. In this country, which professed these ideals, they were not likely to accept discrimination and exclusion. The Six Companies was obviously more powerful and better equipped to deal with self-defense than any individual *huiguan* or other Chinese organization in San Francisco.

The leaders of the Six Companies saw the importance of treaties in the new nation-state system—the concept of sovereignty implies that there is no high power than the authority of the nation-state and that no international law is legitimate unless the state has accepted it. The Chinese leaders' activities in helping to make and later to guard the Burlingame Treaty are unquestionable. Obviously they had learned that treaty inviolability kept nations in comparative safety and security. They also found that in the United States the legal mechanics of the modern nation-state system gave their constituents better protection. In this period the Six Companies began to test the constitutionality of anti-Chinese laws, which would become one of the main themes of the Chinese struggle against exclusion in the later part of the nineteenth century.

The 1860s were also a time of great change in the official identity of the Chinese and the official Chinese approach to foreign relations. Before the 1860s, China believed that no other polity could have equal status with China. After the first Opium War, China slowly yielded to external pressure and moved inevitably toward becoming a modern nation-state. China would send its official representatives abroad, but diplomatic representation, universally common among Western states since the Renaissance, was unknown to China. A totally new international order and new social customs, not to mention language difficulties, proved major impediments for the Qing government in direct Sino-foreign interaction. This may have been one of the basic causes of China's unpreparedness to establish missions abroad in the 1860s and, as never before, the choice of Anson Burlingame in 1868 as the Chinese minister to Western countries. It is also why Americans everywhere acclaimed the trip as "the dawn of a great new era in Sino-American relations" and "the importance of which and the amount of which no man can compute."[106]

CHAPTER 4

• • • • • •

Becoming the Chief Target

The Six Companies in the 1870s

> Chico, March 17th—This morning a terrible feverish excitement prevailed all through town when it became known that a number of citizens had received threatening notices. These notices were all mailed last night after eight o'clock, and read: "get rid of your Chinese help within fifteen days or suffer the consequences," signed, "Committee." An officer received a notice cautioning him that if he took any means to find out who killed the Chinamen he would himself be killed. Talk is common on the street of forming a Vigilance Committee.
>
> —"Latest from Chico"

One question, which first arose at the beginning of the Chinese immigration but has persisted to the present, is whether the Six Companies acted as the chief labor broker for the Chinese during the late nineteenth century. In 1987, for example, Patricia Cloud and David Galenson used the records of the legislative hearings of 1876 to assert that the Six Companies played a central role in importing Chinese laborers. In response Charles McClain branded the charges and the argument as groundless assertions: "No first-person accounts of their experiences by 19th century Chinese immigrants have to my knowledge survived."[1] However logical the arguments may be, they have only skimmed the surface of the problem. This is not an isolated issue, but just one aspect of the Chinese experience in America in the late nineteenth century, especially in the 1870s. The problem requires examination in a wider context.

The Success of the Chinese Business Class

In the 1870s it seemed that Chinese merchants were bound to be successful in the new market economy of California.[2] One single company, Macondrary & Co. of San Francisco, did $500,000 to $600,000 of trade each year.[3]

Their dealings with Simon L. Jones were as high as $1 million a year.[4] The company also transported about $700,000 worth of wheat annually during this period from San Francisco to Hong Kong.[5] In 1878 total imports from China jumped to $18,128,042, while exports to China reached $23,079,586.[6]

Their industries also attained fame along with their success. When Judge Grover Galloway gave his testimony before the Senatorial Chinese Commission that same year, he said that the operations of Chinese miners were often very profitable. "The Chinese for several years worked more men along the banks in the beds of the different forks of the Yuba River than the whites, and made more money than the whites."[7] For example, between 1870 and 1874 Hong Fook Kong & Co., a Chinese mining company, filed claims of 600 feet.[8] In 1876 the *Idaho Statesman* reported that Man See & Company, another Chinese mining company, owned a claim that was worth $20,000.[9]

The Chinese also became factory owners. Many Chinese bourgeois who began their careers as workers used their employment in American factories as a stepping-stone to their own businesses. The *San Francisco Chronicle* of April 4, 1873, described the process: "Our contractors find that as soon as they learn the trade of making boots and shoes they abandon their employers and set up shop for themselves, or go to work for Chinese employers, so that our contractors are constantly engaged in teaching them the trade."[10] In 1876 it was said the cigar industry of San Francisco had passed "entirely" into Chinese hands. The *San Francisco Chronicle* further commented: "Originally knowing nothing about boot and shoe making, they have made such rapid strides in this trade that no other class of workmen are able to compete with them."[11] Like the Chinese merchants, Chinese manufacturing activities went beyond San Francisco. In Virginia City in the mid-1870s, for example, they dominated the woodcutting and peddling businesses.[12]

The Chinese continued their efforts to establish good relationships with Americans. Chinese merchants made donations for the victims of the Chicago fire in 1871. "The contributions thus given by the merchants reached $1290. Not bad for the 'Heathen Chinese.'" The *San Francisco Alta California* continued: "Have the class of beings in human form who beat and maltreat the Chinese, given one dollar to the relief of the Chicago people in their terrible distress?"[13] Tom Quan, a prominent Chinese merchant, hosted a party on February 27, 1877, whose guests included Maj. Gen. Rufus Ingalls, U.S.A., Pay Director John S. Cunningham, U.S.N., Col. Frederick A. Bee, and Messrs. J. G. Kellogg, B. S. Brooks, C. Koopmanschap, and so on. At the banquet, after the chopsticks came knives and forks, and a toast followed. "The health of Caleb Cushing, our first Minister to China, who took an active part in the formation of the original treaty with the Celestial Empire, and of Senator Morton, were duly pledged."[14] In 1876 a number of Chinese merchants donated $500 to the Centennial Fund of California for an exhibition in Philadelphia.[15] It was the first subscription fully paid up, the *San Francisco Alta California* marveled, and furthermore they gave their money to the California fund rather than the Chinese government, which also intended to have its own display at the exhibition. The Chinese merchants, through their contribution, showed "an identification with their adopted home."[16]

The Chinese continued to enjoy a good reputation among some Americans. In 1876, B. S. Gibbs, who had been an adjuster of marine losses in San Francisco for more than twenty-eight years, testified before the Joint Special Committee to Investigate Chinese Immigration: "As men of integrity, I have never met a more honorable, high-minded, correct and truthful set of men than the Chinese merchants of our city."[17] Similarly, Simon L. Jones, an auctioneer for Jones, Benedict & Co. of San Francisco, stated that Chinese merchants were "very reliable" and "honest in their dealings."[18] Frederick W. Macondrary, an American merchant who was a member of Macondrary & Co. testified: "From all our dealings with them here and in China I do not know any class of merchants, I think, who are more honest and upright or who have a better reputation for integrity than the Chinese."[19]

The Effect of the Anti-Chinese Movement on Chinese Merchants

Anti-Chinese sentiment intensified, however, when the depression of 1873 finally reached California in 1876. The fate of Chinese merchants, like that of Chinese labor, was inescapable. An employer of Chinese shoemakers testified at the State Senate Hearings in 1876: "For businessmen to employ Chinese is simply putting nails in their coffins" because, the employer reasoned, they learn quickly and then "go off into their own business," becoming competitors.[20] In 1878 a *San Francisco Post* article complained about the competitive power of Chinese merchants in the trade between the two countries. The American merchants were "losing their foot hold in China" because Chinese merchants, "having acquired our methods," were "monopolizing all the avenues of trade and commerce." The article continued: "If permitted to settle permanently on this coast, [they] will very soon make it impossible for Americans to exist here by industry or commerce."[21] The article warned that it would be only a matter of time before the Chinese monopolized the whole industry.

During the economic dislocations, American laborers were frightened and restless about the danger of any large influx of Chinese. A large Chinese labor market meant lower wages for American laborers as well as greater competition among them.[22] Obviously, white men worried that the Chinese, working for much less than they, would reduce the price of labor so materially that they could not make a living. In the late 1870s there was not much doubt that the Chinese were replacing white labor in many important industries. Therefore, the Caucasian must check the Chinese, or the Chinese would check the Caucasian.

China's famine from 1876 to 1879, "one of the direst calamities that ever afflicted the human race," further troubled and scared American labor. The *San Francisco Call* of March 6, 1878 stated that "after the first famine, if unrestricted immigration was admitted by the United States, California would soon be deluged with Chinamen." It further pointed out, although the reporter had "never seen one of these contracts," the "contracting" party for California was the Six Companies, and it had "imported more than nine-tenths of all the Chinese who have come to this State." Because of this "direct and remorseless competition" with white labor, "the inevitable effect must be to reduce the wages of free labor to that crushing level, and send the white workingman and his family from the house to the hovel, where in a generation or two he will become as abject and spiritless and hopeless a slave as ever tenanted cabin in the Carolinas or hut in the steppes of Russia."[23]

The warning evoked wide repercussions. An article entitled "Chinese Immigration" in the *San Francisco Chronicle* agreed that the famine would be "a spur to emigration," that "without prohibitory measures on our part... within the next half century 100,000,000 Mongols may thrust their ungainly and unwelcome presence upon our posterity."[24] The *San Francisco Bulletin* declared: "Since it is highly improbable that the Chinese Government will carry out internal improvements to remedy the effects of these deadly famines, it is extremely likely that it will encourage emigration."[25] Public sentiment against Chinese immigration became stronger and stronger. Senator James Gillespie Blaine declared: "As soon as the Chinese shall discover that they have a safe and firm footing in California, they will flock here in such vast number as to 'swamp the white race,' because their numbers are inexhaustible and their country over peopled by at least 100,000,000."[26] The *San Francisco Post* asked a rhetorical question: "What is not possible for the Chinese Six Companies to do, with famine-stricken China to recruit from, if the immigration of Chinamen be not absolutely prohibited?"[27]

These arguments carried weight with the American people and trouble for the Chinese ensured. As an illustration of what the newcomers experienced, a story of 1878 may be cited. On May 17, about 250 Chinese arrived in San Francisco after a long voyage and landed with their freights at the foot of Front Street. A large number of express wagons traveled and fro between Chinatown and the pier to transfer the new arrivals, and throughout the morning the wharf was one vast energetic scene. Front Street Wharf was located in the shadow of an outcrop about 200 feet high, upon the top of which was an aggressive anti-Chinese settlement. The wagons containing the Chinese were at the base of the bluff and the upper community "showered down upon each wagon a cloud of stones." Some Chinese were injured by the stones. Two officers named Low and Eaton visited the locality attempting to quiet the aggressors. However, the stones rained more abundantly and soon, the officers also became targets. One stone hit Eaton on the hand and he only evaded a more devastating collision by a lucky ducking of his head.[28]

Major violence against Chinese laborers elsewhere caused large numbers to flee to San Francisco for protection,[29] which placed a major burden on the Chinese merchants because as *huiguan* leaders they had to take care of them. In a conversation in 1876 between Wing How, the president of Sanyi (Sam Yap) Company, and a *Chronicle* reporter, Wing How grumbled that Chinese immigration "hurts us as much as it does you," since there were more "here now than we can find work for, and we can't afford to support them in idleness . . . the wealthiest company will soon grow poor if the drain on its resources is continually increasing beyond the limits of its income."[30]

The anti-Chinese forces repeated old arguments, painting the Chinese as the most vicious heathen, which they published in pamphlets, essays, and other literary products. The rhetoric for exclusion impugned the Chinese business class as well, since the majority of the charges in the anti-Chinese movement were general accusations that made no distinction between laborers and those of higher class. After publication of the report by a joint congressional committee sent to California to investigate the Chinese problem in 1876, the *New York Herald* judged that the report provided Americans with "authentic and incontestable truth of what has been so often related to the beastliness, the filth, squalor, leprosy, venereal diseases, the lawlessness, perjury and violence, the corruption of youth and injury to the laboring classes that make the Chinese quarter of San Francisco a huge festering ulcer which is eating into the morals of the country."[31] Some Americans believed that the nation's bloodstream would be poisoned by Chinese prostitution, a fear given reality in "White Lepers in San Francisco—A Pest Brought from China," in which the *New York Herald* quoted the testimony of a sailor who claimed he had caught leprosy from a Chinese prostitute.[32] In 1878 the *San Francisco Post* painted a picture of the filthy state of the Chinatown: "Hundreds of other buildings far worse than those condemned have been allowed to remain, their fever and disease breeding slums permitted to be unnoticed and unchallenged."[33] The following year the *San Francisco Call* claimed: "They buy women as they do cattle, and sell them when tired of their purchase. Of the many relations which the sexes have sustained to each other in the progress from barbarism to civilization, the Chinese system is about the worst."[34]

Chinese "heathenism" was also highlighted in Congress and became a national question. Senator James Augustus Johnson of California in 1870 charged Chinese immigrants were "a multitude bearing pestilence in their garments and seeping with filth and decay."[35] They were also disturbed by Chinese criminal gangs, or fighting tongs. For example, Senator Aaron Sargent of California complained: "These feuds among the Chinese are frequent and notorious. Can we stand all the vices, all the diseases, all the mischief that infect humanity the world over and retain our American civilization?"[36] In an address at Golden Hill, Nevada, Senator John Percival Jones summarized the Chinese question in one sentence: "They corrupt our youth with their vices, and they starve our men with their virtues."[37] In order to clear the way, the Burlingame Treaty, which granted Chinese free immigration to the United States, must be modified. Senator Sargent therefore sent a letter in November 1877 to William M. Evarts, the secretary of state suggesting that "your department would earn the gratitude of the Pacific Coast and deserve well of the country if it would address itself to the task of remodeling our treaties with China."[38] On December 16, Congressman H. F. Page sent a letter to President Rutherford B. Hayes to call his "early and earnest attention" to the question of Chinese immigration.[39] Congressman Horace Davis had an interview with President Hayes on December 18, 1877, hoping to influence his judgment concerning the Chinese question. In the interview, which lasted two hours, the President at last "significantly outlined his position."[40] In an address to Congress in 1878 he argued that "the opposition to Chinese immigration is not confined to any particular class or race; but that it is the sentiment and desire of all, except the very few whose pecuniary interests are subserved by coolie labor."[41] In January 1878 it was reported that President Hayes, "in a forthcoming message," would urge upon Congress the necessity of some action concerning the Chinese question. The position he would take was "to be highly favorable to the loudly-expressed wish of the people of California."[42] Representative John King Luttrell of California, "one of the most anti-Chinese men in this country," also told a *New York Herald* reporter that he "was satisfied with the view the President takes."[43]

In the 1870s the filth of Chinatown, with its notorious prostitution, opium dens, low-class gambling halls, leprosy, thieving, and murders, exacerbated American frustration that stemmed from the miserable wages for labor during the depression and a possible flood of cheap Chinese laborers fleeing one of the biggest famines in Chinese history. Chinese immigration, which had been systematized by the Six Companies and guaranteed by the Burlingame Treaty, must have awakened a sense of danger among white labor. Perceiving the Chinese multitudes to be creating distress, degradation, and ruin, many Americans simply could not control their temper. Their grievances became explosive, and the Six Companies, the representative of all the Chinese, became the natural target for their outrage. The question was simple: was the right of unlimited immigration of Chinese a danger sufficiently imminent to justify Congress in taking summary measures to restrict it?

The Six Companies as Chief Target

Since the Democrats tended to be pro-labor and anti-immigration, and the Republicans sympathized more with industrialists who wanted import labor but who also opposed slavery, there was no better post–Civil War argument to unite both parties than to charge that the Six Companies had established a slavery government. California and the United States would be completely justified in excluding the Chinese if they were tainted by slavery. In April 1876 Dr. O. M. Wozencraft alleged that the Chinese immigration system controlled by "these six companies of slave traders... [was] more obnoxious than African slavery ever was." The Six Companies was "a government within our government, which defies and defeats our courts of justice in all cases where it conflicts with their interests."[44]

Nineteenth-century San Francisco was filled with Wozencraft's rationale. As the *San Francisco Post* repeatedly stressed, the Six Companies had established "a system of government within the United States in conflict with the spirit and policy of its laws and institutions."[45] In 1878 and 1879 such charges continued. Having "headquarters in this city and in Hong Kong, Canton and Shanghai," a *Chronicle* article of October 28, 1878 stated, the Six Companies enforced laws as a government and punished the coolies under contract with them. They were "a sealed book to the outside world, and are executed with such circumstances of secrecy, certainty, terror, perjury and subornation, as make it impossible in nine cases out of ten to punish in our Courts the worst crimes perpetrated under them." It continued by alleging that if the Six Companies wished someone dead, it was as sure to happen "as the sun is sure to set to-night."[46] The *San Francisco Post* asserted that in "the very heart of San Francisco," the Six Companies ruled "a Chinese empire" numbering "25,000 sojourners from the parent empire" that were "ignorant of our laws and language."[47]

An article of the 1878 *San Francisco Bulletin* argued: "The 150,000 of these people here are ruled almost entirely by the companies," which "set our laws at defense."[48] A few months later it declared: "Now such a system is nothing less than slavery in one of its worst forms. The power of the Chinese Company is as great over the Coolie as that ever held by the southern planter over the

Negro."[49] The *Chronicle* contributed its comment: "The coolie in his hovel subsists on less than was allowed to the African slave—the master [the Six Companies] taking the lion's share of his earnings."[50] The *Bulletin* echoed this: "The Six Coolie Companies... merely bring poor Chinamen across the Pacific and find work for them after they got here. The slave-drivers of the South merely brought poor Africans across the Atlantic and found work for them after they got across."[51]

In addition to being charged as "slave traders" and a "slavery government," the Six Companies was directly threatened. In April 1876, for example, Dr. Wozencraft argued that "their government should be broken up and all their subjects liberated."[52] On May 17, 1876, the "San Francisco Anti-Coolie Secret Society" sent a threatening message to the Six Companies that "unless a system of emigration [is] in full force within twenty-one days from this date and a sufficient number of coolies shipped from this port to satisfy us of your intentions to clean the city of the same, it is our most decided intention to clean the same by force of arms."[53]

Col. Frederick Bee, the spokesman of the Six Companies at the time, was also threatened. He received a postcard dated March 17, 1877, which said: "Take my advice and leave this State in thirty days or you will be killed." The message added, "All of you who are in for coolies and against the whites here are marked."[54] A month later it was reported that a Caucasian, "whose name is well known and whose business is that of janitor at a prominent public place," wanted to raise a fund "for putting Colonel Bee out of the way, in other words, to procure his assassination."[55]

Similarly, an article published in the *San Francisco Post* protested, "First and last, we tell Colonel Bee and the Six Companies that the Chinese labor serfs have got to go.... The fiat has gone forth; and the sooner the Six Companies set their houses in order and make preparations for shipping their human chattels back to China the better."[56] One writer even suggested: "If necessary to protect one victim from the tyranny of these Six Companies, we should call on our army and navy."[57]

To these examples from 1877 may be added a number from 1878 and 1879. In a lecture on August 20, 1878, J. R. Frend stated that the existence of the Chinese Six Companies—a foreign power in the United States—was downright treason to the American government. The American army should "either force the Chinese to loyalty or drive them away."[58] Dr. C. C. O'Donnell made a formal complaint against the Six Companies on July 9, 1879, before U.S. Commissioner James O'Beirne, in which he suggested that the leaders of the organization be arrested. He charged that the Six Companies had violated "Sections 2 and 4 of the United States statutes under which any persons contracting to bring coolies or slaves to the shore of this country for the purpose of selling their labor [is forbidden]." It was liable under Section 2 for a fine of $2,000, or one year's imprisonment, or both, and under Section 4, a fine of $500 and imprisonment of one year, or both. O'Beirne, after hearing the complaint, caused warrants to be issued for the Six Companies.[59]

It is true that the spirit of the American government, which declared the United States a refuge for the oppressed of all nations, was largely welcoming from the earliest days of independence. It is also true that every immigrant group met with hostility and violence. But what was particular about the Chinese was their distinct race, their organization, and the timing of the immigration. Americans could not close their eyes to the radical differences between the Chinese immigrants, who were gathering up under the Six Companies like an invading army, and the European peoples that sought California shores. Under the double pressure of economic dislocation in California and possibility of a large influx of Chinese as a result of a famine in China, some of these differences were exaggerated and twisted, evolving into widespread stereotyping and prejudice. Against this background, we should now examine the charge that the Six Companies was the main labor broker for the Chinese.

Was the Six Companies a Labor Broker?

Americans keenly noticed that most of the Chinese laborers who arrived in San Francisco were almost penniless and that their passage had been paid in advance. The newly arrived Chinese laborers were met at the piers and provided temporary shelter and accommodation by representatives from certain *huiguan*, which were collectively called in English the Six Companies. Partly because of the name Americans gave them, the Six Companies and its member *huiguan* had every appearance of labor brokers.[60] Early in 1869, the *San Francisco Alta California* stated that it was "idle to talk of coolies or Chinese slaves being imported into the United States.... Diligent and searching inquiry in every direction that promises information has failed to show a particle of evidence that any Chinese coolies have ever arrived at any Pacific port of the United States."[61] Even though there was no evidence, Americans just repeated what they had said earlier. When the economic depression of the 1870s finally began racking California, many white Americans feared that an overpopulated China would swamp America with cheap Chinese laborers and undermine their living standards. In the resulting heated charges, there was rarely much effort made to provide proof of accusations. "The Chinese Companies are labor brokers," the *San Francisco Call* proclaimed in 1878, "They do not employ to any large extent on their own account, but they furnish labor to those who want it."[62] In his letters to the governor of California and the editor of the *Chronicle*,

O. M. Wozencraft insisted that "the laboring Chinamen were brought here by the Six Companies and by them held to servitude... our impotency to protect ourselves has but given additional assurance to the Six Companies to continue the aggression."[63] The *San Francisco Bulletin* of 1878 stated: "They [the Six Companies] import them by shiploads, and just as long as they can make immense profits upon the chattels they will bring them."[64] The charge that the Six Companies was a labor broker generally arose for one of the following reasons.

False Assumptions

Because people were ignorant of the nature of the Six Companies, some denunciations were mere conjectures. One article, for instance, described the fact that when the Six Companies telegraphed their countrymen not to come to the United States, the immigration slowed accordingly. Because the writer did not understand the *huiguan*'s close native-place ties, he argued: "We do not know that the Companies were responsible; but as the immigration stopped at their command, it is fair to presume that its returning flow was their work."[65]

Likewise, because most Americans did not understand the judicial power of the Six Companies and its umbrella nature—the fact that almost all the Chinese immigrants were members of the Six Companies—the *San Francisco Chronicle* in 1876 could accuse the Six Companies of being labor brokers simply because the Chinese immigrants were "subject to their rule."[66] One day later the paper again emphasized: "Every Asiatic... is consigned to some one of the Six Companies... [which] are supposed to have almost despotic authority over the Chinese immigrants, compelling a long term of labor after their arrival in return for passage advanced across the Pacific."[67] In an article on July 12, 1789, the *San Francisco Post* posited that Chinese immigration as an invasion directed by the Six Companies because all the Chinese were "consigned to" and "under the control of the Chinese Six Companies."[68]

In an article dated April 2, 1876, the *San Francisco Chronicle* clearly did not understand the inclusive, mutual-aid aspects of a native-place association and therefore assumed the *huiguan* of the Six Companies were labor brokers. "If they don't import coolies, why are the coolies all consigned to the companies? And why are the thousands of emigrants landing here at once taken in charge by the companies and provided with temporary quarters and subsistence?"[69] This kind of ignorance is not rare. The *San Francisco Bulletin* charged on August 30, 1877, that "without their [the Six Companies] aid and support no Chinese of consequence would venture to this coast. It is sufficiently well understood that the mass of the Chinese arriving here are in one form or other under contract to the Six Companies."[70]

Many of the arguments were self-contradictory. In 1876 S. Clinton Hastings, a former attorney general of California and chief justice of the California Supreme Court, testified: "The Chinamen, I think, without any exception, all come here as peons, employed by contractors and these six companies." However, when asked about these matters later, he provided different answers:

> Q. It has been testified here that the Chinese companies do not bring over here any immigrants. Do you know whether the Chinese companies bring over any of their people or not?
> A. I don't think they do; but they take control of them, certainly, when they come here, pay their pecuniary obligations, and settle their difficulties. It is an imperium in imperio undoubtedly.
> Q. Do you know what dues the laborers pay the Chinese companies?
> A. I do not know their compensation.
> Q. You do not know whether they pay a monthly stipend?
> A. No, sir; I do not.[71]

Some Californians thought these issues made it important to learn about China in order to arrive at the truth. Frederick Low, who had served for three years as U.S. minister in Beijing, once stated: "Let the State and city appoint competent men to sift the matter to the bottom." If they learned Cantonese dialect and mingled with the Chinese, he suggested, "they will then doubtless discover that the Coolies who immigrate to this country do so in violation of the United States law, which forbids the importation of Coolies for servile labor."[72] However, no solid evidence was ever cited to show that the Chinese had been imported illegally. William Olmsted, an American merchant who lived in China for years, had wide-ranging contacts with the Chinese for over fourteen years, and said he would have known if the Six Companies were involved in "any mercantile operation."[73]

Labor Contracts

Even though to the best of my knowledge no one has ever seen a contract between the Six Companies and any Chinese laborers, the *San Francisco Chronicle* reported on January 4, 1878: "It is a part of the contract with the Six Companies that if a coolie dies here his bones shall be shipped to his native land."[74] And any researcher exploring the same newspaper files should certainly be struck by an article of June 8, 1878, which charges that "20,000 contracts" had been made, but produces no evidence to back up the assertion.[75]

In August 1878 the *New York Herald* stated that all the boot and shoe manufacturers in Chicago were on the eve of contracting with the "Six Consolidated

Chinese Importing Companies of California" to furnish some 1,500 Chinese to replace striking white men in Chicago.[76] The white laborers wanted $12 per week, and the manufacturers were offering $10.50. The Chinese, the article noted, required only $0.75 a day. "Every incident proves the truth of the charge we have persistently made. . . . The Chicago contract scheme proves and acknowledges it."[77] In an attempt to ascertain the truth, a reporter from the *San Francisco Morning Call* interviewed Ah Nyom, president of the Sam Yup Company, a member *huiguan* of the Six Companies, on August 11, 1878. The companies, Ah Nyom insisted, had no agent in Chicago authorized to make such arrangements. Merchants or employment agents might possibly be negotiating to send shoemakers to Chicago, but he knew nothing about it.[78] The next day the *San Francisco Post* published an interview with all the presidents of the Six Companies. All but two professed to be entirely ignorant of the reported negotiations. The two who were aware of them had either read the news from the newspaper or had learned of it through other channels. "They all ridiculed the idea of Chinamen being found who would be willing to leave here [San Francisco], where they were getting $1.25 to $1.50 per day, and go East to work for such a figure. . . . Some were of the opinion that it was simply a story gotten up by the manufacturers to force the striking men to come to their terms."[79] The evidence thus suggests that the alleged Chicago contracts were nonexistent.

Despite the accusations being groundless, news of contracts by the Six Companies continued into early 1879. The February 10 *San Francisco Bulletin* provided more details: "The agreement is signed in triplicate. One is given to the Coolie entering into it. A second is sent to the Chinese Company in California. The third is retained by the agent in China."[80] Finally, one month later, the *San Francisco Call* recognized it could no longer ignore the fact that no one had ever actually seen any contracts.[81]

Labor Agents

Significant numbers of Californians in this era assumed that Chinese labor brokers were agents of the Six Companies. In 1877 the *San Francisco Post* reported an interview with an agent of the California Cracker Company who charged a Chinese labor broker was an agent of the Six Companies. The charge, however, remained unsubstantiated since he "forgot the name of the broker."[82]

On February 18, 1879, a group of Chinese were leaving for Honolulu. "They were hustled on board the tender like so many cattle," the *San Francisco Bulletin* reported, and two Chinese, "*presumably* [emphasis added] the agents of some of the Six Benevolent Companies," stood at the gangway "holding a bundle of signed and sealed labor contracts . . . [and] a handful of tickets." As each Chinese laborer passed, "his contract was drawn from the bundle and a ticket handed him."[83]

Such evidence should be viewed with skepticism, however, because Californian observers automatically regarded all Chinese labor brokers as agents of the Six Companies. "Chinamen are seldom permitted to hire without paying toll," the *San Francisco Post* stated on August 10, 1877, "generally to the magnates of the Six Companies, but also to white men of the Koopmanschap class."[84] The *Post* charged again in August 1878: "As benevolent institutions, they [the Six Companies] do not import coolies, but the members of these Six Companies [almost all the Chinese in California in late nineteenth century were members of the Six Companies], under a different organization do."[85] Some Californians even linked the Six Companies with the secret societies. An article in the *San Francisco Chronicle* of October 28, 1878, charged that "the Six Companies are responsible for this brutal traffic in women," because whenever a Chinese woman desired freedom from one of these infamous contracts she was pursued by the "highbinder" agents—professional killers of the Chinese secret societies in California.[86] It was natural to think that Chinese labor brokers were *members* of the Six Companies, because in fact most Chinese in the United States were members of the organization, but it would be an error to claim that they acted as *agents* of the Six Companies.

Scholars such as Elmer Sandmeyer, Stanford Lyman, Patricia Cloud, and David Galenson also equate the Six Companies with other Chinese companies that did act as labor agents because they misunderstand instances like the following. In 1853, when asked whether the rumor was true that many Chinese were "hired by Chinese and foreign capitalists" under contract, the leaders of the Six Companies replied that "a large number of the Chinese who come to this State are hired by Chinese and foreign capitalists, and work here under contract for such employers.... Although this was done to some extent at one time, yet it was not found to be as profitable as was anticipated and is now abandoned."[87] Although in this statement the Six Companies confirmed that Chinese contract laborers had existed, they never said that the Six Companies as an organization itself imported labor. However, Sandmeyer uses this statement as evidence that the Six Companies had once imported Chinese laborers, for he states: "The following year members of the Chinese Companies admitted that they had imported men under contract but, finding it unprofitable, had discontinued the practice."[88]

In his "Conflict and the Web of Group Affiliation in San Francisco's Chinatown," Stanford Lyman states: "Though apologists for the Chinese denied that the *hui kuan* [*huiguan*] had anything to do with the labor system that existed among the sojourners, there is evidence that the *hui kuan* [*huiguan*] operated the 'credit-ticket' system (by which Chinese borrowed money to come to America)."[89] This evidence does not withstand close scrutiny. Lyman cites the following from the "Agreement between the English Merchant and Chinaman" (1849) as proof: "The Tseang Sing Hong having now hired the American ship called the Ah-mah-san [Amazon] for voyaging purposes, the mechanics and laborers of their own free will, will put to sea, the ship to proceed to Ka-la-fo-ne-e [California], and port of Fwh-lan-sze-ko [San Francisco], in search of employment for the said mechanics and laborers."[90] But Lyman misunderstands. The Tseang Sing Hong was an individual broker company, not a member *huiguan* of the Six Companies.

Cloud and Galenson use the Yu-chuy-lung Company as evidence to support their argument that the Six Companies played a central role in importing labor. Again the main problem with their argument is that the Yu-chuy-lung Company was a private broker company, not a *huiguan* of the Six Companies.[91]

Early in the 1870s, some Caucasian observers were aware of the distinction between the Six Companies and the companies importing labor. Consul William Lane Booker, a British diplomat in the United States, wrote from San Francisco to the British government in 1875, "The general idea is that the Six Companies control immigration in every way; but, as far as I can learn, they do so only to a very limited extent.... [The Six Companies do] not furnish means to enable Chinamen to come to this country.... [Rather, the funds for passage are] "supplied by parties making a regular business of it, who charge 250 per cent for a loan if unsecured, or 2 per cent per month with tangible security.... Wealthy Chinese houses in Hong Kong are employed in this business of collecting and shipping over these men."[92] The *San Francisco Post* pointed out in 1878: "As we have before stated, Chinese labor importation is done by another and more secret society or cooperation, just as is that of importing prostitutes by another body of Mongolian 'highbinders.'"[93]

Interviews with Chinese Laborers

Some Americans tried to prove their allegations against the Six Companies by interviewing Chinese immigrants. Solid evidence evaded these investigators as well. Ezekiel B. Vreeland, deputy commissioner of immigration from 1873 to 1876, testified that "80% of them [Chinese laborers] are brought out under the auspices of these companies." But when asked how he arrived at this conclusion, he replied, "through the interpreter of the ship, I would ask the question who furnished the money, how they got out, and all that class of information, and, generally, they made replies in that way."[94] Cloud and Galenson offer Vreeland's interview as evidence,[95] which McClain rebuts with the comment that something may have been lost because of poor translation.[96] We should add a number of other points as well. In the 1870s the commissioner was in a position to arbitrarily identify Chinese immigrants as paupers, criminals, idiots, or prostitutes and therefore deny their entry.[97] In addition, Colonel H. Selden Loring, the Vice Consul of the United States for Hong Kong at this time, who had been looking into the matter, interviewed several parties of Chinese emigrants, and he disputed Vreeland's estimate. A "strictest search" was made, Loring said, and "nobody ever admits that he is under any sort of a contract."[98] To this evidence should be added that of Andrew Wilson, who spent years in China and Hong Kong. In April 1861, he traveled with some 400 Chinese emigrants on the American clipper *Bald Eagle* from Hong Kong to San Francisco. He also investigated the widely held charge that the Chinese were imported by the Six Companies and concluded that this allegation was groundless.[99]

The Steamship Company's Agreement

Another reason for charging the Six Companies as labor brokers was an agreement between the Six Companies and the Pacific Mail Steamship Company. This agreement required each Chinese laborer to obtain a certificate from the Six Companies stating that he had repaid his debts before he could return to China. In 1876, for instance, Frederick Low testified before a committee of the California State Senate: "In fact I know they have, with the steamship companies, agreed that no Chinaman can purchase a ticket to return home unless he brings a certificate from the heads of these companies, that he is free from debt; it is very natural that he will pay his pro rata per month until he works out his debt."[100] An article in 1878 condemned the Six Companies with a similar argument: Chinese came to the United States "under contract to labor" and "under the full control of the Companies who advance their passage money." Because no Chinese could return to China until he had "obtained a permit from the Companies with a certificate" indicating he was free of debt, "the Six Companies are labor brokers."[101]

Four years later, in a report submitted to Parliament, Joseph Chapleau, the chairman of a Canadian commission investigating Chinese immigration, offered his conclusion, which was also based chiefly on the agreement with the steamship company. Quoting Low's testimony regarding the refusal of shipping companies to take immigrants back to China without the consent of the Six Companies, Chapleau asserted that the Six Companies were more than benevolent associations. He held that the Six Companies did "bring them to this continent under contract" because no Chinese could go back to China until he was "clear on the books of the company to which they belong." Although there was, as Chapleau said, "no proof of this," the Six Companies "must have quite enough power over the labor."[102]

It is clear that such commentators believed then and now that because Chinese immigrants usually borrowed money to cover passage to the United States, and because the Six Companies demanded assurance that immigrants had paid all their debts before they might return to China, then all Chinese must have incurred debts to the Six Companies, and thus it played a central role in importing Chinese labor.

To assume that debt enforcement is convincing evidence that the Six Companies engaged in labor importation is questionable. The debts the returnees owed were sometimes membership fees owed a *huiguan*. Lwung Cook, an official of the Ningyang *huiguan*, testified in 1876 before the California State Senate committee investigating Chinese immigration. He said that when Chinese from Ningyang district came to California, the Ningyang *huiguan* took care of them and paid "their boarding and lodging expenses." For this service the company collected "five dollars" from each man afterwards to "pay back the amount due the company for the advances, for expense, and its trouble." Upon payment the immigrant could get a permit to buy a return ticket.[103]

In addition, as an organization led by Chinese merchants, the Six Companies sought to protect the interests of Chinese creditors. The constitution of the Yanghe *huiguan*, for example, had detailed stipulations about debt disputes.[104] An article published in the *Oriental* in 1855 emphasized that the collection of debts for its members was one objective of the *huiguan*, "Great facilities are afforded for the collection of debts. . . . If they refuse to pay, complaint is made to our courts of law, they are arrested, and the claim obtained."[105] In 1894 Fong Kum Ngon testified that if any Chinese debtor tried "to go back to China without paying his debt," the creditor usually wrote to the Six Companies about it.[106] The Six Companies also turned to the American courts to collect debts due to them from those Chinese about to depart. These court proceedings should have furnished some evidence that the Six Companies had acted as a labor broker, but none did.[107]

By the early 1870s some Americans had a different understanding of the "exit permit system." An *Atlantic Monthly* story about one Wo Lee declared of the Six Companies: "It does not claim the wages or service of any one, but requires of each member his dues and assessments, as well as a repayment of money to him advanced."[108] From the beginning the Six Companies denied that it was a labor broker, and other Chinese and Americans also vehemently rejected the notion that the organization imported Chinese laborers. In 1877 Ng Choy (Wu Tingfang) told a newspaper reporter: "I wish to say that the Chinese here are not slaves to the Six Companies, nor do those companies, as I understand, pay their passage here."[109]

The Rev. Otis Gibson, for many years a missionary in China and superintendent of a Chinese mission church in the 1860s and 1870s in San Francisco, wrote sardonically in his *Chinese in America:* "What wonderful legislative and executive ability those six Chinamen, the presidents of these companies, must have to enable them to hold so many people in such abject slavery.... These slaves," he wrote, should have "taken advantage of our laws against slavery, and prosecuted their cruel masters in our courts, and obtained a decree of their own freedom.... Why," he asked, "do the hundreds of intelligent Chinese Christians in America constantly assert that there is no such thing known among their people in this country as slavery, or bondage, except in the case of women."[110] In 1877, in response to a question from the chairman of a federal investigating committee as to whether the companies took a percentage of a worker's wages if they found employment for him, Gibson declared: "I never heard of the Chinese six companies—the whole or as one—furnishing employment for anybody...and I never heard of anybody going to the six companies to get employment."[111] Benjamin Brooks, an attorney representing the Six Companies in 1877, testified that he had "never heard of [the Six Companies] importing anybody except in these wholesale charges made against them" and did "not understand them to be mercantile firms in any kind of business."[112]

When interviewed by an *Alta* reporter in 1886, Lyman R. Moaley, superintendent of the Pacific Mail Steamship Company, derided the charge as "ridiculous," a "misunderstanding regarding the Six Companies.... And as for their controlling the Chinese labor market is concerned," he added, "I will wager that you could not go to their office now and secure a contract for a single Chinese laborer.... That traffic," he pointed out, "is all done by mercantile houses."[113]

To these people, who were more familiar with *huiguan,* the charges against the Six Companies were not only simplistic, but also unpersuasive. As a confederation of native-place associations, the Six Companies would, as a matter of course, receive, house, feed, and send laborers off to their various places of employment. It was hardly surprising that an organization established and led by Chinese merchants would protect the interests of Chinese creditors.

At first glance, these arguments may seem convincing, but perhaps, as *outside observations,* they merely echo statements by the Six Companies and skim the surface of the problem. The distinction between funding as a mutual-aid society and acting as a labor importer could become confusing. Even Gibson produced a mixed message when he testified in 1878:

> I am satisfied that the six companies, as such, do not import a man. When a firm wants to employ a large number of Chinese, say one thousand, the manager goes to one of the companies, tells them he wants so many men and

> agrees to pay a certain price. If the companies think they can do better by sending to China, they do so, and induce men to come out.[114]

But denials and counterevidence did not dispel the charges against the Six Companies, which seemed to have great vitality. In 1879 it was reported that Congressman Jones of Nevada would "ask the State Department to cause special inquiry to be made... into the truth of the statement so positively made by Californians that a lien over a Mongolian laborer brought to this country is made effective in China by a system of family enslavement, which the peon has to work out to the Six Companies after his arrival here."[115]

In all the discussions over this issue, including the arguments of contemporary scholars, the key to the puzzle has been overlooked, and that is its function as a mutual-aid society. Because these activities involved money and debt, and because there was a great deal of local hostility, it was easy to disregard the nuances of who was doing what and for what reason. The Six Companies itself acknowledged its role in the immigration. On June 25, 1869, in the rosy and cordial atmosphere just after the 1868 Burlingame Treaty,[116] when interviewing with the Congressional Subcommittee on Ways and Means, Tang Fang (Fung Tang), the Six Companies' spokesman, described the basic functions of the organization:

> The Chinese who come to California to labor are poor men, *so our Companies, which are formed to assist them, and not to oppress them, advance money to bring them here, but no slavery exists here at all among our people,* for every man receives wages for his labor and works voluntarily. Some people in California have said we had slaves here, but it is not true. We make men contribute from their earnings enough to pay their debts, if money has been advanced to bring them to this country [emphasis added].[117]

A Chinese interpreter testifying before the California State Senate in 1878 also said that the Six Companies lent Chinese laborers money to go into the interior. When asked about the Six Companies, he replied: "They are to take care of Chinamen belonging to their own company... when he wants to go from one city to another, the company furnishes money, and he pays it back again."[118]

Attention must also be paid to the voices of the Chinese laborers themselves, the very people about whom everyone was arguing. The *San Francisco Evening Post* of April 5, 1879, has preserved an account by Chan Pak Qwai, a Chinese who came to California when he was fifteen years old and spent seventeen years there as a house servant, coachman, photographer, and assistant to Gibson in his missionary work. Chan joined Gibson on a lecture tour to the East in 1879, that included visits to Des Moines, Iowa City, Davenport, and Chicago. The following is a conversation between Chan Pak Qwai and a *Post* reporter upon their return:

> REPORTER: What were the principal points touched upon in your lecture?
> CHAN: Well, I spoke of a good many things. There has been much said about importing coolies. Now, I do not know what people mean by "coolies." I suppose that they mean those Chinamen who have their passage money advanced by any of the Six Companies who assist immigrants. Well, that practice does prevail to a great extent. I do not call it coolieism. These companies simply advance poor Chinamen so much money. These poor Chinamen agree to work either so long to pay it back when they get here, or they agree to pay it and find their own work. When they first come here they are ignorant of the custom of the people, and would, perhaps, starve to death if they did not have some one who understood the people here to get them work of some kind.
> REPORTER: Then you acknowledge that many Chinamen do come here actually bound to these companies for a term of years, and that these companies can do about what they please with them?
> CHAN: Of course I do. If the men agree to work so long, for so much money advanced, is that any different from some American contracts?[119]

Clearly the Six Companies and its member *huiguan* were native-place associations for mutual aid. It is one thing to claim that the Six Companies provided financial assistance to their poorer countrymen, but it is quite another to say that it was a broker company for importing slaves or coolies.

To assume that the Six Companies "imported almost every Chinaman" in the late nineteenth century is to miss the point.[120] As the preceding chapters have shown, many Chinese and American companies and individuals were impresarios of the Chinese immigration. Recruitment of Chinese laborers by American businessmen occurred right alongside that by Chinese merchants, and these labor brokers continued their activity into the 1870s. On November 11, 1878, the police of San Francisco boarded the *Timandra* and found twenty-one Chinese laborers who declared that they had been engaged by Chung Awa, Seecho Tock Sin, and Parug Park, agents who were planning to send them to Hawai`i for $12 per month. "From the contracts in the possession of the Chinamen it appears that Williams, Blanchard & Co. and C. Koopmanshap were the agents for Thomas Spencer & Co., who were designated masters, and for whom the Chinese were to work for twelve months."[121]

A California shoe manufacturer testified in 1876: "We contracted for... [laborers], for two years, with Yu-chung-lung Company.... We made contracts with them to furnish us so many men for a certain price, and we paid the money to that company."[122] The *San Francisco Alta California* of March 27, 1876, also mentioned, "The firm of Yee Chy Lung & Co.... [which was] composed of Ah Sam, Ah Sue, Ah Jim, Ah Phat and other man... [who were] wealthy and hold extensive contracts for furnishing labor to a number of our city manufactories." In 1876 there were 750 Chinese laborers in the boot and shoe manufactories of Buckingham & Hecht and Kinstein Brothers. The firm had been required to deposit a certain amount of money as guarantee, which it shifted off to the labor.[123] A wealthy Chinese company called the Quong Yee Wo Company of San Francisco was said to "keep an army of men employed on contracts they take.... Agents of theirs are traveling around on the lookout for these contracts."[124]

Chinese brokers were active in providing Chinese laborers to the South and even to Mexico. In the fall of 1871, for example, Fou Loy & Co., a Chinese labor broker company of New Orleans and San Francisco, advertised that it could bring in 1,500 laborers a month from China at a cost of $22 per man.[125] The *Advertiser* of December 5, 1872, reported that one Ah Young, a "successor to Koopmanschap," visited Belleville in December 1872 to arrange for renewal of some Chinese contracts that would expire in a few months. In the late 1880s or early 1890s Quong Ying Kee (Chin Gee-hee?), who was building a railroad in Mexico, sent agents back to China to "advertise for workmen." If any Chinese was too poor to pay his passage, Quong would loan him the money for the ticket and "get the money back by retaining two thirds of his wages every month until the amount was fully paid."[126]

While there is overwhelming evidence that both Chinese and Americans, working as individual brokers or in broker companies, were involved in the importation of Chinese labor, and while the Six Companies did advance money or credit to immigrants, the organization itself did not act as a labor broker. Once again we need to focus on the function of the *huiguan* in immigration. Before and on arrival in a strange land, the immigrants, many of whom were penniless and unable to speak any language but their own dialect, were truly helpless and alone. By assisting financially,[127] by receiving, housing, feeding, and sending off its countrymen to their various places of employment, the Six Companies no doubt facilitated Chinese immigration. But the Chinese in America were not coolies or slaves subject to the Six Companies, which was a confederation of traditional Chinese mutual-aid associations, not labor brokers.

To sum up, in the 1870s Chinese merchants eagerly continued to seek profits and accumulate capital, and they did considerably well in California.

But after the shock of the 1873 depression, many Americans again feared competition from the Chinese, and the hostile attitude the West Coast inhabitants toward the Chinese reached new heights. The lives, properties, and future of the Chinese merchants all became insecure. The press, the people of California, and the politicians discussed the Chinese question with an abhorrence never exhibited before in the history of the state. Many Americans regarded the situation of Chinese laborers as worse than the former system of black slavery and bitterly accused the Six Companies of being an oligarchy of wealth based upon servile labor. Day after day the press published similar exaggerations and misrepresentations. The Chinese question was rapidly assuming national importance. The time seemed to be not far distant when the federal government would take some definite action.

CHAPTER 5

• • • • • •

Setting the Tone and Format

The Six Companies as Spokesman, 1870–1878

> H. H. Ellis, Chief of Police, City and County of San Francisco—Sir: We wish to call your attention to the fact that at the present time, frequent and unprovoked assaults are made upon our Chinese people while walking peacefully the street of this city. The assaulting party is seldom arrested by your officers, but if a Chinaman resists the assault he is frequently arrested and punished by fine or by imprisonment.
>
> Inflammatory and incendiary addresses against the Chinese, delivered on the public streets, to the idle and irresponsible element of this great city, have already produced unprovoked and unpunished assaults upon some of our people, and we fear that if such things are permitted to go on unchecked a bloody riot against the Chinese may be the result.
>
> Regretting that the Chinese are so obnoxious to the citizens of this country, and quite willing to aid in seeking a repeal or modification of the existing treaty between China and the United States, yet being here under sacred treaty stipulations, we simply ask to be protected in our treaty rights.
>
> —"The Chinese Companies"

As the representative of all the Chinese in the United States and the chief target of the anti-Chinese movement in the 1870s, the Six Companies was clearly pushed to its limits. As a federation of *huiguan,* the Six Companies had an obligation, among other services, to defend its members. This practice had begun in China. At the beginning of the nineteenth century, for example, Ningbo merchants in Wenzhou were authorized under an imperial edict to ship rice from any region of China to any other region, and their trade had been successful. Local authorities at Wenzhou, however, detained their vessels and arrested the merchants. The Ningbo *huiguan,* after failing to obtain justice in Wenzhou, took the case to the provincial authorities at Hangzhou. Failing again, they appealed directly to the imperial government at the capital, and here, at last, they got redress.[1] But would this formula, proven in China and in California during the 1850s and 1860s, work for the Six Companies as representative of all the Chinese in the United States? How would the organization respond to the unprecedented anti-Chinese challenges of the 1870s?

Restricting Immigration

Wonderful as the right of free immigration was for the Chinese, it also produced strong public resentment against the Chinese. Because of this, the Six Companies sought to dissuade their countrymen from coming to the United States whenever anti-Chinese hostility heated up. As new tides of Sinophobia swept across the country in the 1870s, urgent dispatches replaced the slow, mildly toned letters of the 1850s and 1860s. The Tung Wah Hospital in Hong Kong received and published the following telegram from the Six Companies in the *Daily Press* on May 30, 1873: "Inform Chinese emigrants must not come; very important, great deal of trouble, much information by telegraph impossible; publish to this fact, Chinese newspapers."[2]

The *Daily Press* echoed the urgency, saying that the large influx of Chinese immigrants had caused anxiety among the Six Companies, "and that this coupled with additional laws of a restrictive character, which it seems have been passed by the state, has been sufficient to induce them to recommend that no further emigrants proceed at present to that port."[3] Partially because of the Six Companies' efforts, the numbers of Chinese immigrants declined from 20,291 in 1873 to 13,776 in 1874.[4]

The organization's attempt to restrict emigration intensified in 1876, when anti-Chinese resentment was at its highest. On March 29, 1876, the Six Companies and the Chinese Merchants' Exchange sent a joint warning message to Tung Wah Hospital: "Day before yesterday we telegraphed you to warn our people of their danger, and if possible prevent any more from coming here."[5] Another letter underscored the need: "Please write out what we have told you and post it in all the conspicuous places in Hong Kong that our people may know the danger they may incur and the hard times they may expect if they come to American shores."[6] Since the organization believed that private letters were more effective than *huiguan* bulletins, the Six Companies called on all the Chinese in San Francisco to write letters to China deterring others from trying to come.[7] The dispatches caused repercussions in Hong Kong. The *Daily Press* announced: "It seems . . . the 'Meeting Hall' [the Six Companies] has requested the Tung Wah Hospital to advise their fellow countrymen not to emigrate to California at present."[8]

All of this was occurring at the very time when the Six Companies was trying to defend itself against charges of labor importation. On April 1, 1876, in a manifesto addressed to the people of the United States, the Six Companies asked rhetorically: "How can such things be said? . . . [Y]ear after year [we have] sent letters discouraging our people from coming to this country . . . [because the expenses of] the poor newcomers . . . [are a continual] drain upon the resources of those already settled here."[9]

Recognizing the limits of what the Six Companies could do as a private, nongovernmental association, the leaders petitioned the Qing government. In 1876 Li Ming Hou, the president of the Sanyi *huiguan*, a member *huiguan* of the Six Companies, sent a letter to Ou Eliang, the Chinese education commissioner in the United States, asking him to urge the Qing government to take action.[10] Richard Dillon comments, "The uneasy presidents of the Six Companies again requested the Government of China to stop further emigration to America of its nationals, fearing mob violence on the *Embarcadero* when so-called coolie ships arrived."[11]

The Six Companies also appealed to the American authorities. Colonel Bee, their agent, in February 1876 sent a letter to Secretary of State William Evarts suggesting a capitation tax of $100 be put on each Chinese immigrant to restrict the immigration. "If carried out by this Government," Bee reasoned it would curb further immigration "most assuredly" and "quite effectively"; alongside that suggestion, however, he also asked for full protection of the Chinese already in the United States and of their property.[12]

The Six Companies even suggested amending the Burlingame Treaty, which had given Chinese immigrants legal right to enter the United States. In a letter dated April 1, 1876, to California Governor William Irwin, the Six Companies suggested "a repeal or modification of the existing treaty between China and the United States."[13] That same day the Six Companies published a manifesto, in which they reaffirmed their immigration restriction policy, asserting that a check to further Chinese immigration would be "very good indeed," because the number arriving was larger than the need, and the presence of new Chinese placed a heavy load on those already settled in the United States. In order to solve the problem, the Six Companies suggested the following: "If the American people do not desire the Chinese to come here, why not go to the Emperor and ask a repeal of the treaty, or why not limit the number of immigrants on each steamer to a very few?" They asked only that the United States guarantee protection for the Chinese already in the country.[14]

The Six Companies wrote San Francisco Chief of Police Ellis, stating that the organization was "quite willing to aid in seeking a repeal or modification of the existing treaty between China and the United States. . . . Being here under sacred treaty stipulations, we simply ask to be protected in our treaty rights."[15] That same day the Six Companies sent a letter to Tung Wah Hospital: "Day before yesterday we telegraphed you to warn our people of the danger, and if possible prevent any more from coming here."[16] Three days later, on April 4, the Chinese leaders wrote the San Francisco Board of Supervisors, asking protection for "the lives and property of [the] thousands [that] might be placed in jeopardy."[17]

The leaders even sent messages directly to President Ulysses Grant suggesting a modification of the Burlingame Treaty. In a letter of May 29, 1876, the Six Companies stressed: "Let there be a modification of the existing treaty relations between China and the United States."[18] On November 23, 1877, Joseph C. G. Kennedy, the representative of the Six Companies at the capital, appealed to President Grant directly: "It would appear to be the duty of the President, before it be too late, to command peace and recommend Congress to provide for such amendment of the treaty as will remove all pretext for outrages predicated upon affected apprehension of a too great influx hereafter of Eastern population."[19]

In addition, the Six Companies hoped that Congress would take action. When Senator Oliver Morton arrived from Oregon in August 1877, the organization complained to him that the Chinese had no assurance that their lives or property would be protected and that Chinese were subjected to insult and outrage, but that they were also as anxious as the Americans to have the treaty amended. Senator Morton agreed to draw up a bill.[20]

In two pamphlets the Six Companies published in 1877, "Memorial to the Senate and House of Representatives of the United States" and "An Address to the People of the United States," it stressed that the organization had "never brought or caused to be brought one of their countrymen to this land under or by any servile or labor contract, verbal or in writing, or in any way binding upon in any manner one of our countrymen or any member."[21] There is a subtle difference in the Six Companies' denials of labor brokering before and after 1877. Before 1877 the organization underscored the fact that it did not import or hold "slaves" or "coolies." After that date the denials expanded to encompass any Chinese laborers at all. The reason for this change is hard to miss—the Chinese Exclusion Act of 1882 was looming.

The Chinese Six Companies also sought to help impoverished and unemployed Chinese to return to China by negotiating with steamship companies for cheap fares. Chinese merchants even chartered sailing vessels to take Chinese back to Hong Kong.[22] The Six Companies developed a plan "to keep the number of Chinamen here at a minimum figure by sending back at least one for every one who arrives from China."[23]

The Six Companies' efforts to restrict immigration continued in 1878. Colonel Bee told a *Post* reporter that at the request of the Six Companies he had sent a dispatch to Secretary of State Evarts, asking him to draw up a bill that would put a tax of $100 on every Chinese coming into the United States. But the dispatch also demanded both indemnity for past losses and a guarantee of protection in the future.[24] However, the $100 per capita tax suggestion received no support from the American public or government. If the United States accepted the idea, the *San Francisco Post* warned: "the lowest and most degrading conditions of human slavery would become part of the administrative system of the United States."[25]

On August 11, 1878, the presidents of the Six Companies published "To the American People" in the *New York Herald*. Again they urged that as "benevolent associations" only, they had "never, directly or indirectly,... brought or caused to be brought one of our countrymen to this country under or by any contract, in written, oral or otherwise, as slave, coolie or laborer or any capacity, under bound, contract or agreement, understanding, influence or advance of money."[26] On February 13, 1879, the companies addressed a similar letter to the *San Francisco Bulletin*. Again they stressed: "We never, singly or collectively, as individuals or companies, ever brought one of our countrymen to this free country, under or by any contract or agreement, made anywhere, as a servant or laborer.... We challenge the proof of the charges contained in your paper from first to last."[27]

On the whole the Six Companies' tireless efforts from 1876 to 1878 were effective. Chinese immigration dropped from 22,781 in 1876 to 10,594 in 1877 and to 8,992 in 1878.[28] What is more, an American diplomatic mission was to be sent to Beijing for treaty revisions in 1880.

Chinatown Reformer

In order to gain acceptance of the Chinese from Americans, the Six Companies expanded its role as reformer of Chinatown in the 1870s. In response to the criticism that Chinatown was dangerous to public health and safety, the organization fought against Chinese criminal activity. In January 1870 the Six Companies published a card in the daily papers of San Francisco "announcing to the world that they disapproved of what was being done by a few of their unprincipled countrymen—that they were willing and ready to do all they possibly could, if proper assistance was rendered, to put a stop to the importation of these women for illicit purposes." It had in addition engaged able counsel and instructed them to have writs issued for the arrest of about forty to fifty Chinese prostitutes who had been detained in houses of ill repute against their will.[29] To break up a gang of Chinese robbers in 1870, the Six Companies employed a counsel named "Mr. Murphy" to bring the offenders to justice.[30] Their efforts were recognized. H. H. Ellis, chief of police for the city and county of San Francisco, made the following statement: "From the more respectable members of the Chinese companies, societies, and merchants, we have had their assistance, from time to time, in apprehending criminals and sometimes in giving evidence, and sometimes in the recovery of property."[31]

The Chinese leaders sought assistance from American missionaries. In 1873, after rescuing a group of girls intended for prostitution, the leaders of the Six Companies visited Otis Gibson and gave him $500 with which to buy the girls' passage back to China. They assured Gibson that if he could devise a plan, they would furnish the means to send all Chinese prostitutes back to China. The *San Francisco Chronicle* in 1873 announced: "This is the most creditable act yet done by this class of people."[32]

The Page Act, which was passed in 1875, forbade the importation of Chinese women for the purposes of prostitution. In addition, the American consulate in Hong Kong was ordered to examine Chinese female passengers and issue certificates indicating their good character.[33] Encouraged by these positive steps, the Chinese leaders sent a petition to President Grant in 1876 to protest a Supreme Court decision that "brought all those women [Chinese prostitutes] on shore again... [to the benefit of] an unscrupulous class of white Americans," who accepted bribes from unprincipled Chinese and benefited from Chinese gambling and prostitution. "The only remedy for this evil," the Six Companies asserted, "lies in an honest and impartial administration of municipal government in all its details, even including the police department."[34]

A story about cooperation between the Six Companies and San Francisco police has been preserved for us by the *San Francisco Bulletin*. It concerned the Lui Sing Tong, "better known to the English-reading public as Highbinders." Wong Wing, an inspector for one of the Six Companies, had taken a lively interest in the capture of these highbinders, since he keenly felt the disgrace of their atrocious acts. Funding the effort himself, he had his subordinate scour the Bay counties in search of them, particularly one Ah Kee. After getting information that Ah Kee was living at a Chinese fishing station in South San Francisco, he immediately reported to the chief of police, who dispatched several officers to arrest Ah Kee. They failed in their attempt, but the fishermen corroborated that the information was correct. Soon afterward, Wong Wing got news that Ah Kee was to depart for China on the steamship *Alaska*. He at once informed the police, and Detective John Coffey and others were dispatched to the Pacific Mail Steamship Company wharf. Ah Kee was arrested, tried, and sent to prison.[35]

In response to the criticism of poor medical facilities in Chinatown, individual *huiguan* established small health agencies on Pine Street, Broadway,

Commercial Street, Bull Run Alley, Cooper Alley, Aleck Alley, Sullivan Alley, Ellick Alley, Clay Street between Kearny and DuPont, and in Montgomery Alley near Broadway.[36] Planning to build a large hospital in 1875, the leaders of the Six Companies reached an agreement that every Chinese returning to China should contribute a dollar to the construction fund.[37] A Chinese hospital committee was formed to raise money for the new hospital, and plans were made to use the Tung Wah Hospital in Hong Kong as a model.[38]

The Six Companies also sponsored edifying lectures. On February 19, 1876, for example, the *Oriental* reprinted a notice from the Six Companies that there would be Chinese lectures every day from 11:00 to 3:00. Hoping the Chinese in the United States would benefit from positive influences, the Six Companies began by inviting Feng Zhipeng to come from China to lecture on the sixteen maxims of the Sacred Edict of Emperor Kangxi.[39]

Defender of Treaty Rights

Enormously heartened by its success in the late 1860s, the Six Companies continued to act as the defender of Chinese rights. In June 1873, after learning of three proposed ordinances pending before the Board of Supervisors of the City of San Francisco designed exclusively to increase the Chinese living and working costs, the Chinese Six Companies asked Otis Gibson to complain to the Board. On June 2, Gibson read his translation of the protest that the heads of the Six Companies had composed, using treaty obligations and justice as arguments: "In the name of our country, in the name of justice and humanity, in the name of Christianity, we protest against such severe and discriminating enactment while living in this country under existing treaties."[40] The result greatly encouraged the Six Companies—William Alvord, the mayor of San Francisco, vetoed the bills because he was convinced by the Chinese presentation and believed that the legislation violated both the Civil Rights Act of 1870 and the treaties between the two countries.[41]

With the anti-Chinese forces continually calling for federal legislation to exclude the Chinese in the late 1870s, the Six Companies again appealed to both the state and the federal governments. On April 1, 1876, the Six Companies sent a letter to Governor Irwin, Mayor A. J. Bryant and Chief of Police Ellis asking "to be protected in our treaty rights."[42] A few days later Mayor Bryant received another communication from the Six Companies: "We appeal to your Honor the Mayor and Chief Magistrate of this municipality to protect us to the full extent of your power in all our peaceful treaty rights against all unlawful violence and all riotous proceedings now threatening us."[43] In August 1877, when Senator Morton arrived in California, some Chinese merchants, introduced by Colonel Bee, requested an appointment with Morton; the merchants complained that the Burlingame Treaty was not being faithfully carried out by the United States.[44] On September 18, Bee, acting on behalf of the Six Companies, telegraphed Governor Irwin in Sacramento: Chinese who were "under solemn treaty obligations" had "a right to demand" that their lives and properties "be protected the same as that of citizens of the most favored nation."[45] Because of continuous anti-Chinese violence, the Six Companies even sent a telegram to President Rutherford Hayes on December 13, calling his attention to the obligation of the United States government for the Chinese security under the treaty.[46]

Given the marked attention attached to the Chinese question in the capital, the Six Companies hired a representative in Washington, Joseph Kennedy, "a man of ability and extensive acquaintance," who undoubtedly exercised "a great deal of influence with the Senators and Representatives."[47] On November 23, 1877, Kennedy asked to see President Hayes and read to him a telegram protesting violation of the treaties and signed by the presidents of the Six Companies. After emphasizing that the Chinese resident in America had been denied the protection guaranteed to them in Articles 1 and 2 of the Cushing Treaty, and Article 4 of the Burlingame Treaty, he appealed to the United States government to maintain and carry out these treaty obligations immediately.[48] Kennedy also read an accompanying letter during the conversation, which he reported would be shown to "the Cabinet at its meeting tomorrow, when the matter is to be discussed." This letter emphasized that the lawless aggression against the Chinese would disgrace Americans as violators of national contracts. In addition, Kennedy called attention to reciprocal justice: "If we expect and require the Emperor of China to protect our people within his dominions, by virtue of a treaty of our own exaction, it is natural that the people of that great empire will expect protection here for their countrymen." Treaty violation, he warned, would "cause retaliation and justify a declaration of non-intercourse, to the destruction of trade and commerce."[49]

Some days later, the Six Companies sent a letter to Secretary of State Evarts stating that Chinese residents had been denied the protection guaranteed them in Articles 1 and 11 of the Cushing Treaty and Article 4 of the Burlingame Treaty. They cited the public threats by large gatherings of people to drive the Chinese out from San Francisco and destroy their property.[50] Kennedy again delivered a communication to the State Department on December 11, 1877, that appealed for the protection according to the "existing treaties" in this "free country."[51]

In February 1878 Colonel Bee sent a letter to Secretary of State Evarts asking for the "protection of the National Government" because it was what the Chinese "supposed solemn treaty obligations entitled them to."[52] After two anti-Chinese bills were introduced in Congress, the Six Companies' representative Joseph Kennedy protested the bills on February 25 before the Committee on Foreign Relations, citing treaty obligations. He stressed an important principle of a modern nation-state system: "It may, as illustrative of the opinions of other nations, be proper to refer to the conclusion on this subject of the congress of Paris in 1856, composed of plenipotentiaries of Great Britain, France, Prussia, Sardinia, and Turkey, that it is an essential principle of the law of nations that 'none of them can liberate itself from the engagements of a treaty, nor modify the stipulations thereof, unless with the consent of the contracting parties by means of an amicable understanding.'" He alluded to the importance of Chinese trade by pointing out that the exclusion policy actually blocked "the wheels of national progress, of which only a faint bluish-tint appears in the $21,111,446 of exports to China in the year 1877 from the single port of San Francisco."[53]

The Six Companies' efforts were successful. Almost all the measures to limit the Chinese immigration in the 1870s failed to pass either body of Congress. Although the Fifteen Passenger Bill did pass both houses in 1879, President Hayes vetoed it on the grounds that it violated the Burlingame Treaty.[54]

Demanding Indemnity

The Chinese in the United States were repeatedly subjected to acts of violence, especially in the 1870s and 1880s. But they were not passive victims. Whenever Chinese deaths occurred, the Six Companies sent agents to investigate. On the night of March 14, 1877, for example, five white men entered a shanty about two miles east of Chico. They shot six Chinese living there and searched for money. Afterward, they poured coal oil throughout the shanty and set it on fire. Soon after, Colonel Bee sent R. B. Hall, head of Hall & Co.'s detectives, to look into the matter.[55] On September 21 of the same year, mob violence erupted in Rocklin. The Chinese buildings were set afire and the Chinese were driven out of town. A reporter for the *Chronicle* asked Colonel Bee what the Six Companies would do about the riot. Bee answered that as soon as news of the affair reached San Francisco, the heads of the Six Companies telegraphed Ah Sam, "a shrewd Chinaman of considerable ability," instructing him to bring charges against the perpetrators at any cost. Ah Sam searched the house where the tragedy happened[56] for the Six Companies was well aware that without evidence, their indemnity claims would fail in court.

Naturally, in addition to its own investigations, the Six Companies appealed to the U.S. government for protection. On April 4, 1876, the organization sent a letter to the Board of Supervisors of San Francisco stating that "moral and legal responsibilities rest with you" when residents ask for protection.[57] An appeal was also sent to Mayor Bryant of San Francisco informing him that anti-Chinese societies had "formed in every ward of the city and in many towns of the State." Though the Chinese were "acquainted with peaceful vocations," the appeal continued, many had lived "long enough in this country to learn that self-defense... [was] the common right of all men." Should "a riotous attack" be made upon the Chinese, the Six Companies had no power "to restrain... [the Chinese] from defending themselves to the last extremity."[58] On September 18, 1877, Colonel Bee wrote Governor Irwin that the Chinese should be protected as citizens of a "most favored nation," he condemned the fact that the U.S. government was failing to make any attempt to suppress the armed mobs intent on driving out Chinese residents and burning their property.[59] The presidents of the Six Companies sent another appeal to the mayor on November 4 complaining that mob violence was occurring "with increasing fury, without any check or hindrance by the authorities" and calling for municipal protection from the violence under their treaty rights. They called his attention to those "who use the most violent, inflammatory and incendiary language, threatening in plainest terms to burn and pillage the Chinese quarter and kill our people unless, at their bidding, we leave this 'Free Republic.'"[60] Soon afterward a gang of toughs attacked a party of 150 Chinese who had just reached San Francisco from Sacramento. In response the Six Companies sent President Hayes a telegram of protest on December 13, 1877, declaring that there had been no intervention by the police and no arrests. It also called the President's attention to an address that the governor of California had made to the State Legislature in which he cautioned that mobs might become too strong to control. The Companies reminded the President of the treaty obligations of the United States government for Chinese security.[61]

The Six Companies also asked the American government to cover Chinese losses. Early in 1876, in a letter to Secretary of State Evarts, Colonel Bee insisted that the Chinese were "entitled to indemnity for past outrages, and those that are here full protection for their lives and property in the future."[62] A year later the Six Companies' spokesman presented a claim against the United States government for indemnity in the case of the Chinese in San Francisco whose property had been destroyed during a riot. Application was made through the British minister in Washington, for China had no diplomatic representative in the United States, and the injured Chinese had emigrated from Hong Kong, a British colony.[63] The Chinese calculated that the cost of damage in the riot of 1877 was $125,000. They expected a payment of $100,000 from the United States government and $25,000 from the city of San Francisco.[64]

The Six Companies also emphasized reciprocal justice and equality among nations. On November 22, 1877, in his interview with the President concerning the Chinese troubles in California, the Six Companies spokesman Kennedy reminded the President that $1 million had been exacted from the Japanese government for "much less injury incurred in 1864 by the Americans [in Japan] than in each year experienced by the Chinese in California."[65] In addition, Kennedy delivered a message to the secretary of state pointing out that since the adoption of the treaty with China, the government of the United States had demanded and received nearly $800,000 in indemnities for malicious acts committed upon Americans residing in China. However, he complained, even though Chinese residents in the United States had experienced robberies and murders for many years, 95 percent of the perpetrators escaped punishment.[66] In January 1878 Colonel Bee dispatched a message to Secretary Evarts citing the case of a Chinese whose store was robbed and burned by a mob. Bee declared that as the American government had required the Qing government to pay an indemnity for American losses in China, "it would be no more than justice" for the American government to "reimburse" the Chinese for their losses.[67] In another letter to Evarts in February, Bee again stated that "the treaty between the two Governments being reciprocal in all its vital parts, they are entitled to indemnity for past outrages, and those that are here full protection for their lives and property in the future."[68] However, each of these requests for compensation failed.

Advocate of Legal Equality

In February 1878 San Francisco enforced the state's Cubic Air Law, which required that the Chinese must have 500 cubic feet of living space for each individual in any rented room, by arresting twenty-nine Chinese. The Six Companies hired "a prestigious lawyer" and petitioned the United States Circuit Court for a writ of habeas corpus on behalf of Ah Wing, one of the prisoners, to test the constitutionality of the law under which the arrest had been made. It was reported the Six Companies had raised more than $5,000 for this effort to test the law. Before Judges Lorenzo Sawyer and Ogden Hoffman, B. S. Brooks, D. W. Douthitt, and Colonel Bee insisted that the law discriminated against certain classes and was unconstitutional. The lawyers hired by the Six Companies argued that the Cubic Air Law was illegal, since it was in violation of Sections 1977 and 1979 of the Revised Statutes of the United States and was also in direct conflict with the terms of the Burlingame Treaty. They also charged that "the law was passed solely for the purpose of enforcing it against [the Chinese], and that there was never any intention to have it apply to those of any other nationality."[69] Although the Six Companies failed to undo the Cubic Air Law in this contest, the court decision emphasized that the city must enforce the law impartially and could not direct it solely at the Chinese.[70]

A month later the Six Companies engaged in another court contest on behalf of Ho Ah Kow, who had had his queue cut off in the county jail, where he had been sent for violating the Cubic Air Law. The Queue-cutting Ordinance mandated that Chinese taken to jail have their long braided queues cut to one inch, even though doing so made it impossible for them to return to China. Once again the Companies raised the constitutional claim, arguing that the queue-cutting violated the rights guaranteed the Chinese by federal laws and treaties.[71] The Six Companies succeeded in this case. The ordinance was, the court declared, "special legislation on the part of the supervisors against a class of persons who, under the Constitution and laws of the United States, are entitled to the equal protection of the laws."[72] Indeed the Six Companies was very active in fighting the Cubic Air and the Queue-cutting Laws. McClain says the following about the legal struggle against the ordinances: "One San Francisco paper was convinced that all three cases—Ah Wing, Ah Yup, and now the attack on the queue-cutting ordinance—were part of a general legal offensive, devised by the Six Companies and their attorney, a belief that is not implausible."[73]

The Chinese Lobby

After maturing for two decades, the Six Companies' lobbying efforts were now fully fledged. In 1873 a Six Companies pamphlet entitled "The Chinese Question from the Chinese Standpoint" was sent to the supervisors of San Francisco. It emphasized that the Chinese were peaceable, industrious, and compliant with American laws; they had no whiskey saloons and faithfully paid their rents, taxes, and debts.[74] That same year, Otis Gibson read a statement by the Six Companies to the Board of Supervisors of San Francisco. The Chinese empire, the statement said, had desired to "remain secluded, and not to admit foreigners or permit the Chinese to leave the country." But it had been forced to "throw off this exclusiveness," and treaties had been made with Western powers. In accord with these treaties, Chinese who were "law-abiding, peaceable, industrious, not addicted to drink" had come to America. Now the Chinese were ready "to propose a speedy abrogation of the treaty and retire from California with their trade and commerce, and drive American settlers from China."[75]

In the late 1870s the rise of the anti-Chinese activity was inevitably followed by an upsurge in apologetics by the Six Companies. In May 1876, the Six Companies sent a letter to President Grant declaring that the Chinese had understood that the whole spirit of American institutions was to welcome strangers from all parts of the world. As before, the Chinese leaders tried to prove that all charges against the Chinese were without foundation, and they provided a picture of the Chinese as peaceful and industrious, conforming to American laws, and respectful of American institutions. The letter refuted the charge that no virtuous Chinese women had been brought to the United States and that the Chinese in the United States had no wives and children. In fact, the Chinese leaders argued, a few hundred Chinese families were in the United States, and the Chinese women were all chaste, pure, keepers of their home, and not known on the public street. There were also a few hundred, perhaps a thousand, Chinese children who had been born in America. The reason why so few Chinese families had come to the United States was because it was contrary to Chinese customs and because the frequent outbursts of violence against the Chinese had discouraged men from bringing their families.

Confessing Chinese prostitutes had indeed been brought to this country by unprincipled men, they emphasized that Chinese prostitutes had at first been brought for the gratification of white men. A few years earlier, the Chinese leaders pointed out, Chinese merchants in California had tried to send these prostitutes back to China, but a certain American lawyer employed by unprincipled Chinese, had procured a writ of habeas corpus and brought all these women back on shore again. The courts had at that time ruled that the women had a right to stay in the country if they so desired. If American officers would refuse bribes, the letter argued, these unprincipled men could no longer purchase immunity from the punishment of their crimes.

Opposing the charge that the Chinese had purchased no real estate in the United States, the letter pointed out, although anti-Chinese sentiment had discouraged many from investing in real estate, other Chinese had already purchased over $800,000 worth of real estate in San Francisco alone. The letter also responded to the charge that Chinese eat only rice, fish, and vegetables. Confessing that it was true that their diet was slightly different from that of the people of the United States, they countered with a question: "But is that a sin on our part of *sufficient gravity* to be brought before the President and Congress of the United States?"

Countering the charge that the Chinese were of no benefit to this country, the letter asked: Were the railroads built by Chinese labor of no benefit to the United States? Were the manufacturing establishments, largely worked by Chinese, of no benefit to the United States? Was it of no benefit to this country that the Chinese annually paid over $2 million in duties at the Custom Houses of San Francisco? Was not the $200,000 annual poll tax paid by the Chinese of any benefit? And were not the hundreds of thousands of dollars of taxes on personal property and the foreign miners' tax of any benefit to this country?

To refute the charge that the Six Companies had secretly established judicial tribunals, jails, and prisons and was secretly exercising judicial authority over their own people, the letter proclaimed that the charge had no foundation at all. The Six Companies was simply a group of benevolent societies organized for the purpose of mutual protection and care of Chinese coming to and going from the United States. Nor did these companies import either men or women into this country.

It rejected the charge that all Chinese laborers were slaves. The letter emphasized that if the Chinese were slaves, then all men laboring for wages, including white workers, were slaves. The letter rejected the charge that Chinese commerce brought no benefit to American bankers and importers by drawing attention to the immense trade carried on between China and the United States by American merchants. Transport by steamers, sailing vessels, even the railroad was carried out by Americans; no Chinese ships were engaged in carrying traffic between the two countries. Finally the letter asked, how was the exchange of millions of dollars annually by the Chinese of this city of no benefit to its banks?[76]

In the same year Benjamin S. Brooks, "a retainer from the Six Companies," sent a pamphlet expanding on the rebuttal to the Committee on Foreign Relations of the United States Senate. Even if the Chinese were filthy in their habits and addicted to vice and shamelessly immoral, Brooks argued, they were not alone in these defects. Plenty of white people were guilty of the same charges. If the Chinese could not assimilate with the white race in the United States, it was because the white people were incapable of appreciating Chinese virtue.[77]

In two pamphlets published by the Six Companies in 1877—"Memorial to the Senate and House of Representatives of the United States" and "An Address to the People of the United States"—the Chinese leaders made clear their purpose: "Your memorialists desire to answer in detail the report of a portion of your Committee, by producing the testimony, thus challenging the correctness of that document and its conclusions."[78] To counterattack the claim that Chinese laborers in California had taken from California not less than $180 million, while they had contributed nothing to the state or national wealth, the Six Companies pointed out: "Its falsity was easily demonstrated," the whole number of Chinese in the United States "at any time did not exceed 90,000, and to credit them with having 'abstracted' $180,000,000 from this State is to allow $2,000 remittance for each individual." The charge was an insult to the common sense of every intelligent person in the United States. Had it not been for Chinese labor, the Chinese leaders continued, California would be far below the condition of prosperity and advancement she could now boast. As to the charge regarding the size of the Chinese population, the Six Companies argued, because California had a voting population of 155,000, no sane person would claim that the adult white foreign population numbered over 125,000.

However, it was asserted boldly by the State Senate Committee that there were 125,000 adult Chinese in California. Obviously, it was an exaggeration.[79]

Once again the address asserted that the Chinese were quiet, peaceful, orderly, temperate, sharp-witted, frugal, philosophical, neat, clean, faithful, honest, and honorable.[80] The Six Companies emphasized the importance of trade between the two countries, which reached tens of millions of dollars annually. Other foreign countries, they added, were looking jealously at the steady divergence of Chinese traffic toward the United States; the United States should therefore cherish the trade relationship between the two countries.[81]

On January 9, 1878, the Six Companies dispatched Joseph Kennedy with copies of the address to give to members of Congress. The organization hoped to find greater favor in Washington than California, for they reasoned that Congress would naturally shrink from any exclusionist action. The address pointed out flaws of the report of the Legislative Committee of the Senate of California in 1876, which had just been presented to the President.[82] In stark contrast to the widely accepted belief that Chinese immigration was not a benefit to the states, Colonel Bee compiled a statement for the Committee providing proof of the business transactions by the Chinese population of San Francisco. He also furnished the trade statistics to the *San Francisco Post* for publication.[83]

Joseph Kennedy addressed the House Committee on Education and Labor on February 18, 1878. He compared Chinese laborers with white workers: if the Chinese were a dishonest people, why was it that the Chinese merchants enjoyed better credit in San Francisco than Americans did? Their habits were thought to be filthy and dangerous to health, yet the Chinese were capable of doing more work than white laborers. It was claimed that a Chinese man was a slight, fragile being, debased by numerous vices, yet the Anglo-Saxon could not compete with him; he worked for nothing, but had sent $180 million to China; he added nothing to the wealth of the country, but supplied labor for California; he ought to be expelled, but this would derange industrial pursuits; his habits were such as to make people loathe him, yet he was received into almost every family as a domestic servant. Kennedy also emphasized that the Chinese were not Sabbath breakers, criminals, paupers, ballot-box stuffers, Molly Maguires, or conspirators against the public schools. Then turning to the charge of nonassimilation, he argued that the Chinese would assimilate with Americans if they were kindly treated, but the desire to assimilate would undoubtedly vanish like smoke if they were maltreated.[84]

Three days later Kennedy continued his testimony. He denied that Chinese labor in the United States consisted either of coolies or slaves; the Chinese were free men who had borrowed money and were simply under legal and moral obligation to repay it. After comparing the contracts of the Chinese to those made by white people in the early days of the Gold Rush, he remarked that the only noticeable difference between the Americans and the Chinese was that the Chinese had more scrupulously fulfilled their contracts. People who claimed that the Chinese impoverished the country by sending their earnings to China were ignorant of political economy, for they ignored the wealth the Chinese created. While it was natural to think that the wages earned left the country, it was foolish to claim that the Chinese impoverished the country. The improvement of the land, bringing it to a productive condition, for example, was a direct addition to the country's wealth. How trifling were the wages sent abroad compared with the enormous productivity of California due to Chinese labor, which had cultivated a million acres of land originally worth between $1 and $3 and now worth $100 an acre. It would also be wrong to believe that Chinese laborers damaged the employment opportunities of white workers. Because of the Chinese, better employment was available to white labor. The congressmen were asked to consider the employment opportunities and the value created by the railroads that the Chinese had built, of which there were 2,150 miles in California alone. Because of Chinese labor and industry, wages were higher and the cost of living lower in California than in the other states.[85]

Kennedy also addressed the Committee on Foreign Relations. Referencing material in a Senate report that placed the Chinese beneath the Caucasian by comparing the size and angle of their skulls, he argued that the report was self-contradictory. He pointed out that the author spoiled his entire theory by claiming: "Like wine and water, we will never mix, and in the great struggle for existence, the Chinamen *will come to the top every time* if left to free and equal competition." Before America's ancestors even existed, Chinese were familiar with the compass, the printing press, glass, and gunpowder.[86] To highlight the benefits of the Chinese immigration in industry, agriculture, and railroad construction, Kennedy pointed out that the Chinese contributed $17 million annually into San Francisco manufacturing; they shipped $18.5 million worth of wheat from the city; they recovered $100 million worth of gold and silver in 1877. He argued that American "trade with China is a valuable interest, which should not be relinquished for a people who care nothing for the national honor like the anti-Chinese people of California."[87]

Kennedy argued again before the Committee on Foreign Relations on February 25, 1878. To oppose the bills "To restrict the immigration of the Chinese to the United States" and "To regulate Chinese immigration," he first recalled America's treaty obligations and then turned to the importance of trade between the two countries. He asked rhetorically: "Should we experience the loss of the vast and rapidly-growing commercial advantages which the observance of common honesty in living up to our obligations is sure to guarantee us in the immediate, and augmenting with the distant future?"[88]

No doubt in part because of the Six Companies' lobbying efforts, almost all measures to limit Chinese immigration in the 1870s failed to get enough votes to pass either body of Congress.

Promoting the Establishment of a Chinese Legation

In the 1870s the effect of the anti-Chinese movement was so serious that the Six Companies decided to seek help from the Qing government. But this was not an easy task. Not only was the Qing government unprepared to establish modern foreign relations, but the Chinese merchants also had to overcome a sort of indifference on the part of almost all Qing officials, for they were universally trained in Confucian classics and thus suffered from the Confucian bias against commercial activity.[89]

The efforts of the Six Companies were a key factor in shaking the Qing government out of its lethargy. Starting in the 1870s, whenever China had natural disasters, the Six Companies offered financial and material assistance. During the north China famine in 1876 and 1877, for example, Chinese merchants in California donated nearly $10,000 for famine relief.[90] Recognizing their low social status in China, the Chinese merchants in California took pains to choose Chinese scholars as their leaders. This was not a temporary measure. From the beginning of *huiguan* in California until the end of the nineteenth century, the presidents of the *huiguan* were usually selected from "the scholarly men from the various districts"—holders of Jinshi and Juren degrees, successful candidates to the civil service examinations at metropolitan and provincial levels.[91] Whenever important Qing officials visited or passed through California, the Six Companies always seized the opportunity to entertain them. During their visits in California, Qing officials concluded that due to the efforts of the Six Companies the overseas Chinese were Qing loyalists. Zhang Deyi noted in his diary that San Francisco Chinatown looked "surprisingly like the city of Canton" and that of all Chinese in San Francisco, "those who are dressed in Western clothes are less than 1%." The Chinese leaders had posted a notice at the front of the hotel where the delegation stayed, which said: "No Chinese who wears Western-style clothes should see the Imperial Commissioners dispatched by the Emperor."[92] Such actions and the attitudes they indicated must have narrowed the gap between the merchants in the United States and the mandarin officials, and they may have been a key factor in changing the Qing's lassitude.

More important, the Six Companies asked protection from the Qing government and strongly promoted the establishment of a Qing legation in Washington, DC as well as a consulate in San Francisco. In August 1874 the Six Companies approached a Chinese government official who was in California en route to Washington and urged him to petition the imperial government to dispatch a consul to safeguard their interests. The Companies would be willing to pay at least part of the expenses involved.[93]

At the end of 1874 the Qing attitude toward making use of Chinese merchants in future diplomatic missions was reinforced. Li Zongyi, governor-general of Liangjiang province and superintendent of trade for the Southern Ports,[94] sent a memoir to the court on December 20, which dealt with the choosing of diplomatic and consular representatives. He pointed out that a large number of Chinese lived in such foreign ports as Singapore, Penang, Old Gold Mountain (San Francisco), and New Gold Mountain (the goldfields in Victoria, Australia). He noted that they had organized *huiguan* and elected "head men," called presidents, who were generally well known and longing for home, and who always entertained Chinese who passed through the ports. Since all the presidents were able persons, they should be appointed irrespective of their background. Chinese envoys should not only make friends with the presidents of the Chinese *huiguan* and persuade them to act together, but also award them official positions.[95] This memoir is too important to be neglected, and as we will see, the Qing government did eventually accept Li Zongyi's suggestions.

In 1875 the Six Companies not only sent a letter to Li Hongzhang, governor-general of Zhili and superintendent of trade for the Northern Ports, Li Zongyi's counterpart in China, that detailed the abuses and intimidation the Chinese faced in California, but also enclosed in the letter a number of threatening newspaper statements in order to show Li how serious the situation was.[96] Such letters evidently convinced the Qing government that a permanent mission had to be appointed to protect the Chinese in America.[97]

Soon after the appointment of Chen Lanbin as the first Chinese minister to Washington in December 1875, some Cantonese in Guangdong, who claimed to be relatives of the Chinese in California, petitioned Governor-General Liu Kunyi in Canton for the establishment of a Chinese consulate in California. Like the arguments of the Six Companies, the petitions stated that the Chinese in California could collect enough money to support the Chinese consuls. On August 29, 1876, Liu Kunyi reported the request to the Zongli Yamen and sent similar letters to Li Hongzhang and Chen Lanbin, in which he suggested the establishment of a consulate in California to help protect the Chinese in California from harassment.[98]

The Six Companies held a meeting on April 2, 1876, at the Sanyi Company in San Francisco. A merchant named Ah Pak delivered a long address indicating that the situation was pressing. A communication must be sent to the Qing government about establishing a consulate. If a consul was appointed, another merchant emphasized, "money should be raised on the Coast sufficient to pay him a handsome salary tax would be made on the Chinese government."[99] The Six Companies then sent a letter to Ou Eliang, the Chinese education commissioner, explaining the plight of the Chinese immigrants and asking him for advice.[100] Ou passed the information on to Yung Wing, the founder of the Chinese Educational Mission in the United States.[101] Yung Wing sent the Six Companies' letter on to the Zongli Yamen. Its contents subsequently formed the substance of the Yamen's exchange with U.S. Secretary of State William Seward.[102] On October 28, 1876, Li Hongzhang sent a letter to Chen Lanbin concerning Yung's letter and reiterated the need for a consul in San Francisco.[103]

In the 1870s anti-Chinese sentiment rapidly escalated and took on a national character, so the Six Companies rose up in self-defense on several fronts. The Six Companies clearly understood and used elements of Western ideology as a means for defending "Chinese" rights. As the champion for all the Chinese, the Six Companies expanded its crusade from California to Washington, where the organization attempted to safeguard the rights of the Chinese as citizens of an equal nation, as had been established by the Burlingame Treaty and endorsed by the federal government. Violations of the treaty stipulations, the organization claimed, would disgrace the United States and make the country infamous in the eyes of other nations. Invoking the most-favored-nation clause and established modern international practices, the Six Companies was also the first modern Chinese organization to demand indemnity for losses they suffered in violence and robbery. As a modern Chinese fighter for legal equality, the organization unhesitatingly tested the constitutionality of the discrimination against Chinese in American courts. The Six Companies also suggested that stopping the influx of Chinese was against the whole spirit of American institutions, which sought to welcome strangers from all parts of the world. Publishing articles, making speeches, and sending pamphlets to Congress to correct repeated charges and the deep-rooted unfavorable image of the Chinese that had been presented to American people and legislatures, the Six Companies worked at its role as a modern Chinese lobbyist. The organization hoped this American mode of addressing the public would have a positive effect on the actions of Congress and the general sentiment of the country. Ultimately the Six Companies also petitioned the Qing government for protection, which eventually led to the establishment of the first Chinese legation in the United States.

On the surface, it suggested that the Six Companies and the Chinese were motivated by self-interest—with a Chinese legation in the United States they would be better protected and would face fewer discrimination laws, harassment, and humiliation. But upon further investigation, we find that it had more profound messages. By identifying their interest with the presence of the Qing consulate and bounding themselves and the legation closely together, the Six Companies and the Chinese in California also distinguished themselves from the rest of the immigrants who were assimilating. Further, this provided the evidence that the Six Companies promoted and facilitated the Qing government's acceptance of foreign relations defined by the Western nation-state system. Therefore the importance of the Six Companies' diplomacy in the 1870s, as before, is self-evident: it was not Chinese culture as such that was defended, but Chinese rights. The acceptance of Western ideologies and means distinguished the Six Companies' diplomacy from traditional Chinese culturalism and the tributary system. Thus, the role of the Six Companies in the development of modern Chinese nationalism is of critical importance.

CHAPTER 6

"Superseding the Six Companies"

The Qing Legation, 1878–1890

> The coming of this Embassy is quite a surprise and the question—Why have they come? is in everybody's mouth. We cannot answer by the card otherwise than as the diplomatic Chin Mook answered a *Chronicle* interviewer. He said they were going to supersede the Six Companies, establish consulates, and look after the interests of the race generally in Cuba, Peru and this country, with headquarters at Washington.
>
> —"Why Have They Come?"

On July 26, 1878, San Francisco's Chinatown was aglow with excitement. Chen Lanbin, the first minister plenipotentiary from China, accompanied by a full diplomatic corps, was about to arrive. The news was received with outbursts of delight among the Chinese in the city and rapidly spread throughout the state. The prominent Chinese merchants immediately hired nearly forty carriages to be driven to the wharf. Chen Lanbin remained secluded in his cabin on the Pacific Mail Steamship Company's steamer *City of Tokio* until Shuck Pun, the delegate of the Chinese merchants, arrived and went in to meet him. Each dropped onto his right knee and bowed in salutation. No words were exchanged. Shuck Pun left the cabin after a servant came up and whispered something to him, and Chen Lanbin, with the five of his entourage next highest in rank, went into another cabin and prepared to meet the formally attired presidents of the Six Companies. They were led in by Shuck Pun. Each *huiguan* leader went first to Chen Lanbin, and the two men then dropped to the right knee and bowed. After salutations were exchanged, they took the carriages to the Palace Hotel where the national dragon flag of China was flying on the Market Street side and the American flag on the New Montgomery Street front. On arriving at the hotel, the members of the embassy were settled into the twenty rooms on the second and third floors. After a rest of half an hour, Chen Lanbin received visitors. The first to be introduced was Col. Frederick

Bee, the representative of the Six Companies. Then prominent Chinese merchants, newspaper reporters, and others were invited in. It was the first day of the Qing legation in the United States.[1]

After the establishment of consular offices in San Francisco, Sit Ming Cook, one of the Chinese consuls in San Francisco, told a reporter for the *Chronicle* outright that it would "supersede the authority of the Six Companies" because the Six Companies had in reality been exercising authority of a governmental character in the United States. In a different interview Minister Chen Lanbin assured the reporter that the embassy would to a great extent "supersede" the authority and influence of the Six Companies.[2] How, exactly, did the Chinese government do this?

The Chinese Merchants: Victims of the Anti-Chinese Movement

To understand what happened requires a review of the challenges the Chinese faced in this period. After the depression of 1873, which finally reached California in 1876, and the depression of 1885–1886, California was brought to the verge of bankruptcy. Her industries, prostrated and ruined, made paupers of the working population. The economic dislocation meant there was no more room for the Chinese, and it is quite natural that they encountered stronger discrimination, opposition, violence, and forcible expulsion. By the late 1870s popular sentiment and all the rhetoric expressing it held that the Chinese laborers must go, even if Chinese trade went with them. A story from 1878 illustrates this clearly: the Marin County supervisors advertised for bids to build a road from Bolinas Bay to Fairfax. One Chinese merchant's proposal was $1,500, lower than that of any other bidders, but the supervisor awarded the contract to the next highest bidder, a white man, "out of deference to the anti-Chinese sentiment."[3]

In the 1880s a movement to boycott the employment of Chinese and the purchase of goods they made was spreading. As a result, Hop Kee & Co., then the largest boot and shoe manufacturer on DuPont Street, declared bankruptcy in August 1885.[4] At the end of 1885 the *San Francisco Alta California* reported that many Chinese cigar-making factories had to close down due to lack of orders caused by the boycott of Chinese manufacturers.[5] Quang Sing & Co., one of the largest Chinese boot and shoe manufacturing factories, noted that from the withdrawal of one retail store alone since the beginning in January 1886, they had lost at least $1,000 per month.[6] When discussing the effects of the anti-Chinese agitation, the *San Francisco Alta California* also stated: "The general uprising against the Chinese throughout the state and coast, especially in Seattle and other portions of Washington Territory of California, has an exceedingly depressing and dispiriting effect on trade in Chinese-made goods."[7] As a consequence a large number of Chinese firms suspended business and the failures continued "with alarming frequency."[8]

The experience of Chin Kit, a Chinese merchant in San Francisco, exemplifies the chain reaction. The failure of the firm of Ma Lee & Co. of Portland, Oregon, put him $6,000 in debt, and the expulsion of the Chinese caused him to lose an additional $5,000. In order to recover from these losses, he borrowed large sums from other Chinese merchants and then engaged in wheat and flour speculation, all the while paying a high rate of interest on his loan. However, his speculations failed, and he was forced into bankruptcy, and three of the Chinese companies that had advanced him nearly $50,000 were also forced to close.[9]

Chinese merchants faced other insecurities due to the anti-Chinese violence. In 1885 Consul Bee told a reporter of the *Daily Times-Telephone:* "Many of them [the Chinese] are peaceable merchants, whose business has been broken up by their expulsion."[10] When the worst of the anti-Chinese riots, at Rock Springs in the Wyoming Territory and Seattle in the Washington Territory, were over in February 1886, they had caused more than $500,000 in property damages. Chinese merchants in the Washington Territory alone suffered additional losses of more than $300,000.[11]

These two most violent upsurges against the Chinese had created large flows of Chinese laborers into San Francisco and thus placed a huge burden on the merchants,[12] for the *huiguan,* as mutual-aid associations, had to take care of these Chinese laborers forced to seek refuge.[13] The *Chronicle* reported on January 16, 1886, that the great number of unemployed Chinese driven from towns in the interior was "becoming a serious matter to the Chinese Six Companies."[14] On February 6, 1886, an association in Chinatown posted the following notice: since the soup kitchen erected by the Six Companies was not large enough for all the poor in the city, "we have accordingly made arrangements with the Tung Yee restaurant to supply those of our district—the Tung Kun—who are really extremely poor, without charge."[15]

The moral component of the crusade against Chinese immigration also continued. The *San Francisco Post* in 1878 complained: "No white laborers anywhere in modern city life would be allowed to herd and horde together as the Mongolians are."[16] An editorial in the *American Journal of the Medical Science* in 1881 made clear that medical professionals were disturbed by the crowded conditions, alleged filth, and strange germs in Chinatown, and it warned of epidemics as a result.[17] "There is an absolute necessity that the Chinese quarter should be brought as fully under the domain of the laws as any other section of the city," the *San Francisco Bulletin* demanded. "Its streets must be cleaned, its premises inspected and its dens of vice suppressed."[18]

Chinese merchants were looked upon with more and more disfavor. Complaining about their "non-assimilation," the *San Francisco Post* in 1878 argued that Chinese merchants were "most prominent as examples of the very evils the presence of their people brings to our life and institutions.... [N]onassimilation is not only an ingrained fact,... it is fast becoming an aggressive policy on the part of the 'Chinese merchants' who control their countrymen on this coast."[19]

At last, it seemed, the Chinese would have to bow to the inevitable when the United States Congress took action. Prior to the establishment of the Qing legation, anti-Chinese legislation was generally confined to the West Coast. But slowly yielding to public pressure, which was inevitably moving in one direction, Congress passed the Chinese Exclusion Act in 1882, which suspended Chinese labor immigration for ten years. Thus Chinese laborers became the first group to be denied entry into the United States on the basis of nationality. Then the mid-1880s boycott against Chinese merchandise essentially drove Chinese merchants out of the American market. By 1890 the meeting of the old Cantonese market economy and American capitalist market economy on the West Coast had virtually come to an end.[20]

The Qing Legation Enlists the Six Companies

Despite their dreadful difficulties, the Chinese nonetheless had reason to be excited in 1878—an official Qing legation had finally arrived in the United States to look after their welfare. The *San Francisco Alta California* wrote: "There need be little doubt that the unsatisfactory position of Chinese emigrants in California has been the main cause of the departure of the mission for Washington."[21] The Chinese looked to this new diplomatic representation for relief and leadership. But how could the Qing legation, which was without modern diplomatic experience and was just becoming established in the United States, deal with the anti-Chinese movement?

While he was still in San Francisco, Chen Lanbin was again told by the Six Companies that the Chinese immigrants were easy targets for attacks because they lacked protection. They were especially assaulted and plundered by the Irish in California.[22] On September 19, 1878, Chen memorialized the emperor requesting establishment of a Chinese consulate in California. "His sense of urgency was probably promoted by what he had seen and heard about the Chinese in San Francisco."[23] His request was granted, and San Francisco's first Chinese consulate, located at No. 917 Clay Street, opened on December 12, 1878. Along with its regular duties, the consulate also served as "a school of diplomacy where young Mongols will study the American life and people."[24]

Because the Six Companies knew the condition of the Chinese in the United States and the steps necessary for their protection, it is not at all strange that one of Chen Lanbin's first actions in the United States was to appoint Colonel Bee, the spokesman of the Six Companies, as a consul of the Chinese consulate in San Francisco.[25] In a joint memorandum with Yung Wing to the throne in early 1879, they urged that consuls be appointed to protect the Chinese in California. When suggesting Colonel Bee as a Chinese consul, they emphasized that the assistance of an experienced American was especially indispensable as the consulate was being established. Previously Bee had often helped Chinese immigrants in disputes with Americans and, therefore, he was qualified to act as Chinese consul.[26] Consul Bee accompanied the Qing diplomats to Washington and after a few months went back to San Francisco.[27] He would stay on the staff of the San Francisco Chinese Consulate until his death in 1892.[28]

In addition, the Qing legation enlisted all the presidents of the Six Companies as advisers.[29] On November 28, 1888, Minister Zhang Yinhuan asked Thomas Bayard, the secretary of state, to admit Lum Tang Ying "who engaged to be the director of the Gang Chow club [Gangzhow *huiguan*] in that port [San Francisco] and to assist him [the Chinese consul] in the discharge of his consular duties."[30] Lee Hon Fun, the president of the Ningyang *huiguan* in 1889 was reported to be employed by Liang Tingzan, the Chinese consul-general, "to assist him in the discharge of his consular duties in the connection with the Chinese affairs."[31] On September 12, 1889, Zhang notified the new secretary of state, James G. Blaine, again that Cheong Hew Choe, the new president of the Sanyi *huiguan*, would help the Chinese consul-general in San Francisco.[32]

In 1888 the Chinese legation also hired two retiring officials, one from the Ningyang *huiguan* and the other from the Gangzhou *huiguan*. On approving the request, the Chinese minister commented that "in the Gold Mountain, where Chinese and foreigners live together... their knowledge of the people and place can help to resolve disputes."[33] When Liang Lianfang completed his term as the president of the Sanyi *huiguan*, he became a diplomatic attaché at the Chinese consulate in Hawai`i.[34]

The Qing government also enlisted the Tung Wah Hospital, the Six Companies' information center in Hong Kong, as its own information clearinghouse. In 1882, when Minister Chen Lanbin set up a bureau in Canton to help people establish contact with their relatives abroad, he asked Tung Wah Hospital to transmit the letters to major foreign cities where the *huiguan* and Chinese consulates would distribute them. The Chinese ministers in Washington came to depend heavily on the hospital to provide and disseminate information.[35]

To choose suitable diplomats to serve in the United States, the Qing government turned to people from Guangdong, who understood the Cantonese dialect that almost all Chinese in California spoke. This action especially encouraged communication and cooperation between the legation and the Six Companies. Five of the seven ministers and the only associate minister to come to Washington from 1878 to 1907 were from Guangdong; this was not the case in other countries where the Qing sent envoys. None of the eight ministers to England between 1875 and 1907, and only one of the eleven ministers to Japan from 1876 to 1907, was a native of Guangdong.[36] The Qing government furthermore deliberately sent low-level diplomats originating from Guangdong to the United States. For example, fifteen of the twenty of Chen Lanbin's diplomatic corps were from Guangdong province.[37]

The Qing government formalized its relations with the Six Companies. After a joint petition from the leaders of the Six Companies, in 1882 Zheng Zaoru, the second minister sent to Washington from China, gave the Six Companies the formal name of Jinshan zhonghua zong huiguan (Gold Mountain National Chinese General Native-place Association) or Chinese Consolidated Benevolent Association-San Francisco (CCBA-SF) and requested that their presidents take turns serving as director of the organization's council.[38] The Qing government not only engraved an official seal for the Six Companies,[39] but it also turned the Six Companies into the assembly place for Qing consuls and leaders of the Six Companies when they wished to discuss important issues.[40] Following the founding of Jinshan zhonghua zong huiguan, Chinese diplomatic officials used it as an example to encourage the formation of CCBAs in other large Chinese communities. They were established in New York City in 1883, Honolulu in 1884, Lima (in Peru) in 1885, and Portland sometime before 1887.[41] Zhang Yinhuan, Zheng's successor, not only began to ask the governor-general at Canton to investigate the background of any president employed by the Six Companies,[42] but he also initiated the practice of issuing official passports to these men.[43] Beginning in 1888 the Chinese ministers began to recommend the presidents of overseas Chinese associations for awards after the presidents had served for three years.[44]

The Qing Legation as Chinatown Reformer

It is not surprising that the Qing legation policy with regard to Chinatown reflected that of the Six Companies. First, it was of vital importance to remove any firewood from under the cauldron of anti-Chinese sentiment, and hence the legation sought to curb anything disgraceful and infamous within the Chinese community. Here again the Qing legation simply "superseded" the Six Companies, carrying on the fight the Six Companies had begun and employing its strategies. In the early 1880s, for example, Consul-General Huang Zunxian in his formal reports to Minister Zheng Zaoru suggested that the honesty of any Chinese women bound for the United States be vouched for by Chinese merchants in San Francisco and a Chinese consul. Only those who had guarantees from the consul could apply for their passports.[45] Zhang Yinhuan's diary also reveals that Chinese consuls sent Chinese prostitutes back to Tung Wah Hospital in Hong Kong for repatriation.[46]

The tong wars, which escalated in the 1880s, began to replace Chinese prostitution as the biggest problem in Chinese settlements. In order to control the Chinese immigrant underworld and monopolize the profits from prostitution, gambling, opium smoking, and Chinese labor smuggling, the notorious tongs employed highbinders or hatchet men to assassinate each other. In 1883 Ouyang Ming, the Chinese consul in New York, issued a proclamation to the Chinese in that city asking them to refrain from conflicts, opium smoking, and gambling.[47] Immediately after a serious San Francisco tong feud in 1886, Zhang Yinhuan announced: "It is my responsibility to protect the Chinese,... [but] all the Chinese have to live in harmony in order not to be mistreated by Americans." The appalling deeds of a small group of gangsters would taint the whole Chinese community. He warned that if there was any more violence, the troublemakers would be severely punished.[48]

To enhance the effectiveness of any reform activities, the Chinese legation and the Six Companies cooperated closely. To curb fighting between two tongs in the early 1880s, Consul Huang Zunxian not only sent an admonishing letter but also dispatched Zhao Wengong, the president of the Six Companies, and Zhou Bangli, secretary of the Sanyi *huiguan* to mediate the dispute.[49] In 1886 two violent clashes between tongs occurred, and the Six Companies appealed to Ouyang Ming, the Chinese consul-general in San Francisco, to issue a proclamation against violence among the Chinese. After receiving the petition from the consulate, Zhang wrote a proclamation warning that any crimes that tong members committed in the United States would lead to the punishment of their relatives in China. Instead of fighting each other, Zhang suggested, the Chinese should bring their arguments before the Six Companies or Consul Ouyang Ming for arbitration.[50] Zhang also asked the consul-general in San Francisco to select about two hundred hooligans, racketeers, gangsters, and gamblers for punishment in China. In cooperation, the Six Companies accumulated more than $7,000 for passage fees, but because this activity contravened American laws, which said that crimes committed in the United States had to be resolved in American courts, they had to give up the effort.[51]

Like the Six Companies, the Chinese diplomats realized the limited effectiveness of their reform efforts, and so they tried to get extraterritorial rights to punish Chinese criminals. In 1887, in negotiation for a new treaty to restrict Chinese immigration, one article of Zhang Yinhuan's draft treaty provided for the legation's right to deport Chinese criminals to China.[52] Because the United States had signed treaties with many countries over the extradition of criminals, Zhang argued, this article should also be included in the new treaty with China.[53]

The Six Companies' moral exhortation policy was also handed on. In the early 1880s Huang Zunxian, the Chinese consul-general in San Francisco, and the leaders of the Chinese community assembled at the Six Companies several times to discuss the possibility of having a Chinese school to teach classical Chinese morality to the children of the immigrants in San Francisco.[54] After Minister Zhang Yinhuan instructed the Chinese consulate in San Francisco to establish a Chinese language school in April 1886, the Six Companies gave strong backing both by donating $34,000 for construction and by contributing regularly afterward to the upkeep of the school to teach the Sacred Edict of Guangxu.[55]

Finally, the Chinese legation continued the practice of the Six Companies to set up new hospitals. On May 30, 1886, several *huiguan* leaders told Zhang Yinhuan that the Chinese in San Francisco needed their own hospital because if the Chinese went to American hospitals, the Americans would force them to change their way of dressing. The minister immediately donated $100 to initiate a hospital fund.[56] In late 1887 and early 1888, promising to contribute $14,000, the Six Companies asked Liang Tingzan, the consul-general, to raise more funds for the construction of a bigger Chinese hospital.[57] Liang Tingzan supported the project and requested that the *huiguan* leaders cooperate closely.[58] After a piece of land was purchased in Liang's name, Consul Bee announced that the Six Companies would build the 100-bed hospital and offer free medical care to all Chinese. However, the project failed because there was an outcry from residents in the area, and the San Francisco Board of Supervisors refused to grant the necessary permission.[59] To make matters worse, the city health authorities closed down nearly all the other Chinese medical facilities, but provided no alternative, and so Chinese patients were simply driven out into the streets.[60] On May 15 Consul Bee expressed his frustration to a *Chronicle* reporter: "How about the French hospital, the Sisters of Mercy hospital, the German, the Italian, and last, but not least, the City and County hospital? . . . If it be illegal to maintain a Chinese hospital in the city and county, it is most certainly illegal to maintain any other hospital." After giving this statement, the consul seized his hat and excused himself on the ground that he had an appointment at his lawyer's office.[61]

The Qing Legation Fights for Chinese Legal Equality

Like the Six Companies, the Chinese consulate in San Francisco also tested the constitutionality of actions by the Sinophobic white majority in the courts. Soon after the passage of the new California Constitution in 1879, which prohibited corporations from employing Chinese, the president of the Sulphur Bank Quicksilver Mining Company filed a petition for a writ of habeas corpus in the United States Circuit Court. Delos Lake, a representative of the Chinese consulate, argued in court that the California statute denied to the Chinese the right that others had and therefore violated the Fourteenth Amendment. The argument received sympathetic responses from Judges Lorenzo Sawyer and Ogden Hoffman, who ruled that California did not have the power to limit Chinese employment rights.[62]

The Chinese won other cases as well. On May 22, 1880, a few days after six Chinese fishermen had been arrested in Vallejo for violating the law prohibiting Chinese from fishing in the waters of California, Consul Bee, Delos Lake, and Thomas Riordan, representatives of the Chinese consulate, filed a petition for a writ of habeas corpus in the federal circuit court on the fishermen's behalf. The lawyers argued that the arrest was illegal since the law ran counter to the Burlingame Treaty, the Fourteenth Amendment, and Section 1977 of the Revised Statutes. Again their efforts were rewarded, and the court ruled that any law singling out the Chinese violated the Fourteenth Amendment.[63]

The successes must have been inspiring for the newly established Chinese consulate. In May 1880 another anti-Chinese ordinance was passed that made it unlawful for any person to maintain a laundry in a frame building without the consent of the Board of Supervisors. A Chinese laundryman was tried for violating the new law. This again was made a test case. Thomas D. Riordan, counsel for the Chinese consulate, argued in the court that the ordinance was unconstitutional for the following reasons: in addition to the fact that the Consolidation Act did not empower the Board to pass the ordinance, it was unreasonable, unjust, and oppressive because it was directed solely at the Chinese and therefore violated the Fourteenth Amendment. In addition, it deprived the defendant of both his vested rights and his property without due process of law. In this case the Chinese succeeded again; the court ruled the ordinance invalid.[64]

Heartened, in 1882 the Chinese consulate filed a petition for a writ of habeas corpus in the Federal Circuit Court on behalf of several Chinese crewmen who were denied entry into the United States by the collector of customs in San Francisco.[65] They argued again that the action of the collector of customs violated both the Constitution of the United States and the Burlingame Treaty. And again the court decided in favor of the Chinese: the 1882 act could not be applied to the petitioner since an American ship was deemed to be part of American territory.[66]

In 1883 Chin Ah Ki, Chin Man Chow, and Chin Ah On, three Chinese merchants returning from China, were not allowed to land. The legation brought their case to the United States District Court. The *San Francisco Bulletin* of

October 29, 1883, noted that "Thomas D. Riordan and A. P. Van Duzen appear as attorneys for the petitioners and they are seated by the side of Colonel Bee, the Chinese Consul at this port, and Tsing Hoy, the vice consul and interpreter of the Legation." They maintained that the Chinese were "unlawfully deprived of their liberty to which they were entitled" by the Burlingame Treaty and the treaty of 1880. The court delivered its decision that the Exclusion Act of 1882 could not be applied to Chinese who had left the United States before the law went into effect.[67]

In 1884 a Chinese girl born in the United States was denied enrollment in a public school by the San Francisco school superintendent. Consul Bee sent a strong letter to the superintendent emphasizing that the denial was inconsistent with the Constitution, the laws of the United States, and the treaties. William F. Gibson, the son of Otis Gibson, warned that the Chinese would go to court if the consulate's petition was refused. Then in the California Supreme Court, William Gibson argued that not only did Section 1662 of the Political Code stipulate that the schools should be open to "all children," but also the most-favored-nation provision of the Burlingame Treaty guaranteed that Chinese children should share the same privileges as the children of other aliens. Their effort, another success, made it possible for the girl to gain admission to the school by order of the Supreme Court.[68]

Also in 1884, Look Tin Sing, a fourteen-year-old Chinese boy who had been born in California and sent to China for education, was denied reentry and detained aboard his ship pending deportation to China. A lawyer took out a writ of habeas corpus on Look's behalf, "very probably with the financial support of the [Chinese] consulate or some domestic Chinese organization [*huiguan*]."[69] According to Section 1 of the Fourteenth Amendment, the lawyer argued, Look Tin Sing was a U.S. citizen and therefore was entitled to enter the country. The court ruled that Look Tin Sing should be allowed to land.[70]

In 1886, in a case concerning the Nicolaus riot, Consul Bee informed the court that he had retained Hall McAllister to represent the Chinese in the case. He argued that all treaties between the two countries guaranteed the Chinese the right to reside and trade in the United States and that the Angell Treaty of 1880 further secured measures of protection for the Chinese in the United States. The Supreme Court again voted in favor of the Chinese.[71]

While Congress continued to try to tighten the screws against the Chinese after 1888, the Chinese consulate and the Six Companies together fought exclusion in the courts. Soon after the Congress passed the Scott Act on September 18, 1888, which provided that Chinese laborers who left the United States would not ever be allowed to return, the Six Companies raised about $100,000 to test the constitutionality of the act in the case of *Chae Chan-pin v. the United States.* The attorney for the Six Companies was Thomas Riordan, who "may in fact... [be] under joint retainer to the Six Companies and the consulate."[72] This time, however, the Chinese did not succeed. Although admitting that the act contravened the treaties, the Supreme Court held that the act was constitutional because the United States had the plenary power to exclude aliens from its territory.[73]

The Qing Legation as a Lobby

The Six Companies ceased its lobbying efforts after the establishment of formal relations between the United States and China, leaving it to the Chinese diplomats to produce propaganda. rebut anti-Chinese charges, and emphasize the importance of Chinese trade. The chief Chinese legation lobbyist in the late 1870s and 1880s was Consul Bee, the former spokesman of the Six Companies. On November 22, 1878, soon after his appointment as consul, Bee delivered an hour-long speech to the Joint Congressional Committee at the Palace Hotel in San Francisco. Consul Bee refuted many charges and painted a rosy picture of the Chinese. He stressed that the Chinese immigration was in fact a benefit rather than a burden to Americans. The Chinese filled a vacuum of cheap labor and were especially needed in California. To refute the charge that the Chinese were like a cancer, slowly but surely eating into the every vitals of California and the United States, he pointed out that the Chinese had been brought here under a solemn treaty, and the Chinese laborers, by their willing industry, had contributed greatly to the present wealth of California. He highlighted the importance of trade between the two countries. Before the Burlingame Treaty, he said, trade of the Orient had been controlled by other nations, especially Great Britain. "Our fast clippers plying between here and China could be counted on our fingers." In order to catch up, Congress subsidized the Pacific Mail Steamship Company to the amount of $5 million, but, he complained: "This year has witnessed a demand for a modification or a complete abrogation of the Burlingame Treaty."[74]

Also in 1886 Consul Bee published a monograph entitled *The Other Side of the Chinese Question,* which gave an extended presentation of his support of the Chinese.[75] The Chinese have many vices, he argued, but they are industrious, frugal, temperate, and peaceful, and they pay their debts at the close of the year. Their white brothers have all of their vices, but few of their virtues; hence, it was absurd for the United States to compel Chinese to adopt the ways of the white race.[76] Against the charge that the Chinese had impoverished the country, he pointed out, that the only foreign currency circulating in China was Mexican dollars and that the Chinese did not send U.S. dollars directly back to China. America's fear of Chinese cheap labor was actually a delusion.

He further discussed the benefits of the Chinese immigration by quoting an article published in the *Overland Monthly:* "The employment of Chinese has enabled capitalists to invest money in factories with safety, and to promptly dismiss white laborers who would not work faithfully, and to give high wages to others." The result was that "gradually the proportion of whites increased."[77] Once again he stressed the importance of trade between the two countries. After the Burlingame Treaty was concluded, he pointed out, California began to introduce flour into China, first as an experiment but since then the trade had increased continuously until it reached 460,000 barrels in 1885. The increase in exported cotton cloth, ducks, and drills drove out the English manufacturers. Bee asked in closing: "Is it necessary to put 'embarrassing restrictions' upon this growing commerce?"[78] However reasonable, these lobbying efforts of the 1880s did not produce a successful outcome, for the anti-Chinese movement was swinging into full gear.

The Qing Government's Treaty Policy

The Chinese diplomats also inherited the Six Companies' emigration restriction policy. Consul Sit Ming Cook stated on July 27, 1878, that the Qing government wanted no more Chinese to come to the United States than could find work. But he nevertheless regarded the United States as bound by treaty to protect those Chinese who were already in the United States.[79] In 1879 the Qing government informed George F. Seward, the U.S. minister in Beijing (Peking), that China might cooperate in restricting the emigration of undesirables, such as the diseased, paupers, criminals, and prostitutes.[80] When former President Grant visited China in the same year, the Qing government suggested Chinese emigration restrictions on all "the laboring classes."[81]

Just before James B. Angell's mission to China in February 1880, the Six Companies sent a telegram to the Tung Wah Hospital Committee calling again for the restriction of Chinese emigration. The dispatch announced that a bill had been passed requiring U.S. citizens employing Chinese laborers to dismiss them and that over a thousand Chinese were consequently unemployed and homeless.[82] However, the repeated messages from the Six Companies had by now become annoying, and many people in Hong Kong and Guangdong province regarded them as insensitive; Chinese immigration more than doubled, from 5,802 in 1880 to 11,890 in 1881.[83]

It needs to be emphasized that the negotiation to modify the Burlingame Treaty in Beijing (Peking) was no doubt a success for the Six Companies. First, the talks went smoothly and quickly, so much that Angell wrote in his diary: "We signed treaties in 48 days from our first business meeting." Such expeditiousness when dealing with the Chinese had "rarely or never been known," and the foreign ministers in Beijing were "surprised."[84] Just two years before, a *San Francisco Call* reporter had commented that the Chinese government might not consent to modify the treaty: "Some years may be occupied in the preparation and transmission of documents in which the question will be discussed in all its bearings, but without practical result."[85] Second, the Six Companies' recommendations regarding immigration restriction and protection were fully incorporated in the four articles of the Angell Treaty of 1880: though the Government of the United States might regulate, limit, or suspend the arrival of Chinese, it would not prohibit such immigration or residence. Before the American government adopted measures limiting Chinese immigration, it would first inform the Chinese government. The treaty also assured the right of Chinese to come freely to the United States as teachers, students, and merchants; all Chinese residing in the United States were promised protection from any maltreatment. In any case where these measures induced hardship for Chinese immigrants, the Chinese government could bring the instances to the attention of the American government.

The Angell Treaty of 1880 did not, however, ease the problem; the anti-Chinese movement accelerated and by the mid-1880s had developed to the point of crisis. In a riot in 1886 more than forty Chinese were killed, and over $500,000 of property was damaged.[86] The Chinese once again had become the scapegoats in California for the industrial upheavals that racked the nation in the mid-1880s.

Once again the Six Companies intensified their advocacy of emigration restriction. On March 4, 1882, the Chinese leaders sent Tung Wah Hospital a telegram: "Great excitement against so many Chinese coming here; you must stop them or great trouble for us."[87] In 1885 the *Xunhuan ribao* (Daily circle), one of the first modern-style Chinese newspapers in Hong Kong, repeatedly published—on December 8, 10, 12, 13, and 14—a telegram sent by the Six Companies to Tung Wah Hospital: "Those who don't come to California will be benefited greatly; those who discourage their countrymen to California will have endless happiness."[88]

The ongoing efforts of the Six Companies must finally have had an impact on Minister Zheng Zaoru, who sent a memorial outlining the following to the Zongli Yamen in January 1886. If China banned all Chinese labor emigration, he argued, the Americans might stop assaulting those Chinese already in the United States, and the American government might effectively protect the Chinese, and the properties of Chinese merchants might, as a result, be saved from damage. If the Qing government posted notices in Hong Kong about the dangerous situation in the United States to warn off possible immigrants, potential immigrants might take heed and obey. The Zongli Yamen should ask the

British government in Hong Kong to prohibit any vessels from carrying any Chinese laborers for the United States. Although the Zongli Yamen informed the United States of its intention to ban all Chinese labor immigration, the Yamen needed to ensure the Chinese laborers remaining in the United States and those Chinese who were not laborers would enjoy all their treaty rights. Finally, Zheng suggested that the Qing government should ask the American government to permit individual Chinese to cross the United States in transit to other countries.[89]

The Six Companies, in the meantime, tried to send surplus Chinese back to China. In early February 1886 the Six Companies negotiated with the Occidental and Oriental Steamship Company and the Pacific Mail Steamship Company to carry Chinese back to China at the reduced rate of $25 per person. Chinese at or near age sixty were given a free ticket and $15, and those below age sixty who were in extreme poverty were also given free passage and $10.[90]

A Six Companies' petition promoted the self-restriction policy of the Qing government that came to be embodied in the Bayard-Zhang Treaty of 1888. On February 13, 1886, Lee Kim-wah, president of the Six Companies, sent telegrams to both the Chinese minister in Washington, DC and the Zongli Yamen in Beijing asking for protection. He stated the situation in the United States was "deplorable in the extreme"—Chinese laborers flocked to San Francisco "in a destitute condition" while Chinese merchants also "suffered greatly." If the expulsion of Chinese from various towns and cities continued, he warned, Chinese merchants would be "irretrievably ruined."[91]

Alarmed by the Six Companies' telegram, the Zongli Yamen asked the opinion of Chinese diplomats who had served in the United States. The long-standing immigration restriction policy of the Six Companies, along with what they themselves had seen and heard in the United States, undoubtedly had influence on these men. All suggested that China should take the initiative to prohibit Chinese emigration to the United States. Ouyang Ming, consul-general of San Francisco, for example, suggested that the Qing government should ban all Chinese laborers from moving to the United States because the United States did not favor Chinese immigration, and a continuous trickle of Chinese entering the United States could only cause more trouble and ill-feeling. But once the Qing government decided to prohibit Chinese emigration, it should make a treaty to guarantee the protection and safety of those Chinese already in the United States.[92] Chen Lanbin and Zheng Zaoru echoed and supported the emigration restriction policy.[93] Indeed, the Qing government and the Six Companies shared feelings of frustration. Without any effective means to ensure their treaty rights, they could only adopt a self-restriction policy in exchange for the protection of the Chinese who were already in the United States.

The Zongli Yamen followed the recommendations, and on April 3, 1886, notified Charles Denby, the American minister in Beijing, of China's intention to prohibit the emigration of Chinese laborers to the United States: since the American government had not carried out the stipulations in the treaties for the protection of the Chinese in the recent anti-Chinese violence, China would prohibit all Chinese laborers from going to the United States. All Chinese laborers already in the United States and other Chinese who were allowed to enter the United States should be protected by the United States government according to the treaties between the two countries, and the United States should allow Chinese to cross the country in transit to other countries.[94]

On August 3, 1886, the Zongli Yamen again notified the American minister in Beijing of China's decision to prohibit emigration of Chinese laborers to the United States.[95] In addition it was writing to the British government to prevent any vessel of any nationality from carrying any Chinese laborers as passengers to any port in the United States, and the Yamen urged Zhang Yinhuan to negotiate a new treaty with the State Department.[96]

On March 12, 1888, Secretary Bayard and Minister Zhang signed the new treaty. It prohibited the immigration of Chinese laborers for a period of twenty years, but the prohibition did not prevent the return of any Chinese laborer who had "a lawful wife, child, or parent in the United States, or property therein of the value of one thousand dollars, or debts of like amount due him and pending settlement." In addition to allowing Chinese "officials, teachers, students, merchants, or travelers for curiosity or pleasure" to enter and reside in the United States, the treaty assured that the United States would devise measures for the protection of the Chinese in the United States. The United States further agreed to pay a sum of $276,619.75 to the Chinese government to indemnify the Chinese victims of mob violence. The Senate ratified the treaty with amendments: all Chinese laborers who were not in the States at the time of ratification of the treaty, "whether holding return certificates under existing laws or not," were prohibited from returning to the United States.[97]

It is especially important to emphasize that even though it promoted immigration restriction, the Six Companies did not want a total prohibition on immigration since the business of the Chinese merchants depended on serving the laborers.[98] Early in September 1877, for example, Colonel Bee provided information concerning immigration restriction to the *Chronicle:* the Six Companies had arranged a plan to return the idle and indigent surplus of Chinese that it was supporting, and to keep the number of Chinese in the United States at a minimum by sending back at least one for each new arrival from China. But he also argued that Chinese immigration should not be totally prohibited, and in support of this he furnished a large number of letters he had received from Americans relating to the need for Chinese labor.[99]

The prohibition period of twenty years and the amendments in the new treaty touched off a wave of protest. The Six Companies in San Francisco sent letters and telegrams to Guangdong province and Hong Kong concerning the new treaty.[100] A number of merchants in Guangdong and Hong Kong who had business ties with the Chinese in San Francisco collectively cabled the Zongli Yamen and Zhang Zhidong, the governor-general at Canton, to help prevent the court from ratifying the treaty. The Six Companies also sent Zhang Yinhuan a letter to oppose the treaty.[101]

The most important part of the merchants' petition was an article entitled "A Tentative Proposal on Business," which highlighted the possible damages the treaty could bring to China. It pointed out that the prohibition was a suicidal act because the Chinese population in the United States would disappear completely after twenty years. Chinese laborers in the United States obtained all their daily necessities from China, and hence the more Chinese laborers in the United States, the more revenue the Chinese customs would obtain. If the United States was allowed to ban the Chinese totally, other countries, such as Canada, Australia, Hawai`i, and other islands in Southeast Asia, might follow suit. Consequently, destitute Chinese might have to stay without means of livelihood in Guangdong and Fujian and therefore become a source of potential trouble for China.[102]

In response to the petitions, Li Hongzhang and Zhang Zhidong, two powerful officials who had been active in matters relating to the Chinese in America, recommended that the government not ratify the new treaty. Li Hongzhang reminded the Zongli Yamen of the "public outrage," while Zhang Zhidong reiterated the views expressed in the petitions and emphasized their implications.[103] Due to their efforts, the Zongli Yamen did not ratify the new treaty. In response to China's rejection of the treaty, the United States Congress hastily passed the Scott Act, which prohibited the return to the United States of Chinese laborers who had left the country for temporary visits abroad.

The Qing Legation as Treaty Defender

As an organization the Six Companies ceased to complain to the American government against discriminatory laws after the establishment of the Chinese legation in Washington, DC. However, its previous use of arguments concerning "treaty obligations" and "justice" must have impressed the Qing legation. If a nondiplomatic organization could use this weapon so successfully, there was no reason for the Qing government to doubt its effectiveness. Although the Chinese legation was now the official defender of Chinese treaty rights, it made use of the same arguments the Six Companies had as it continued the struggle.

From the beginning of 1880 the Chinese faced more and more discriminatory legislation. California changed its constitution to prohibit the employment of Chinese, while the California School Laws established a segregated education system for Chinese children. Impatient with ineffectiveness of the new legation's counterblows, the Six Companies decided to petition the Qing ministers in complaint. On March 2, 1880, the *San Francisco Bulletin* reported that representatives of the Chinese Six Companies were on their way to the capital and intended to get "an explicit answer" from the Chinese legation as to whether the United States meant to protect the Chinese.[104] Then in a long letter to Secretary of State Evarts on March 9, 1880, Yung Wing recounted the sufferings the Californians had caused the Chinese and reminded the secretary of the treaties between the two countries. That California had changed its constitution to prohibit the employment of Chinese, Yung stated, violated Article 6 of the Burlingame Treaty, which guaranteed the Chinese in the United States the same privileges enjoyed by citizens of "most favored nations." He proclaimed that "the 'Treaty of 1868' is practically a dead letter."[105] Although Secretary of State Evart did nothing in practice to ease anti-Chinese agitation in California (the election of 1880 was near), he did state in his reply to Yung Wing that the United States would protect the Chinese treaty rights.

Subsequently the Chinese legation usually complained of discriminatory laws without having to be prodded by the Six Companies. In early 1882, soon after Sen. John F. Miller of California introduced a bill in Congress to suspend the immigration of Chinese laborers, Minister Zheng Zaoru complained to Secretary of State Frederick T. Frelinghuysen that the American government "strangely misunderstood" the character of the treaty of 1880.[106] Zheng's effort was quite heartening for the Chinese. A few days after his complaint, President Chester A. Arthur vetoed the bill by citing almost exactly the reasons suggested by Zheng.[107]

However, the revised bill passed both the Senate and the House soon after the failure of Miller's bill, and on May 6, 1882, President Arthur had no choice but to sign it because the revised bill had changes designed to meet his objections.[108] Xu Shou-peng, who was in charge of the business of the Chinese legation during Zheng Zaoru's absence from Washington, protested that ten years' suspension of immigration was too long and an infringement of the spirit of the 1880 Angell Treaty, but his reasoning fell on deaf ears.[109]

In 1884, as the U.S. Congress was discussing another bill to strengthen the restriction, Zheng Zaoru protested that the proposed bill was a violation of the treaties and contradicted America's claim to be a country of justice.[110] Even though President Arthur signed this 1884 amendment to the Chinese Exclusion Act, he nevertheless requested Congress be "more in harmony with the provisions of the treaty."[111]

After 1886 the tightening of congressional legislation against Chinese immigration is exemplified by the Scott Act. The Qing legation's protests intensified accordingly. The Chinese diplomats did not realize that their tactics were no longer adequate, and that both Congress and the President were under intense popular pressure. On January 26, 1889, after the passage of the Scott Act in 1888, which prohibited the return of all Chinese laborers who had left the United States, Minister Zhang Yinhuan sent his first note to Secretary of State Thomas Bayard. "I beg respectfully to represent to you that this act is in plain violation of the treaty of 1880," he began, which gave the United States only the right to regulate, limit, or suspend the immigration of Chinese laborers, not to restrict the return of the Chinese laborers who had already once arrived in the United States. The Scott Act was a violation of the treaty of 1880 because the new bill had no time frame and prohibited Chinese immigration completely.[112] Although President Grover Cleveland, who was engulfed in the 1888 Presidential elections, had signed the bill, the Chinese legation fight still elicited hopes for success. Zhang's arguments had convinced Secretary of State Bayard, and he had urged President Cleveland to veto the bill at a time when the President was still unresolved about his decision.[113]

Even though the Supreme Court of the United States upheld the Scott Act on the grounds that the United States had the plenary power to exclude aliens from its territory, on July 8, 1889, Zhang Yinhuan sent a protest to the new secretary of state, James G. Blaine, expressing his amazement that the United States "could release itself from treaty obligations without consultation with or the consent of the other party." The violation of the existing treaties, he warned, was "an invitation to China to terminate all diplomatic and commercial relations."[114] Nonetheless, Zhang failed to undo the anti-Chinese law.

Cui Guoyin, who replaced Zhang Yinhuan as head of the Chinese legation, also tried to stop the enforcement of the Scott Act by using the treaties as a weapon. His note to the State Department on March 26, 1890, protested that the Scott Act violated the treaty rights of almost all the Chinese in the United States. He further emphasized reciprocal justice by indicating that China had strictly observed every stipulation of the treaty in dealing with Americans in China. He threatened that China could retaliate against American missionaries and merchants in China, but American officials ignored his request, appeared unconcerned about his threats, and did not want to discuss the matter further.[115]

The Qing Legation Pursues Indemnity

The calls in the 1870s by the Six Companies for protection and indemnity also set the precedent for complaints by the Chinese legation over mob attacks on Chinese. Here again the Chinese legation simply "superseded" the Six Companies as the official demander of indemnity and protection and followed the path first blazed by the Six Companies.

On October 31, 1880, a serious anti-Chinese riot took place in Denver, Colorado. As a result of a mob attack, a Chinese laborer named Look Young was killed, many others were wounded, and property with an estimated value over $50,000 was destroyed. Minister Chen Lanbin sent a note to Secretary of State Evarts demanding the arrest and punishment of the guilty persons and compensation for the Chinese losses.[116] Consul Bee was ordered to go to Denver to investigate.[117] On January 21, 1881, Chen Lanbin sent another letter to Secretary Evarts, enclosing Bee's report. Chen argued that the United States government was responsible for the riot because the Chinese "who were subjected to the wanton outrage of the mob, came to this country under the right of the Treaties," And thus the United States government should compensate the Chinese for their losses since the local authorities had known about the violence but had not done their best to stop the mob.[118] Secretary of State Evarts replied that the federal government could not interfere with the authorities in Colorado and Denver, and it was also not "the principle of national obligation" to compensate the Chinese victims.[119] Minister Chen had to drop the case at last.

Despite earlier failures to win indemnities, the Chinese legation was not discouraged. In early 1885 an outburst against the Chinese in Eureka, in which the Chinese were robbed of their property and expelled, was brought to the attention of the Chinese consulate. Consul Bee told a reporter that because the Qing government had paid America nearly $500,000 for damage to the property of Americans in the riots at Canton, Americans could not complain if they were asked to do the same for the Chinese in the United States. "The Eureka case," emphasized Consul Bee, "will establish a precedent, and if America will not indemnify Chinese, China will not indemnify Americans."[120]

On September 2, 1885, with the support of the Knights of Labor, the most brutal mob attack against the Chinese occurred at Rock Springs in the Wyoming Territory.[121] Twenty-eight Chinese miners were killed, and fifteen others were wounded; the total property loss was estimated at $147,748.[122] Zheng's indemnity request this time was much more comprehensive. Instead of ordering an investigation by his own people only, he asked the State Department to send an official to accompany the Chinese group to inspect the scene.[123] He also requested that the Zongli Yamen send information relating to China's payment of indemnity to American victims in China directly to the State Department; he urged the Yamen to be firm on the indemnity issue.[124] In addition he cabled Li Hongzhang and Zhang Zhidong, the two powerful Qing officials, for support.[125]

After acquiring the necessary evidence, he delivered his letter of protest concerning the Rock Springs riot to Secretary Bayard on November 30, 1885. Emphasizing that the government of the United States had demanded and received $735,258.97 indemnity for outrages committed upon Americans residing in China in the year 1858 alone, he argued, on the basis of reciprocal justice, that the United States government should compensate Chinese losses. In closing, he reminded Secretary of State Bayard of the assurance in the treaty of 1880 that the Chinese in the United States "should have ample protection guaranteed to them."[126]

The depression of 1886 fueled more anti-Chinese outbreaks and made the Chinese merchants extremely uneasy. On February 11, 1886, the president of Kwong Lun Hing & Co. notified Zheng Zaoru that "the Chinese have already been driven out of many towns... without any attempt being made by the officials to prevent the same, and threats are now being made to drive them out of nearly all the towns and cities in this state."[127] Two days later Lee Kim-wah, president of the Six Companies, asked the Chinese minister to contact the American President to demand that federal troops be sent to protect the Chinese, since the Chinese "are absolutely terrorized, and are flocking to San Francisco, where great destitution now exists among them."[128] Several days later, Zhang called on Secretary Bayard and laid before him a collection of telegraphs and newspaper articles from California; he complained that the Chinese residents were being deprived of the protection and rights guaranteed to them by treaty and reminded Bayard that Chinese merchants had invested a large amount of capital in the United States under the guarantees provided by treaty.[129]

The incidents led the Six Companies to appeal directly to the Zongli Yamen as well. "At the present time the condition of our countrymen on the Coast is deplorable in the extreme," the organization wrote. "We earnestly and respectfully request... [that the Zongli Yamen ask the President of the United States] to send troops to protect all the Chinese."[130] Shortly thereafter the Six Companies sent a letter to Zhang Zhidong, the governor-general of Liangguang, the administrative center in Guangdong, detailing their miseries in the United States.[131] In addition to listing numerous instances of violent attacks on Chinese by white mobs, they further asserted that the Chinese in San Francisco had "ten miseries" with regard to accommodation, "six unjust items" for laundrymen, and "seven difficulties" for Chinese laborers and merchants. Zhang not only reported the letter, especially the miseries and difficulties, in a memorial to the Qing court, but also took the initiative to meet with Charles Denby, the American minister in China, to discuss punishment of the criminals and protection for the Chinese in the United States. Zhang also presented a note to Charles Seymour, the U.S. consul in Canton, that an unsatisfactory solution to the indemnity issue would lead to repercussions against the Americans in Guangdong.[132]

China's effort was successful. President Cleveland sent Congress a message demanding compensation for Chinese losses in the riot on March 2, 1886. The Rock Springs massacre claim was settled, and in February 1887 the Chinese were paid $147,748.74.[133]

However, anti-Chinese violence continued. Only a month after the Rock Springs riot, three Chinese in Seattle were murdered.[134] So once again, in March and April 1887, while negotiating a new treaty with Secretary Bayard, Zhang Yinhuan requested indemnity. Bayard replied that he could not promise there would be such a provision in the new treaty.[135] In June 1887, at Log Cabin near the Snake River, a group of white Americans killed ten Chinese and stole gold dust worth between $5,000 and $10,000. On August 16, Zhang sent another note to Bayard in which he insisted that protection and indemnity articles be part of the draft treaty. He again underscored the fact that whenever American residents in China suffered injury because of conspiracy or mob violence, the Chinese government punished the guilty promptly and made full pecuniary indemnity.[136]

After ignoring Zhang's stand on indemnity and suspending negotiations for almost four months, on December 28, 1887, Secretary Bayard sent a note to Zhang to resume negotiation for a new treaty.[137] In January 1888 Zhang replied that he was ready to sign a new treaty if the United States would take into consideration his demands about protection and indemnity because they were of "prime importance."[138] Once again Zhang was successful. On February 29, 1888, Bayard finally agreed to incorporate the protection provision and the Snake River murder indemnity into the new treaty.[139]

Because of the Six Companies' ability to provide meaningful assistance to the nascent Chinese legation, the Qing government actually turned it into a special branch of the legation and accordingly appointed the presidents and merchant trustees as advisers or other officers of the Qing government. What is more striking is that the Six Companies' diplomacy established the parameters for the legation's fight against the anti-Chinese movement. Although changes did occur with the passage of time, the changes were not enough to alter the essence of the pattern. It can be said, therefore, that in the 1880s the Six Companies and the Qing government formed a united nationalist front against exclusion.

CHAPTER 7

• • • • • •

"As Skilled in Dialectics"

The Qing Legation, 1890–1906

> Next, perhaps, to the Indian question, but in any case only next to it, comes the Chinese question in the discredit that it has brought upon the Government of the United States. The difference between the two questions for practical purposes is that the Indians, whom we have been persistently and quite shamelessly wronging since the expulsion of the Cherokees, in violation of the faith of the Government, have not been able to plead their own cause, and that such statements of it as have from time to time appeared and affected the public mind have been the work of sympathetic whites, in large part of the sympathetic sex. The Chinese officials, on the other hand, are quite as skilled in dialectics as the officials of the United States, are as keenly aware of their rights and as much disposed to insist upon the same.
>
> —"The Chinese Correspondence"

After a decade's practice in modern diplomacy, the Qing legation finally won acclaim from Americans as this chapter's epigraph from the *New York Times* demonstrates. Unlike the Indians, the Chinese diplomats were "as skilled in dialectics as the officials of the United States," and "as keenly aware of their rights and as much disposed to insist upon the same." It is apparent that the activities of the Qing legation in the 1890s deserve close attention.

The Qing Legation and Its Advisers

In the 1890s the Qing legation continued to enlist the services of the Six Companies. This development had a psychological as well as political significance. The leaders of the Six Companies must have felt that they were becoming part of the Chinese legation, for whenever Cui Guoyin, Zhang's successor, asked the State Department to admit newly engaged presidents of the Six Companies, he informed the secretary of state that the presidents were consulting directors attached to the Chinese consulate general in San Francisco. On September 12, 1892, for example, he informed Secretary John Watson Foster that Chun Nang, the new president of the Sanyi *huiguan*, was also a member of the board of consulting directors for the Chinese Consulate General in San Francisco.[1] The next two ministers, Yang Ru and Wu Tingfang, also made newly appointed presidents of the Six Companies into ex officio members of the advisory board of the San Francisco consulate.[2] On April 19, 1901, Enkai *huiguan*'s newly arrived president, Fang Maochi, carried an official passport as an ex officio member of the consulate issued by Wu Tingfang.[3] A photograph taken at the celebration of the 1902 Chinese New Year shows all the presidents of the Six Companies wearing the robes of Qing officials.[4] In a similar move, Minister Liang Cheng appointed Huang Yinheng, former president of the Ningyang *huiguan*, as a diplomatic attaché for the Chinese consulate in Mexico in 1906.[5]

While the Qing legation continued to employ leaders of the Six Companies, the practice of hiring Americans as Chinese diplomats ended. On May 26, 1892, Consul Frederick Bee died suddenly of a heart attack, after serving many years as spokesman for the Six Companies and as a consul for the legation. There was sadness in the Chinese community over the loss of Bee, who had been decorated three times by the Qing government. "The flag of the consulate and flags on various houses in Chinatown were at half-mast for half an hour after Consul Bee's death."[6] There was speculation about who would take his place as the next white consul, but in an interview T. D. Riordan, who had acted for many years as an attorney for the Chinese, said there was "no present necessity for a white Consul to represent the Chinese."[7]

Indeed, after years of dealing with Americans and immigrants from other nations, the Chinese had gained confidence. In 1902, for example, Wu Tingfang dismissed an American lawyer named Costello who had been with the legation more than twenty years. "In the past," Wu wrote, "a foreign adviser has been essential because neither the minister nor his Chinese staff was familiar with foreign relations and they needed outside assistance.... [T]he new minister Liang Cheng [being sent to Washington as Wu's successor] is an experienced diplomat and may not need a foreign adviser and if he does the Counselor of [the] legation can get one for him."[8]

A Champion for Chinese Treaty Rights

During the 1890s, just as the Six Companies had before them, the Qing diplomats continued to assert the principles of the modern nation-state system, which rested on the sanctity and inviolability of treaties. Although the legation had failed to undo the Scott Act in the late 1880s, their hopes still rested with treaty obligations and justice.

In 1892, with the Chinese Exclusion Act of 1882 about to expire and an election coming, Thomas J. Geary of California introduced a new and more stringent bill restricting Chinese immigration, the Geary Act, which President Benjamin Harrison signed into law in May 1892. No Chinese except diplomats and their servants could now enter the United States, and all Chinese already in the United States were required to register with American authorities. Immediately after the proposed Geary Act was introduced in Congress, Minister Cui sent a protest to the State Department arguing that the proposed law violated every article of the treaty of 1880. In addition to breaching Article 1, by "making [an] absolute prohibition [on] the coming of Chinese laborers," the act violated Article 2 by banning the immigration of nonlaboring classes and forbidding the return of Chinese laborers who left the country temporarily. Nor was the proposed legislation consistent with Article 3 in its requirement that all Chinese obtain a certificate of residence.[9]

A few days later, Cui sent another note to Secretary Blaine, asking him to notify the President of the treaty violations. He had, he emphasized, "already protested to you against it as a violation of the treaty of 1880 ... [and now wanted] to bring the matter to your notice in the most urgent manner." The bill, which also denied Chinese the right of bail in habeas corpus suits, violated Articles 2 and 3 of the treaty of 1880. There was no denying that the registration provision would place an additional hardship on Chinese laborers. Finally, he pointed out that the bill's provision that allowed Chinese to be arrested without a warrant obviously disregarded American legal principals and practice.[10]

Not satisfied with the legation's efforts, Chen Dazhao, president of the Six Companies, went to Washington, and on August 15, 1892, he and Minister Cui paid Secretary of State Foster a visit during which they argued that the Geary bill violated existing treaties between the two countries and the Constitution of the United States. The Geary bill "proposed to treat Chinamen like animals," Chen at last told Secretary Foster, and "we would petition our Government in China to prevent it." But this effort, like that of the Chinese legation, failed.[11]

On August 5, 1892, armed with the treaties of 1868 and 1880, the Zongli Yamen took the matter up with Charles Denby, the American minister in Beijing.[12] When Denby visited Li Hongzhang, a leading statesman of the late Qing dynasty, Li complained that the United States had again violated the treaty agreements by passing the Geary Act. When Denby asked how the act violated the treaty, Li did not reply, but he warned that China would treat the Americans in China as the United States had treated the Chinese in the United States.[13]

Even though it became evident that citing treaty obligations and the demands of justice would no longer work, Minister Cui and his successors could find no better arguments. As a *New York Times* article pointed out in 1893: "It is certain, nevertheless, that any European power of the first class would find itself forced, in like circumstance, by the public opinion of Europe, to adopt that mode of redress or abdicate its position, because we have repeatedly offered China what would be recognized between civilized nations as ample cause of war."[14] One may argue that China had little alternative, given the fact that China had declined as a power and lacked gunboats to back up its demands. In November 1892 Cui Guoyin again presented Secretary Foster a letter arguing against the Geary Act by stressing that the bill was inconsistent with the principles of justice and the treaties between the two countries.[15] The "unjust, unfair, and discriminating legislation of the Congress" was in violation of "the solemn treaty stipulations" now in force between the imperial government and the government of the United States; the Act was "a violation of every principle of justice, equity, reason and fair dealing between two friendly powers."[16] But these persistent efforts still failed to get the Geary Act repealed.

When Wu Tingfang was appointed as the Chinese minister in 1897, he was to experience a breadth of Chinese exclusion his predecessors had not even imagined. With the American annexation of Hawai`i and the Philippines, Chinese immigration to both territories became a problem. Although the prospect was not encouraging, treaty obligations and demands of justice remained the best bet for fighting exclusion laws. In order to oppose exclusion from the Hawaiian Islands, Wu wrote to Secretary of State John Hay on December 12, 1898, arguing that all the treaties between the two countries and the legislation based on those treaties that excluded Chinese laborers from the United States did not apply to the Hawaiian Islands.[17] Two months later, in a follow-up note, Wu highlighted the demands of justice: "To single out the Chinese alone for exclusion from the islands is to lower the whole nation in the eyes of the world, particularly if there is no discriminating legislation against any other Asiatic people."[18] Wu's efforts ended in failure. In September 1899, when the exclusion laws were extended to the Philippine Islands, Wu complained again to Secretary Hay that the extension was "contrary to international law, . . . in violation of the spirit of existing treaties, and in utter disregard of the friendly relations which should exist between the two Governments."[19] On November 15, he sent yet another note to Secretary Hay protesting extension of the exclusion laws to the islands: "I have to ask that instructions be sent to Major-General Elwell Stephen Otis to cease the violation of the treaty of 1894 by the exclusion of merchants and others of the exempt classes mentioned in article 3 of the said treaty."[20] Even though Secretary Hay replied that he had sent instructions to the military officials to observe the treaty and admit the privileged classes, the exclusion policy continued to apply in the Philippines as it did on the mainland.[21]

Fighting for Chinese Legal Equality

Since all modern nation-states hold individual rights and national equality sacred, the Qing legation confidently continued the approach set by the Six Companies in demanding legal equality for the Chinese. In fact the Six Companies and the legation cooperated in a legal battle against the Geary Act—the biggest court engagement the Chinese had ever faced. Soon after the Geary Act was signed into law, Attorney Thomas Riordan was again employed to fight the act.[22] The Six Companies also posted a proclamation calling on all the Chinese to stand together against the Geary Act: "The United States does not treat the Chinese right, because it compels no other nation to do such things, and no other nation in the world treats Chinese like the United States does."[23]

The Six Companies drew up a petition to the emperor of China and to the Chinese government asking for them to help, on behalf of "your children in this country," and to challenge the "cruel and unjust" act. The petition asked the Qing government to remind the American legation in Beijing that Americans in China might "be treated as the United States" now proposed "to treat Chinamen here."[24] In an interview with the *San Francisco Call,* King Owyang, the Chinese vice-consul in San Francisco, said, "I consider that the reasons adduced by the Six Companies are unanswerable, and I believe the love of justice, of which this nation boasts, will lead your people to see the injustice of the Geary bill."[25]

On March 13, 1893, Minister Cui informed Secretary of State Walter Gresham that the Chinese would challenge the constitutionality of the Act and asked him to assure that the matter would be resolved promptly by the U.S. Supreme Court.[26] On March 24, the Six Companies issued a circular "to all Chinese in America" detailing its plans for challenging the Geary Act in court. It declared that five famous and competent lawyers had been employed to fight the unjust law in the Supreme Court and that the Chinese minister had already required the U.S. government to arrange for a speedy hearing. The Supreme Court, the Chinese leaders assured their countrymen, would find the Geary Act unconstitutional.[27]

A Chinese vice-consul provided a *New York Times* reporter with more details of their plan to challenge the act. They would first order all Chinese to disobey the Geary Act, and then urge any Chinese arrested to comply peaceably with imprisonment and they would take the matter to the United States Supreme Court to test the constitutionality of the law. In court, he stated "the United States may be asked some questions by the nations of the earth that will be hard to answer."[28]

On May 6, 1893, the day the Geary Act went into effect, three Chinese laborers were arrested for not having certificates of residence. The Chinese immediately launched their attack on the law's constitutionality.[29] The lawyers argued that the Geary Act violated several constitutional provisions and that the arrest violated the Fifth Amendment's prohibition against taking liberty or property without due process of law. However, the temper of the court had changed, and the majority of the Supreme Court justices upheld the Geary Act on the grounds that a sovereign state had plenary and unconfined power over immigration.[30] The Fifth Amendment to the Constitution, they held, applied only to naturalized and native-born citizens of the United States, and therefore any action taken by virtue of this law by America against aliens, especially against the Chinese, who could not become citizens, would not conflict with that amendment. Immediately after the decision, the attorney Riordan sent the following message to John J. Quinn,[31] asking him to inform the Six Companies and the consulate: "Decision against us. Five to three. The three ablest Judges, Fuller, Field and Brewer, with us. Tell Brown, Consulate and companies."[32]

Justice Stephen Johnson Field, who dissented from the decision, said that "brutality, inhumanity and cruelty can never be recognized as elements in any form of procedure adopted in the administration of the laws of our Government." Judge David Josiah Brewer gave his verbal opinion to a *San Francisco Call* reporter and notified the court that he would submit an extended written opinion on the subject. In his opinion, though there was no question about the general power of the government to enact laws keeping people out of the United States, "this act dealt with persons who were lawfully in the United States."[33]

After their failure to overturn the Geary Act, Chinese diplomats were no longer as active in court contests as they had been before. In 1898 Minister Wu sent a note of protest to Secretary Hay concerning the interpretation that James E. Boyd, the acting attorney general, was placing on Article 3 of the 1894 treaty. In answering Wu's protests, Secretary Hay suggested that the whole matter be submitted to the courts for judgment.[34] Wu, however, opposed the suggestion because in his opinion the Chinese government should not be a party to a suit before the courts of the United States, for decisions made in the courts of the United States had no binding force on the actions of China.[35]

But the Six Companies and the San Francisco consulate continued the legal fight. Thomas Riordan was not the only American lawyer who was under joint retainer to both the Six Companies and the Chinese consulate in San Francisco. A retainer agreement, signed by the Six Companies, the Chinese consulate in San Francisco, and Oliver Stidger, stipulated that Stidger would represent Chinese already in the United States and those Chinese seeking to enter by defending their constitutional, legal, and treaty rights.[36] Former judge James G. Maguire, a counsel for both the Chinese consulate in San Francisco and the Six Companies in 1900, was another.[37]

On May 24, 1900, the Six Companies petitioned the federal court in California to challenge a mandated inoculation of all residents of Chinatown. The lawyers for the Chinese were James Maguire, who represented the Six Companies, and John E. Bennett representing the Chinese consulate. Again, they argued that the rights of Chinese guaranteed by both treaty and the Constitution were being violated.[38] The Chinese were determined to resist enforcement of the order: "This was decided upon at a meeting of the Six Companies yesterday. This was announced by the Chinese Consul last evening." This time they succeeded; the court finally ruled that forcible inoculation was a clear violation of the equal protection clause of the Fourteenth Amendment.[39]

Chinese Lobby

The Qing diplomats continued to follow the Six Companies' lead by adopting an American-style rhetoric effort—and like their diplomacy this was in sharp contrast to their traditional tributary system. The economic depressions of the late nineteenth century had led to a general consensus among American decision-makers, the business elite, and the leading journalists as to the root cause of the economic problems and their solution. They believed that the most serious domestic crisis was overproduction, which among other things threatened to produce serious social unrest. The challenge faced by the Americans was overproduction and the need to stabilize the society. Exporting to large foreign markets seemed to be the answer.[40] To this end Secretary of State John Hay articulated the Open Door policy in 1899 and 1900. Showing great sensitivity to the politics of the time—and the national interests of the United States—the Chinese legation now renewed their lobbying on a large scale. For the first time, the Chinese legation began to utilize its own Chinese lobbyists, all of whom were Western-trained. Minister Wu Tingfang, a British-trained scholar who was also the first Chinese admitted to the bar in Great Britain, was the legation's top lobbyist. On February 23, 1899, he addressed the members of the New York Southern Society in the large banquet hall of the Hotel Savoy where "an American flag and a Chinese flag were draped together." Wu, as the principal guest of the society, wore "silken robes of yellow and drab, with a black cap, or fez, modestly jeweled, on his head." After discussing the American occupation of the Philippines, Wu turned to the topic of trade. Chinese merchants had carried on trade between China and the Philippines for centuries, he said, and pointed out that the United States could now take advantage of this: "Your trade would be greatly increased and to your benefit. Aside from this the American trade in China has been increasing largely in the last few years." Then he turned to the immigration laws: "I hope that you may see your way clear to modify your Chinese exclusion laws, then our relations could be closer. We are constructing railroads which will open the whole of our country to you, and we shall be glad to have you enjoy the full benefits."[41]

This instance is typical of many. On October 18, 1899, about a month after Secretary Hay had sent his Open Door message to the powers, Wu addressed the International Commercial Congress: "China always favors the open door. China opens her doors to the peoples and the trade of every country, without distinction as to race or color." He used statistics to enhance his message about China's trade and prospects. After several other delegates read papers, Wu spoke again, this time alluding to the Geary Act: "I believe that to get the trade of China, it is worthwhile to repeal this objectionable statute."[42]

On January 26, 1900, Wu spoke at the second annual dinner of the American Asiatic Association to an audience of more than one hundred, including Senators Addison Gardner Foster of Washington and John Lowndes McLaurin of South Carolina.[43] He pointed out that China's huge population made it the greatest potential market in the world: "You all know that China is a great market with her 400,000,000 population, which has to be fed, clothed, and provided with all the necessaries of life." China wanted the wheat of the Platte, the cotton of the Carolinas, and the steel of Pennsylvania and Alabama. In addition, China needed to build railroads, manufacture steel, develop electric power, and hundreds of other things. "There is a fine field for you," said Wu, "It is for you to realize it." And then he made an obvious connection: "If you want to have a share of China's trade, a good deal depends upon the kind of treatment you extend to my countrymen in this country, and especially in your new possessions." At the end of his speech he warned that Chinese merchants would boycott American goods if America continued the ill-treatment of the Chinese.[44]

Wu made full use of any opportunities to influence the American public. On February 8, 1900, he once again made an address against exclusion at a banquet of the Silk Association of America. Among the 300 members and guests were Gov. Foster M. Vorhees of New Jersey, Lieut. Gov. Timothy L. Woodruff, George Wurtz, the secretary of state of New Jersey, William L. Strong, the former mayor of New York, William R. Merriam, director of the Twelfth Federal Census, and Congressman James A. Tawney.[45] "If you come to China to buy raw silk from us," Wu declared, "we embrace you with open arms. We do not legislate against your coming. Our doors are open to you; we treat you as we treat all other people—not as you treat us."[46]

Wu made a similar speech at a banquet sponsored by the National Association of Manufacturers in Boston on April 26, 1900, which brought together nearly three thousand people, two-thirds of whom had to stand in the hall to hear the speeches.[47] As Wu rose from his seat, "in Oriental costume amid a sea of American dress coats, he was greeted with a burst of cheers which lasted for some minutes." In his address he repeated his argument for better trade relations: "We need the cotton manufacturers of Lowell, . . . and the food products of the West." China, he said, had immense natural resources to be developed, which needed modern American mechanical equipment to supplant China's slow processes of production. China needed thousands of miles of railroads, which required American rails, locomotives, and iron bridges. "It is needless for me to go on with the enumeration," he concluded, "the market is vast enough for every line of American goods." And all these made clear "the importance and necessity of allowing Chinese merchants and traders to have free and friendly intercourse with the manufacturers and merchants in this country."[48]

In addition to public speeches, Wu published his trade argument in popular magazines. In 1900 he reiterated his opinion in an article entitled "China and the United States" in the March issue of *Independent Magazine*.[49] He showed statistics that trade between the two countries had been increasing rapidly and steadily. "A report recently prepared by the United States Department of Agriculture states that during the years 1889–1899 there was a gain of $13,293,168 in the commerce of the United States with China." He then complained that the exclusion bill had been extended from Chinese laborers to include other classes. At last he asked, "How can you expect Chinese merchants to give you much business in the face of these facts?"[50]

In July 1900, Wu published "Mutual Helpfulness between China and the United States" in the *North American Review*. After warning about the "constant danger of overproduction" in the United States, he pointed out: "It is imperative for the farmers and manufacturers of the United States to seek an outlet for their products and goods in foreign markets. . . . But on the other side of the Pacific lies the vast Empire of China, which in extent of territory and density of population exceeds the whole of Europe."[51] The Chinese market cannot be realized, however, if the United States keeps its anti-Chinese policy. "Her door is wide open to the people of the United States, but their door is slammed in the face of her people."[52]

Wu Tingfang also lobbied the American government and Congress to prevent the possible renewal of the Chinese Exclusion Act in 1902. On December 10, 1901, he sent Secretary Hay a fifty-eight-page note and requested "that a copy of this note be transmitted to the honorable Congress."[53] He challenged four standard arguments used to stop Chinese immigration to the United States. To refute the charge that the Chinese would work for lower wages than American workers and cause wages to decline, he presented statistics that proved the reverse was the case. The average wage for labor in California in 1870 was $2 per day and remained at this rate until 1884 when, under partial restriction of

Chinese immigration, it was raised to $2.31 per day. Immediately upon the passage of the 1884 amendments to the Chinese Exclusion Act of 1882, however, the average wage dropped to $1.70; following passage of the Geary Act, the average wage for labor in California declined steadily until in 1898 it was only $1.59 per day. It was therefore absurd to claim that exclusion of the Chinese raised wages.[54]

To refute the second charge, that China's 400 million people would overrun the United States and destroy its institutions if immigration was unrestricted, Wu argued that the fear was groundless, for most Chinese were not interested in immigrating to the United States. Moreover, immigration statistics demonstrated that all the Chinese immigration to the United States had come from a few districts, which had only about 5 million inhabitants.[55]

To rebut the accusation that the Chinese were not interested in becoming American citizens, Wu noted that American laws rather than Chinese attitudes prevented their naturalization. If they were accorded the same privileges to become naturalized as the people of other countries, he argued, many would become citizens; but even if they did not, it would not be against the interests of the United States.[56] He also stated that the Chinese were law-abiding people: The census of 1890 showed that the Chinese had the smallest percentage of criminals and paupers of any nationality within the United States.[57]

Nor could the charge that the Chinese had a low standard of living be sustained. Statistics showed that Chinese purchases were increasing more rapidly than those of the inhabitants of any other country; and it could be proved that the Chinese consumed in proportion to their means as much as the people of any other nation.[58]

Yet again Wu pointed out that the exclusion laws actually damaged American commercial interests. "On account of the exclusion act, the American people are not securing the share they would otherwise have in the profits of this period of Chinese progress."[59] And finally, he expressed the hope that "the honorable Congress of the United States will deal with the import question at hand in a spirit of fairness and equality."[60]

He You (Ho Yow), a graduate of Oxford University and the Chinese consul-general in San Francisco, and Minister Liang Cheng, a graduate of the Phillips Academy in Andover, Massachusetts, and Wu's successor, were also Chinese lobbyists who wrote to influence American public opinion. In the *Forum* of June 1900, Consul He published "The Attitude of the United States towards the Chinese." Like Wu Tingfang, he emphasized trade and produced statistics as evidence: "From computations to date the figures indicate that the imports will exceed $22,000,000, an advance of $3,000,000 since 1894, and that the exports will be over $12,000,000, an advance of $6,000,000 since the same year." But there were yet "some dark spots on the disk of trade"—the laws of this nation toward Chinese immigrants.[61] He, too, highlighted the benefits of Chinese immigration: the Chinese had added $289,700,000 to the wealth of California in the redemption of desert lands alone. In fact, he noted, because of Chinese exclusion California was a billion dollars poorer than she would have been.[62]

Soon after the Boxer Uprising in China, He You sent the United States Chamber of Commerce a communication expressing his regret over what had happened in China. He said the trouble was especially unfortunate coming at this particular time when the United States was poised to reap the benefits of trade with China. After stating the importance of China in the business world and the abilities of Americans to benefit from its trade, he moved to his goal: "And as our Government and the influences which attend it are, and will hereafter be, alert to suppress anti-Caucasian bias, so must you here resist, discountenance, and denounce all anti-Mongolian prejudice, and feeling in order that amity and comity may prevail, which is a condition absolutely necessary to precede and abide with any volume of trade between people whatsoever."[63]

In 1901, in an article entitled "Chinese Exclusion, a Benefit or a Harm?"[64] He You conceded that the Chinese were indeed cheap labor; that they lived cheaply; that they sent their money to China; that most of them had no intention of becoming American citizens; that after a few years they returned to China with their money; and that they did not assimilate American customs, but resided in Chinatowns. But then he argued that all these traits were actually to the highest advantage of the United States, especially to those who opposed the presence of the Chinese laborer. The exclusion laws were a mistake because Americans did not understand their effect. They were a costly error, not only to China, but also to the United States, because they deprived the country of millions of dollars annually. In fact, Chinese immigrants to the United States had been in all respects as beneficial as European immigrants, and in some respects, much more so. There were no Chinese paupers, criminals, or insane immigrants, whereas these undesirables comprised a considerable percentage of the European immigration.[65]

In "The Chinese Question," in the October 1901 issue of *Overland Monthly,* He You again answered many charges against the Chinese. Concerning the Chinese working for lower wages, he argued: "It is now generally known throughout the country that the Chinese demand higher wages than even the best of the white laboring class, notwithstanding which there is still a great demand for Chinese labor."[66] That the Chinese sent their money back to China was actually to the advantage of the United States. By doing so, their relatives in China became wealthy enough to consume many of the luxuries and products from the United States. As for the question of cleanliness, the Chinese laboring class was just as clean as the corresponding class of any other nationality. "It is unfair to compare the Chinese laboring classes with the white middle or higher classes." Answering the charge that the Chinese took work away from the American laboring class, He You argued that the Chinese took lower sorts of jobs than the great majority of white workers. To refute the contention that the Chinese would swamp the country if the restrictions against them were lifted, he pointed out all the Chinese in the country had come from the province of Guangdong, and no Chinese from other provinces would migrate to the United States, nor had they ever done so. Furthermore, it was unfair to charge that the Chinese had brought their vices to the United States because there were vices among the whites, too. If the Chinese gambled at all, they gambled among themselves, and in any case gambling gave little cause for criticism because life itself was a gamble. He concluded with the importance of China trade for the United States: "The demand in China for your products will, in time, be equivalent to about one-half of your total export trade to the world."[67]

Minister Liang Cheng, Wu Tingfang's successor, gracefully accepted the relay baton with an article entitled "Commercial Relations between United States and China" in *Harper's Weekly* of December 23, 1905.[68] Because "the industrial expansion of the country" seemed to have reached "the limit of home consumption," Liang wrote, a foreign market needed to be found for American goods. "There is no doubt that China is just the market required." However, close commercial relations between the two countries were not possible if the United States kept its exclusion policy.[69] By concentrating on the same argument and publishing in different popular magazines, the Chinese diplomats obviously hoped that the argument would reach a wide range of the American public and exert a far-reaching influence.

The tireless efforts of the Chinese ministers "made a marked impression" on many Americans. Speaking in the Senate in 1906, Senator Benjamin Tillman said that almost all who heard Wu Tingfang's addresses "can recall... the way his mustache fairly got four or five additional kinks or curls in it when he alluded to the indignities and outrages put upon his countrymen."[70] Wu's lobbying also caused a panic among labor leaders. Samuel Gompers wrote anxiously to the head of the International Typographical Union and other labor leaders to call their attention to the activities of the Chinese minister: Wu mingled with politicians "making himself agreeable to everyone"; he met southern manufacturers and cotton farmers to whom he stressed "the market of northern China"; he urged American bankers establish American banks in China. "All this activity... is plainly for the purpose of making friends in every direction against the time when there shall be a renewal of the efforts to keep Chinamen out of this country."[71]

The lobbying effort secured support from some American pressure groups. The Rev. Nathan R. Johnson not only wrote to the President in 1901 protesting the violation of treaties but also tried to get 100,000 signatures in various states to petition the U.S. government to amend the discriminatory laws. In 1902 the American Asiatic Association passed a resolution to establish a fund to influence public opinion and promote trade with China; John Ford, the vice president of the association, even established an office in Washington to lobby politicians.[72] The Portland Chamber of Commerce, the Merchants' Exchange in San Francisco, and the San Francisco Chamber of Commerce, along with the Philadelphia Board of Trade and New York Chamber of Commerce, all urged Congress and the President to moderate the exclusion laws.[73] However, despite their efforts, Congress passed the Exclusion Act of 1902, and President Theodore Roosevelt signed it into law.[74] The last Qing lobbying effort was made by Minister Liang Cheng in 1905. On November 11, at the banquet for the Chicago Merchants Club, he delivered the principal address. "In discussing commercial possibilities between the United States and China," he said, the exclusion question and how exclusion was administered were "matters of vital importance to the Chinese directly concerned."[75]

Chinatown Reformer

In the 1890s the Qing legation continued, often in cooperation with the Six Companies, to attempt to reform Chinatown. In November 1890, after two Chinese factions had gotten into a violent fight with each other, Zuo Geng, the Chinese consul-general in San Francisco, issued a proclamation asking the Chinese to live in peace with each other and forbidding further fighting among them.[76] Just as the Six Companies had done, the Chinese consulate not only kept watch for criminals and informed the city police about them, supporting their arrest and conviction,[77] but the consulate also offered rewards for the arrest and conviction of any Chinese guilty of murder.[78]

On another occasion in the early 1890s, when two Chinese gangs were at war with each other, Consul-General Chang Yintang tried to stop the violence by ordering the Six Companies to locate and arrest the criminals. In a proclamation he declared: "The criminal element cannot be allowed to go on unchecked... no criminal arrested for robbing or shooting will be bailed out."[79] In March 1893, in the midst of violence sparked by the Supreme Court's failure to declare the Geary Act unconstitutional, the Six Companies posted proclamations on street corners in San Francisco's Chinatown, warning that all Chinese merchants who were members of street or highbinder societies and who did not give up their memberships would be classed as highbinders and arrested by the police. Posted beside the Six Companies proclamations were notices from the consulate stating that it would deport highbinders to China for severe punishment: "You will not only be beheaded but you will bring disgrace on your own family, fathers, brothers and sisters."[80]

In further evidence of the cooperation between the consulate and the Six Companies, on April 4, 1893, certain judges of the courts of San Francisco requested that the Chinese consulate try to stop the continuous violence and murder among the Chinese. The consul turned to the Six Companies, asking the leaders to find a way to end the lawlessness. The Six Companies called a meeting of all Chinese merchants in San Francisco, and together they decided on twelve rules to curb the highbinders; the Six Companies posted these throughout Chinatown in a proclamation entitled "Notice to All Subjects of the Chinese Empire."[81]

In 1894 Minister Yang Ru sent the Zongli Yamen a memorandum entitled "Relating to an Overall Policy for Dealing with the Protection of the Chinese in the United States." Considering that much anti-Chinese sentiment was caused by the vices of the Chinese themselves, he suggested seeking a solution to the anti-Chinese movement within the Chinese community. The key to solving the problem, he asserted, was to reform the Chinese community by cooperating with American officials to ban such activities as opium smoking, gambling, and gang violence that was causing so much trouble in the United States. Many-time offenders would be returned to China for severe punishment.[82]

The legation's battle was not confined to prostitution and tong wars. In 1895 Minister Yang Ru issued a proclamation urging the Chinese not to participate in any illegal or immoral activities. The proclamation pointed out that the Chinese in the United States experienced discrimination in part because of their own vices, such as opium smoking, gambling, and feuds. If the Chinese could cease such pernicious conduct, he stated, Americans would stop discriminating against them and would not pass additional anti-Chinese laws.[83]

In response to a clash among the secret societies in San Francisco in early March 1900, both the Six Companies, on March 5, and Consul He You (Ho Yow), on March 10, issued proclamations asking the Chinese to end all violence. After reiterating the analysis that the American people discriminated against the Chinese and treated them badly because the Chinese often settled disputes through feuds, He You declared: "If this trouble is not settled without further blood, I will invite the aid of the Six Companies and the Merchants' Association, and bring the offenders to American justice."[84]

Even though the Six Companies and the Qing ministers had failed to get extraterritorial rights before the 1880s, the idea took root in their successors' minds. Minister Cui Guoyin believed, for example, that American punishment of these Chinese criminals was too light to stop their vices; if China had extraterritorial rights, the Chinese ministers could have punished these Chinese criminals severely and effectively.[85] While Minister Yang Ru was negotiating a new treaty with Secretary of State Walter Gresham in December 1893, he expressed China's intention to secure from the U.S. government the right to extradite Chinese criminals for punishment in China.[86] On September 30, 1897, Minister Wu Tingfang, Yang's successor, continued to urge the United States to deliver Chinese criminals to the Chinese consulate so that they could be returned to China.[87] He You, the Chinese consul in San Francisco, on April 4, 1900, also demanded that the United States grant extraterritorial rights to the Chinese consulate.[88] But neither the Chinese legation nor the Six Companies succeeded in this effort; the United States thought that an extradition convention between the two countries was impractical.[89]

On March 17, 1894, Minister Yang Ru in a message to the Zongli Yamen reported his plan to order the Chinese consuls, with the help of the *huiguan,* to offer lectures twice a month on the Sacred Edict of Emperor Kangxi. He hoped such lectures would reduce vice among the Chinese and therefore make the Americans dislike the Chinese less.[90] Soon after the memorial, he instructed the Chinese consul in New York to hire a Chinese representative to explain the Sacred Edict to Chinese residents in that city; the Chinese consul selected Zhao Jiabi, a clerk at the consulate, to give such lectures at the Chinese Merchants' Association.[91]

Generally speaking, the measures of the Qing legation and the Six Companies seemed to work. The 1870s had seen a sharp decline of Chinese prostitution in both numbers and percentage, while violence within the Chinese community dropped dramatically by 1900.[92] By the beginning of the twentieth century, newspaper stories of Chinese crime became less and less frequent; the efforts to bring "peace and stability" to the Chinese community "more or less succeeded in 1913."[93]

The Qing Government and New Treaties

In the 1890s and early 1900s it again becomes apparent that the Six Companies was the driving force behind all the immigration treaties between Qing China and the United States. Soon after the passage of the Scott Act in 1888, the Six Companies petitioned Minister Zhang Yinhuan to use a treaty renegotiation as a remedy.[94] In January 1892 the Six Companies again appealed to the Chinese legation to renegotiate with the United States government for less restriction on Chinese immigration. It demanded that Chinese laborers holding reentry certificates should be allowed to return and that Chinese presently residing in the United States should be permitted to come and go between the two countries.[95] In 1893 Chinese merchants submitted a joint petition to the Zongli Yamen, the superintendent of trade for the Northern Ports, and the superintendent of trade for the Southern Ports, pleading strongly for new treaty negotiations and the abrogation of the Geary Act.[96]

Responding to the petitions, the Zongli Yamen advised Yang Ru, the new Chinese minister, to work to repeal the Geary Act and negotiate a new treaty that would ensure better protection of the Chinese. The Yamen instructed that if the negotiation was not smooth, Yang Ru could use the substance of the abortive treaty of 1888 as the basis for a new treaty.[97]

Although Yang sought the repeal of the Geary Act, Walter Gresham, the secretary of state, informed him that the President had no authority to repeal acts already passed by Congress. So on December 16, Yang cabled a summary of his efforts to Zongli Yamen and concluded that China should begin to negotiate a new treaty.[98]

Yang tried to negotiate with the American government for fewer restrictions on Chinese immigration. His first draft was based on the failed treaty of 1888 and was sent to the State Department on January 11, 1894. In addition to reducing the period for the prohibition of Chinese immigration from twenty to ten years, the draft asked the United States to allow the wives and minor children of those who were entitled to stay in the United States to enter the country.[99] Yang visited Gresham in person on February 17 to add an additional provision that would allow a Chinese laborer who possessed a reentry certificate to return if he had a wife, child, parent, or property valued at more than $1000 in the United States.[100] The negotiations completed, the Gresham-Yang Treaty was signed on March 17, 1894, and promptly ratified by both the United States and Qing governments.

As the Six Companies had petitioned, the treaty was based on the substance of the abortive treaty of 1888, with some modifications. The period of prohibition of Chinese laborers was reduced from twenty years to ten years. Any Chinese laborer who had "a lawful wife, child, or parent in the United States, or property therein of the value of one thousand dollars, or debts of like amount due him" could return to the United States after a temporary absence abroad, if he had secured a reentry certificate before leaving. The treaty allowed officials, teachers, students, merchants, or travelers to enter and reside in the United States. Chinese laborers also won the privilege of transit across the United States. Though granting the Chinese in the United States protection, the treaty also specified that registration of Chinese residing in the United States would continue.

Discrimination against the Chinese in the United States did not improve after enactment of the new treaty. Instead, the administration of the exclusion laws became increasingly callous, especially after Terence V. Powderly, a former labor leader, was appointed as the commissioner-general of immigration in 1897.[101] American authorities not only refused to classify Chinese restaurant owners as "merchants," but they also, in early 1903, further tried to remove the status of "merchant" from the owners of tobacco, broom, and clothes factories. The exclusion laws were also extended to the Hawaiian and Philippine islands.[102]

The year 1904 was very important because the Gresham-Yang Treaty of 1894 was due to expire in December. Both governments had to give notice of termination of the treaty six months before the expiration date; otherwise, the treaty would be good for another ten years. In October 1903, therefore, representatives of all the Chinese in the United States assembled at the Six Companies, where they reached a consensus to petition the Qing government to terminate the treaty.[103] The petition was sent to seven Chinese authorities: the Ministry of Foreign Affairs, the Ministry of Commerce, the Chinese minister in Washington, DC, the deputy minister of Foreign Affairs, the governor-general of Liang Hu (Hunan province and Hubei province), and the governor-general of Liang Guang (Guangdong province and Guangxi province).[104]

The petition began by tracing the history of the Chinese immigration, the restriction laws, and especially the miseries the Chinese had experienced. The perpetrators of the Chinese sufferings, it pointed out, were men of low origin and a small segment of American society, who had stirred up the anti-Chinese movement for their own selfish gains. Because the United States was a democratic country, workers could use their votes and political parties to further their interests. Although many American merchants and manufacturers favored Chinese laborers, they had to restrain their support due to the threat from American laborers.[105] The time was ripe for China to speak out because the United States was evolving from an agricultural to an industrialized country, with an increasing demand for access to the China market. The Qing government should take advantage of the opportunity to gain concessions on the immigration issue from the United States. A weak country would be subjected to endless bullying and humiliation if it continuously yielded, but it would gain respect if it rose in resistance. Since a great part of the merchandise imported to the United States by Chinese merchants depended on Chinese consumption, if no Chinese laborers were allowed to enter, Chinese merchants would also suffer. If all Chinese in the United States were driven back home, China would lose 25 million taels annually in remittance and export, and the loss of annual income could reach 50 to 60 million taels if other countries followed the example of the United States. But worst of all, the sudden increase in China of more than a million unemployed vagrants would cause social and political chaos. Failure to take a hard line, the petition concluded, would let slip this golden opportunity and result in fatal consequences for the empire.

The petition must have shaped the Qing government's decision on the exclusion issue. In a telegram to the Ministry of Foreign Affairs at the end of 1903, Minister Liang advised the government to terminate the existing treaty and renegotiate certain important provisions.[106] Following Liang's suggestion, on January 24, 1904, Prince Qing of the Ministry of Foreign Affairs informed Edwin H. Conger, the American minister in Beijing, of China's intention to terminate the 1894 treaty when it expired.[107] Liang further gave Secretary Hay a warning on January 7, 1905, that there would be retaliation against many American bankers, accountants, and company directors if the United States continued the exclusion policy.[108]

There is no stronger proof of the influence of the Six Companies than the appendix of its petition, which outlined eight items requiring urgent attention if the Qing government could not overturn the Exclusion Law: (1) opposition to the extension of the Exclusion Law to Hawai`i and the Philippines; (2) the right of nonlaboring classes to enter the United States; clear definition of the exempt classes; (3) clear definition of the term "merchants"; (4) cessation of the maltreatment of the Chinese upon their arrival; (5) improvement of the visa inspection system; (6) cessation of merchant registration and better protection of Chinese residents in the United States; (7) the right to transit the territory of the United States; (8) and the elimination of ambiguous clauses in previous treaties to avoid abuses.[109]

Evidence suggests that all these items were reflected in Liang's draft of the new treaty. With regard to the Six Companies' first requirement, Liang insisted that the Exclusion Law should not be applied to the newly acquired territories and that Chinese laborers should be allowed to go to Hawai`i and the Philippines.[110] Concerning the right of nonlaboring Chinese to enter and reside in the United States and clear definition of "merchants," Article 1 of the proposed treaty required that "laborers" should mean both skilled and unskilled laborers, such as Chinese employed in mining, fishing, huckstering, peddling, and laundry work. Only Chinese laborers should be included in the prohibition.[111] To address the Six Companies' demand to improve the visa inspection system, Article 5 suggested that certificates of identification in both English and Chinese that had been issued by Chinese local officials should be considered reliable evidence for entry and residence in the United States. These visas should be authorized by representatives of the United States in China on the basis of the certificates of identification.[112] The draft treaty requested that no Chinese seeking entry into the United States be confined, and any adverse decision by an American official affecting a Chinese citizen should be reviewed judicially. Chinese subjects in the United States should not be physically abused or harassed by administrative officials.[113]

The State Department turned down the first draft, but Minister Liang sent Secretary Hay a second draft on January 7, 1905, which restated most of the provisions in the first draft and further inserted additional requirements for protecting the interests of registered laborers and the exempt class. Not surprisingly, it was also declined by the Roosevelt administration.[114] In 1904 Congress had made the exclusion of Chinese indefinite with the Chinese Exclusion Extension Act. It would be approximately forty years—only when China became an ally of the United States during World War II—before Congress reconsidered this policy of exclusion.

The turn of the century marked the climax of the tremendous Chinese fight against exclusion. The policy that the Qing legation adopted in America, was simply a continuation, with minor variations, of the unofficial Six Companies diplomacy, but by 1900 the legation had demonstrated its mature understanding of the modern nation-state system. For the first time, the spokesmen and lobbyists were all highly qualified Western-trained Chinese diplomats. Minister Wu Tingfang, a British-trained international lawyer, was the most eloquent and persuasive when writing and speaking to awaken public sentiment in favor of the Chinese. For the first time the proclamation of the Six Companies in 1892 directed *all* Chinese in the United States to resist the Geary Act. Even though the joint fight of the Qing legation and the Six Companies against the Geary Act failed, it was the greatest court challenge the Chinese ever had in Chinese-American history. The Qing legation, backed by the Six Companies, suppressed or silenced almost all vice and immorality within Chinatown. As a result, after 1900 the Chinese were less pained by lurid stories in American newspapers. In 1903 the Six Companies called an assembly of representatives of all the Chinese in the United States and sent its most comprehensive petition to the Qing government to terminate the Gresham-Yang Treaty. Following the petition completely, the Qing legation refused to compromise in the negotiation.

We must recognize that the official Chinese spokesmen were not in the dark about American politics or the modern nation-state system. They were indeed "as skilled in dialects as the officials of the United States." The Chinese well understood that a treaty is an international agreement concluded between sovereign nation-states and governed by international law, which holds it to be binding on any nation-state that is party to it. The Chinese insisted on making immigration agreements and demanded that any laws in conflict with these treaties should be null and void. In addition to the sanctity of treaties, modern nation-states of the time adhered to the principles of national development and equality. "Nation-states are remarkably uniform in defining their goals as the enhancement of collective progress and individual rights and development," John Meyer, John Boli, George Thomas, and Francisco Ramirez reminded us in

1997. "This occurs in constitutions, which typically emphasize goals of both national and equitable individual development."[115] In the United States—whose stated mission was to ensure equal rights and which professed to speak for the oppressed of all nations of the world—the Chinese legation and the Six Companies understandably decided to test the constitutionality of anti-Chinese laws. They also argued that American trade with China was a valuable interest for the national development of the United States and therefore that anti-Chinese sentiment was an impediment to fulfilling the country's global vision. The Chinese began at the foundation and utilized almost every crucial element of the nation-state system in its fight against discrimination and for "Chinese rights." However, the United States was (and is) governed by the majority of its citizens. Theirs was the voice of power that had to be obeyed. The Chinese failed because they fought against impossible odds at a particular time in history, not because they could not make the best use of circumstances.

If it is true that the Six Companies and Qing diplomacy were defeated at last by a coalition of anti-Chinese interest groups, it does not follow that they left no legacy. Good did come out of this half-century collision, however. In response to American racism, the Six Companies first developed, and the Qing legation then elaborated, a novel form of Chinese nationalism, one distinct from the older forms of Chinese identity—profound attachment to native place and culturalism. And this modern nationalism is simply "the biggest change in the Chinese three thousand years' history."[116]

Conclusion

The diplomacy of the Six Companies provides a framework for connecting the elements that made up one of the most important developments in nineteenth-century Chinese-American history, modern Chinese history, and the early history of Sino-American relations. It is evident that modern Chinese nationalism first emerged in California from the *huiguan* or native-place associations and that the Six Companies' modern nationalist diplomacy set the tone and format for late Qing-U.S. policy and piloted China's turn toward modern nationalist foreign relations. Viewing the Six Companies, rather than the Chinese government, as the center of modern Chinese diplomacy during its crucial beginnings, this study remaps the intellectual landscape of the culturalism-to-nationalism thesis and of China's entrance into the modern family of nations.

The traditional Cantonese market economy played a crucial role in Chinese emigration to the United States. This particular group of Chinese, steeped in a knowledge of market economics, were willing to leave their homes and families far behind just for the benefits of trade. Chinese merchants, the spearhead of Chinese emigration, brought the tradition of the *huiguan* or native-place association with them to the United States for the purposes of liaison, mutual aid, and protection. Around 1860 the *huiguan* in San Francisco united into a confederation known as the Six Companies. One major reason for this union was the fact that an overall association was needed to address affairs that affected all Chinese in the United States, not just those from a particular city or region. In the years following, this new organization would prove to be of critical importance.

One perennial puzzle is whether the Six Companies acted as the chief Chinese labor broker during the late nineteenth century. In the 1870s especially, this question attracted general attention and furnished prolific material for newspaper comments. The charges Americans made against the Six Companies were uninformed conjectures. No concrete evidence was ever found that the Six Companies acted as a labor broker, but the accusation became a part of the anti-Chinese movement all the same. The Six Companies repeatedly denied that it had trafficked in any bound labor. Evidence exists, however, that the Six Companies advanced the cost of passage to Chinese laborers. To understand what the organization was doing here, we must consider the fact that the Six Companies and its member *huiguan* were acting as native-place associations, and providing mutual aid. It is not surprising that they advanced money to their poorer countrymen. As Goodman says in her recent study of the Shanghai *huiguan*, "These ties [native-place sentiments] were most frequently economic as well as sentimental, for local communities assisted and sponsored individual sojourners, viewing them as economic investments for the community."[1] As other *huiguan* with the same functions within China, they were not acting as labor brokers. Various other Chinese and Americans as well did act as individual brokers or worked for broker companies involved in the importation of Chinese laborers.

It is evident that the Six Companies' function with regard to immigration demands a more complete explanation. The Six Companies did not just advance the cost of passage to their poorer countrymen when the United States needed cheap laborers, but it also actively tried to dissuade potential Chinese immigrants from coming when the anti-Chinese movement shifted into full gear. The Six Companies not only met the new immigrants at the piers and took care of them in this strange setting until they found employment, but it also, through the "exit permit system," checked the financial status of departing Chinese so that no Chinese returned to China until they were clear of debt. The Six Companies not only arbitrated internal disputes, but it also defended the community against threats from the Caucasian world outside. It therefore acted as a safety valve for the Chinese immigration mechanism in the nineteenth century.

It is not surprising that as the focal point of all Chinese in the United States, the Six Companies both suffered and resisted the main pressure of Sinophobia. It became the generalized target for the anti-Chinese movement; in the eyes of some Americans who did not understand the *huiguan* tradition, the Six Companies was an evil organization directed by Chinese merchants undermining American institutions and civilization. But it was also both spokesman for all Chinese in the United States and the main challenger of the anti-Chinese movement before the establishment of the Chinese legation in Washington. The way the Six Companies played its role in diplomacy clearly piloted a turn in China's foreign relations from the traditional tributary system to the modern nationalist world order of the late nineteenth century.

This study is therefore also a critique of the culturalism-to-nationalism thesis, which is generally accepted as the authoritative explanation for China's changing approach to foreign relations. Good as this generalization is, it has one distinct lacuna: it neglects the fact that prior to the twentieth century Chinese identity arose not only from the country's embracing culture but also from the profound attachment of each Chinese to his particular native city or region. The affection of the broad population for their native place was no less important than the elite's allegiance to traditional Chinese culture. Scholars have long recognized the centrality of native-place identity to the Chinese self-image, and I can think of no better description than William Rowe's conclusion that "geographically determined subethnic distinctions . . . constituted the most important distinguishing feature between individual Chinese in the late imperial period."[2] It is evident that the function of native place in the development of Chinese nationalism demands considerable emphasis. The anti-Chinese movement in America served as the catalyst for the transition from attachment to a particular native place to Chinese nationalism.

Although cheap Chinese labor and Chinese merchants helped to build the railroads and otherwise enabled Americans to acquire many other desirable results that would have been hard to accomplish except at immense cost, the Chinese were also undermining and replacing white labor and businesses in important industries. Americans, moreover, could not close their eyes to the radical differences between the Chinese and every other nationality that had come to the Pacific slope. It was quite natural, especially under the pressure of the Chinese famine (1876–1879) and American economic dislocations in the 1870s and 1880s, that white labor wanted the Chinese out of the country before they themselves were overwhelmed. Their solution was to prevent the Chinese from coming in the first place. Irish and German immigrants had also experienced discrimination in the United States, but nearly all the native and foreign-born citizens were united in their prejudice against the Chinese, who became the first population excluded from the United States altogether, despite the country's fine rhetoric about equal rights and claims of a promise to open its doors to all who had knocked. When total discrimination against the Chinese as Chinese occurred, the time for modern Chinese nationalism had clearly arrived.

The effect of the anti-Chinese coalition was felt so powerfully that the individual *huiguan* hastened to join together to shoulder the burden. Since the anti-Chinese movement linked together Chinese from every group, the Chinese in America needed to reconceptualize their understanding of native place; it was no longer just a district or a small region, but a much larger entity—a motherland. Of particular significance here is the formal name taken by the Six Companies—*Zhonghua huiguan,* the Chinese national *huiguan*. It is one of the most important milestones in Chinese history, for it conceptualized the awareness of "Zhonghua" or the Chinese nation. Modern national identity came to the "Gold Mountain guests" in the late 1850s, well before a Chinese national identity came to Chinese intellectuals in China at the turn of the twentieth century, as the culturalism-to-nationalism thesis has it. The indisputable evidence is that the Six Companies' struggle in nineteenth-century America in defense of "Chinese" rights is the first demonstration of modern nationalism in Chinese history.

The Chinese leaders in America were astute politicians. Though they had no vote or any meaningful protection, these leaders fought against the anti-Chinese movement simultaneously on several levels. The rise of modern Chinese nationalism in California came about largely because the leaders of the Six Companies had to deal with the new ideologies and methods they found in the United States, ones not familiar or readily available to people living in China. These new ideologies and methods quite naturally became the foundation of their remedy against exclusion.

In the United States the Six Companies discovered the sanctity and inviolability of treaties, one of the key principles of the modern nation-state system. They therefore became the first Chinese defenders of their treaty rights by complaining to the American government that the United States was not faithfully carrying out its obligations. The leaders held that the Burlingame Treaty was beyond the reach of state legislation and that anti-Chinese laws should be void because they were in conflict with the treaty. They argued that the treaty was international law, which the United States could not repeal or modify without the consent of the other party to the contract. Quoting treaties and established diplomatic practice, the Six Companies was also the first Chinese group to demand indemnities from the American government for losses caused by the anti-Chinese riots on the grounds that the government had not done its duty.

The Six Companies also discovered and utilized the paramount power of the Constitution of the United States, which typically emphasizes equitable individual rights. The organization frequently tested the constitutionality of discriminatory measures in American courts by pointing out that exclusion of the Chinese violated the Fourteenth Amendment of the Constitution, the treaties, and America's own claim to be a country of freedom and justice. These men deeply believed that the anti-Chinese resolutions and laws would be found unconstitutional.

Since the Chinese had no ballot, they could not instruct the senators or representatives to help them. But the leading men of the Six Companies knew that through lobbying efforts they might influence the actions of those congressmen who owed no allegiance to the constituencies of California. Publishing articles, making speeches, and sending pamphlets to the U.S. Congress to help create a different image of the Chinese, the Six Companies not only denied anti-Chinese charges but also highlighted the benefits of Chinese immigration and trade between the two countries. The leading Chinese thought the national legislature would find it very difficult to see any desirable reason to drive out an industrious and law-abiding race of people. By aligning its own commercial interests with those of the United States, the Six Companies especially hoped that the benefits of a large Chinese market and national development would swing public opinion and the actions of Congress in their favor. The importance of the China trade was therefore emphatically employed as a principal argument by the lobby.

One way the leaders of the Six Companies developed their effectiveness was by employing American advocates and legal talents. By so doing, they came to understand the American national character a good deal better than the Americans understood the Chinese. Americans also helped them learn what means could be applied to secure protection for their rights.

The Six Companies candidly acknowledged Chinese vices and was the first organization within the Chinese community to attempt to solve the issue of Chinese criminals. In an exceptional effort to remove the exclusionists' excuse for excluding all Chinese because of a small group of criminals, the Six Companies spared no pains to cooperate with government entities to end misbehavior by the Chinese. The determination to reestablish a positive Chinese reputation and image was at the heart of the Six Companies' reform efforts.

Finally, it was the Six Companies' petition to the Qing government for protection that led directly to the establishment of a Chinese legation in the United States. While it is true that self-interest motivated the petition, it also signaled the organization's recognition that they could not go it alone, that is was necessary to engage in government-to-government foreign relations as defined by the European nation-state system.

"What is novel about modern nationalism is not political self-consciousness," Prasenjit Duara tells us, "but the world system of nation-states."[3] As a nongovernmental organization, the Six Companies came to realize that real power and final remedies lay in the hands of official national representatives. But the evidence does suggest that it was the Six Companies that persuaded the Qing government to join in a nationalist anti-exclusion united front.

To assume that official representatives from China could better protect the Chinese was very wide of the mark in reality, for modern diplomatic representation was totally new to Qing China. In addition, Chinese officials were not proficient in English and were ignorant of American customs and international law. As a consequence this period witnessed the difficult process of China's adaptation to membership in the modern family of nations.

The Qing government was keenly aware, however, of the value of the Chinese merchants and the Six Companies. When the legation announced that it would "supersede" the authority of the Six Companies, the statement indicated a sharp break with traditional Chinese government attitudes toward any popular organization, for it suggested that the Qing government would enlist the services and follow the example of the Six Companies. Evidence of the linkage between these two defenders of the Chinese is now clear and unassailable. To average Americans of the time, the Six Companies ceased to be the spokesman for the Chinese after establishment of the legation, but these ingenious *huiguan* leaders remained active in the background, and the legation continued to operate on all fronts in precisely the same fashion as the Six Companies had.

The influence of the Six Companies is particularly evident in the immigration treaties between China and the United States. The Burlingame Treaty of 1868, the Angell Treaty of 1880, the Bayard-Zhang Treaty of 1888, and the Gresham-Yang Treaty of 1894 can, without exception, be traced back to petitions of the Six Companies. There is no better proof than the appendix of the Six Companies' 1903 petition, which became the original draft version of China's new treaty.

In analyzing the concept of modern nationalism, Joseph Levenson states: "A culturalism bars foreign ideas, but it may actually invite or not actively oppose foreign material force. Nationalism reverses these relations; it may admit foreign ideas, but it will blaze against foreign material incursions."[4] Benjamin Schwartz has a similar formula: "Where the commitment to the preservation and advancement of the societal entity known as the nation takes priority over the commitment to all other values and beliefs, . . . where other values and beliefs are judged in terms of their relevance to this end rather than vice versa, nationalism in a precise sense is already on the scene."[5]

By adopting a Western way of thinking and Western means for seeking their ends, the Six Companies and later the Qing legation certainly qualify as modern nationalists. As this study has pointed out, these two groups were quite apparently the best nineteenth-century Chinese students of the modern nation-state system. It is plain that they no longer viewed China as the center of the world or Confucianism as the universal value. On the contrary, the anti-Chinese movement forced them to fight for equality with Americans who denied them this status. All the evidence confirms that modern nationalist diplomacy was the main instrument in their struggle. Their arguments were based on the principles of legal equality among nation-states as embodied in the Westphalian system rather than the hierarchical tributary system. In other words the fight did not lack the core propositions of nationalism in diplomacy: international laws, legal equality, standing diplomacy, and so on. The activities of the

Six Companies and the Qing legation stood as a radical departure from the traditional Chinese world order. It was the Six Companies who established the tone and format for the subsequent struggles of the Qing government and who helped pilot China's transition from the tributary system to modern nationalist diplomacy. A diplomatic revolution—a transition to modern nationalist diplomacy—was taking place from the bottom up in the traditional Chinese world order.

The political significance of the Six Companies and its struggles on behalf of all Chinese in America has not been generally appreciated, but I believe that no other popular minority nonvoting political body in American history, or any other overseas Chinese organization, ever fought a campaign with more diplomacy, astuteness, and influence. The Six Companies was simply one of the oldest and most influential international nongovernmental organizations in the nineteenth-century United States.

Notes

Introduction

1. Akira Iriye, "The Transnational Turn," *Diplomatic History* 31:3 (June 2007): 376.

2. Ibid., 374.

3. Lyman Cromwell White, *International Non-Governmental Organizations* (New Brunswick: Rutgers University Press, 1951).

4. J. J. Lederer, *International Non-Governmental Organizations and Economic Entities* (Leyden: A. W. Sythoff, 1963); James A. Field, "Transnationalism and the New Tribe," *International Organization* 25:3 (Summer 1971): 353–372; Kjell Skjelsbaek, "The Growth of International Nongovernmental Organization in the Twentieth Century," *International Organization* 25:3 (Summer 1971): 420–442; Johan Galtung, *The True World* (New York: Free Press, 1980); Harold Jacobson, *The Network of Interdependence* (New York: Alfred Knopf, 1984); Robert Keohane and Joseph S. Nye, *Power and Interdependence* (New York: Longman, 1989); Paul Diehl, ed., *The Politics of Global Governance* (Boulder, CO: Lynne Rienner, 1997); Margaret E. Keck and Kathryn Sikkink, *Activists beyond Borders* (Ithaca, NY: Cornell University Press, 1998); Jeremi Suri, "Non-Governmental Organizations and Non-State Actors," in *Palgrave Advances in International History,* ed. Patrick Finney (London: Palgrave Macmillan, 2005); Akira Iriye, "A Century of NGOs," *Diplomatic History* 23:3 (Summer 1999): 421–435; and Iriye, "The Transnational Turn," 373–376.

5. Prasenjit Duara, "Transnationalism and the Predicament of Sovereignty: China, 1900–1945," *The American Historical Review* 102:4 (Oct. 1997): 1030–1051. Aihwa Ong and Donald Nonni, eds., *Ungrounded Empires* (New York: Routledge, 1997); Aihwa Ong, *Flexible Citizenship* (Durham: Duke University Press, 1999).

6. Madeline Hsu, *Dreaming of Gold and Dreaming of Home* (Stanford: Stanford University Press, 2000); Yong Chen, *Chinese San Francisco 1850–1943* (Stanford: Stanford University Press, 2000); Sucheng Chan, *Chinese American Transnationalism* (Philadelphia, PA: Temple University Press, 2005).

7. Jonathan D. Spence, *The Search for Modern China* (New York: W. W. Norton & Co., 1999), 212.

8. Michael Hunt, *The Making of a Special Relationship* (New York: Columbia University Press, 1984), 68; David Anderson, *Imperialism: American Diplomats in China, 1861–1898* (Bloomington, IN: Indiana University Press, 1985).

9. Roger Daniels, *Asian America* (Seattle: University of Washington Press, 1988); Ronald Takaki, *Strangers from a Different Shore* (Boston: Little, Brown and Co., 1989); Sucheng Chan, *Asian Americans* (London: Twayne Publishers, 1991).

10. See Betty Lee Sung, *The Story of Chinese in America* (New York: Collier Books, 1975); Zo Young Kil, *Chinese Emigration into the United States, 1850–1880* (New York: Arno, 1978); Shih-shan H. Tsai, *The Chinese Experience in America* (Indianapolis: Indiana University Press,1986); Sucheng Chan, *This Bitter-Sweet Soil* (Berkeley: University of California Press, 1986); Renqiu Yu, *To Save China, To Save Ourselves* (Philadelphia, PA: Temple University Press, 1995); Min Zhou, *Chinatown* (Philadelphia, PA: Temple University Press, 1992); Judy Yung, *Unbound Feet* (Berkeley: University of California Press, 1995); Zhu Liping, *A Chinaman's Chance* (Niwot, CO: University Press of Colorado, 1997); Huping Ling, *Surviving on the Gold Mountain* (Albany, NY: SUNY Press, 1998); Madeline Hsu, *Dreaming of Gold;* Yong Chen, *Chinese San Francisco 1850–1943* (Stanford: Stanford University Press, 2000); Jean Pfaelzer, *Driven Out* (New York: Random House, 2007).

11. Him Mark Lai, "Historical Development of the Chinese Consolidated Benevolent Association/Huiguan System," *Chinese America: History and Perspectives,* 1987 (San Francisco: Chinese Historical Society of America, 1987), 13–52; Him Mark Lai, *Becoming Chinese American: A History of Communities and Institutions* (Walnut Creek, CA: Alta Mira Press, 2004), 39–76.

12. Sucheng Chan, *Asian Americans,* 207.

13. I have found only a few articles and one slim booklet (thirty-two pages) that deal primarily with the Six Companies. Almost all the literature before 1980 was primarily intended to oppose prejudice under the favorable political climate that existed in 1868, 1894, and 1942. In the rosy days after the Burlingame Treaty of 1868 gave Chinese immigrants the legal right to enter the United States and promised most-favored-nation treatment for China, A. W. Loomis published an article entitled "The Six Chinese Companies" in the first volume of the *Overland Monthly* (1868). In 1894, following decades of anti-Chinese feeling and laws, another treaty gave China some concessions, such as reducing the operation of the Exclusion Law from twenty to ten years and reaffirming the protection of Chinese residents in the United States. The same year, Walter Fong published an article entitled "The Six Companies" in *Overland Monthly* 23 (May 1994). In 1942, in the more sympathetic climate of World War II, William Hoy's *The Chinese Six Companies* (San Francisco: Chinese Consolidated Benevolent Association, 1942) was published, the only book on the Six Companies until this volume. But these early works are neither scholarly nor substantial.

Not until the late 1980s did the Six Companies begin to receive scholarly attention. In 1987 Him Mark Lai published "Historical Development," but he focused on its role as a *huiguan*, not on its activities in opposition to the anti-Chinese movement. In addition, a debate arose between Patricia Cloud and David Galenson on the one hand, and Charles McClain on the other. In 1987 Cloud and Galenson published "Chinese Immigration and Contract Labor in the Late Nineteenth Century" in *Explorations in Economic History* 24 (1987). They argued that the Six Companies was the major labor broker importing Chinese laborers for American businesses during the late nineteenth century. McClain argued against their assertions in a 1990 critique in the same magazine entitled "Chinese Immigration: A Comment on Cloud and Galenson." Cloud and Galenson rejected McClain's criticism in "Chinese Immigration: Reply to Charles McClain," published in 1991. Finally, in 1995 Ellen Katz published "The Six Companies and the Geary Act," *Western Legal History* 8:2 (1995), a useful study because it explores the activities of the Six Companies even though it concentrates on one case only.

14. *Xinning* magazine is the original *qiaokan* (overseas Chinese magazine) published in China.

15. "Jinshan zhonghua huiguan shenshang cheng tao junwang daizou sukai guohui qingyuanshu," *Xinning zazhi* 15 (1910): 13–21.

16. *Chinese World (Shijie ribao),* Nov. 11, 1909.

17. Ibid., Feb. 23, 1915. Also see Shehong Chen, *Being Chinese,* chap. 3.

18. *Chung Sai Yat Po,* Sept. 16, 1915. Also see Shehong Chen, *Being Chinese,* chap. 4.

19. *Chinese World,* June 10, 11, and 14, 1919. Also see Shehong Chen, *Being Chinese,* chap. 4.

20. *New York Times,* Sept. 29, 1972, 12. Also see Stanford M. Lyman, *Chinese Americans* (New York: Random House, 1974), 34.

21. William Speer, "Democracy of the Chinese," *Harper's New Monthly Magazine* 37 (Nov. 1868): 844; Tsai, *China and the Overseas Chinese,* 31.

22. Tony Platt, "Reign of Terror against Chinese," *San Francisco Chronicle,* June 3, 2007. Also see Pfaelzer, *Driven Out.*

23. Yuk Ow, H. Mark Lai, and Philip P. Choy, eds., *Lumei sanyi zonghuiguan jianshi.* (San Francisco: Sanfan shi lumei sanyi zong huiguan, 1975), 62.

24. Madeline Hsu, *Dreaming of Gold,* 4.

25. James Townsend, "Chinese Nationalism," *The Australian Journal of Chinese Affairs* 27 (January 1992): 99; Joseph Levenson, *Liang Ch'i-ch'ao and the Mind of Modern China* (Berkeley: University of California, 1967). For more discussions of Chinese nationalism, see, Paul Cohen, "Wang T'ao and Incipient Chinese Nationalism," *The Journal of Asian Studies* 26:4 (Aug. 1967): 559–574; John Fairbank, ed., *The Chinese World Order* (Cambridge, MA: Harvard University Press, 1968); Joseph Levenson, *Confucian China and Its Modern Fate* (Berkeley: University of California Press, 1968); James Harrison, *Modern Chinese Nationalism* (New York: Hunter College of the City of New York: Research Institute on Modern Asia, 1969); Benjamin Schwartz, "Culture, Modernity, and Nationalism—Further Reflections," in *China in Transformation,* ed. Tu Wei-ming, (Cambridge, MA: Harvard University Press, 1993); Chen Zhimin, "Nationalism, Internationalism and Chinese Foreign Policy,"

Journal of Contemporary China 14:42 (Feb. 2005): 35–53; Suisheng Zhao, "Chinese Nationalism and Its International Orientations," *Political Science Quarterly* 115:1 (Spring 2000): 1–33; Zhao, Suisheng. *A Nation-state by Construction: Dynamics of Modern Chinese Nationalism* (Stanford: Stanford University Press, 2004).

26. Harrison, *Modern Chinese Nationalism,* 2.

27. Joseph Levenson, *Confucian China and Its Modern Fate: A Trilogy* (Berkeley: University of California Press, 1968), 98-103; also see Henrietta Harrison, *The Making of the Republican Citizen* (Oxford: Oxford University Press, 2000), 7.

28. Akira Iriye, *China and Japan in the Global Setting* (Cambridge, MA: Harvard University Press, 1992), 32; also see Immanuel Hsu, *China's Entrance into the Family of Nations* (Cambridge, MA: Harvard University Press, 1960), 13.

29. Chen Zhimin, "Nationalism, Internationalism and Chinese Foreign Policy," 38.

30. Townsend, "Chinese Nationalism," 101; also see Levenson, *Confucian China and Its Modern Fate,* 98–104.

31. Levenson, *Liang Ch'i-ch'ao and the Mind of Modern China,* 110. Benjamin Schwartz also states it "represents a fundamental 'turn' in modern Chinese culture"; see Schwartz, "Culture, Modernity, and Nationalism," 247.

32. Zhao, "Chinese Nationalism," 4.

33. J. K. Fairbank "A Preliminary Framework," in his *The Chinese World Order,* 2; Yongjin Zhang, "System, Empire and State in Chinese International Relations," *Review of International Studies* 27 (Special issue) (2001): 53.

34. *Qianlong huidian* 56. 1–8b; J. J. L. Duyvendak, "The Last Dutch Embassy to the Chinese Court (1794–1795)," *T'oung Pao* 34 (1838): 1–137; J. K. Fairbank, "Tributary Trade and China's Relations with the West," *The Far Eastern Quarterly* 1:2 (Feb. 1942): 134.

35. *Qinding da Qing huidian* (Kangxi), 142–143; John Fairbank and Ssu-Yu Teng, *Ch'ing Administration* (Cambridge, MA: Harvard University Press, 1960), 158–159.

36. Fairbank, "Tributary Trade," 133.

37. *Qinding da Qing huidian* (Qianlong), 56: 1–8b; Fairbank and Teng, *Ch'ing Administration,* 170. For examples of royal appointments, see *Qinding da Qing huidian* (Qianlong), 31, 2–4; Fairbank and Teng, *Ch'ing Administration*, 183–184.

38. Mark Mancall, quoting *Kham-dinh Viet-su thong-giam cuong-muc,* in "The Ch'ing Tribute System: An Interpretive Essay," in *The Chinese World Order,* ed. J. K. Fairbank, 64–66.

39. Fairbank, "Tributary Trade," 135.

40. Bryna Goodman, *Native Place, City, and Nation* (Berkeley: University of California Press, 1995), 4; also see G. William Skinner, "Introduction: Urban Social Structure in Ch'ing China," in his *The City in Late Imperial China* (Stanford: Stanford University Press, 1977), 538–548.

41. For more discussions of *huiguan,* see D. J. MacGowan, "Chinese Guilds or Chambers of Commerce and Trade Unions," *Journal of the China Branch of the*

Royal Asiatic Society for the Year 1886; Hosea Ballou Morse, *Guilds of China* (London: Longmans, Green & Co.,1909); Ho Ping-ti, *Zhongguo huiguan shi lun* (Taipei: Xuesheng shuju, 1966); William Rowe, *Hankow: Commerce and Society in a Chinese City, 1796–1889* (Stanford: Stanford University Press, 1984); William Rowe, *Hankow: Conflict and Community in a Chinese City, 1796–1895* (Stanford: Stanford University Press, 1989); Him Mark Lai, "Historical Development"; Goodman, *Native Place;* Wang Rigen, *Xiangtu zhilian: Ming Qing huiguan yu shehui bianqian* (Tianjin: Tianjin renmin chubanshe, 1996).

42. *Wuhu xianzhi* (Minguo), vol.13 "Jianzhi."

43. Dou Jiliang, *Tongxiang zuzhi zhi yanjiu* (Chongqing: Zhengzhong shuju, 1943), 22. For more examples see Liu Yuanbo and Sun Chengxiu, *Jinzhoufu zhi* (Guangxu), vol. 4, "Xiangzhen."

44. MacGowan, "Chinese Guilds," 135.

45. Ibid., 137.

46. Dou, *Tongxiang zuzhi zhi yanjiu.* Five *huiguan* in Dazhu county of Sichuan province also formed a confederation to handle local affairs in 1879. See *Dazhu xianzhi* (Minguo), vol. 2, "Jianzhi."

47. Rowe, *Hankow: Conflict and Community,* 106. For more examples, see *Dazhu xianzhi* (Minguo), vol. 2, Jianzhi; *Guanxian zhi* (Minguo), vol. 16, Lisuzhi and G. William Skinner ed., The City in Late Imperial China (Stanford: University of Stanford Press, 1977).

48. Wang Rigen, *Xiangtu zhilian,* 247–261, 331; Morse, *Guilds of China,* 38.

49. Dou, *Tongxiang zuzhi zhi yanjiu.* Also see Rowe, *Hankow: Conflict and Community,* 106 and 334.

50. Wang Rigen, *Xiangtu zhilian,* 99–103.

51. Guangdong sheng difang shidi bianzhuan weiyuanhui, *Guangdong sheng zhi: Huaqiao zhi* (Guangzhou: Guangdong renmin chubanshe, 1996), 81–82. For other *huiguan* in this small island country, see Yen Ching-hwang, *A Social History of the Chinese in Singapore and Malaya 1800–1911* (Singapore: Oxford University Press, 1986), 96–108, 322–326.

52. Shanghai bowuguan tushushi, *Shanghai beike ziliao xuanji* (Shanghai: Shanghai renmin chubanshe, 1980), 244. Also see Rowe, *Hankow: Commerce and Society,* 308.

53. Morse, *Guilds of China,* 37–38. As to the reason why Chinese liked to be buried in their hometown, Fang Tang, a famous Chinese merchant in San Francisco, stated, "Our people are accustomed on the 3rd of March and 9th of Sept to visit the tombs of their relatives. There are frequently twelve of fifteen generations or many more, lying close together in the same vaults"; Bancroft Library, University of California, Berkeley, Bancroft Scraps, vol. 6, 223

54. Shanghai bowuguan tushushi, *Shanghai beike ziliao xuanji,* 235–236.

55. Morse, *Guilds of China,* 39. Also see Rowe, *Hankow: Conflict and Community,* 177.

56. MacGowan, "Chinese Guilds," 133–192; Morse, *Guilds of China,* 43–44.

57. MacGowan, "Chinese Guilds," 141.

58. Ibid., 136; also see Stanford Lyman, *Chinatown and Little Tokyo* (New York: Associated Faculty Press, 1986), 118–119.

59. MacGowan, "Chinese Guilds." 136.

60. Ibid., 135, 150; also see Morse, *Guilds of China,* 36.

61. Morse, *Guilds of China,* 38; also see *Decennial Reports of the Chinese Imperial Maritime Customs, 1892–1901* (Shanghai: Statistical Dept. of the Inspectorate General of Customs, 1893–), 114, 158.

62. Morse, *Guilds of China,* 37; also see Dou Jiliang, *Tongxiang zuzhi zhi yanjiu,* 24.

63. Goodman, *Native Place,* 313–314.

64. Generally speaking, before decolonization—that is, before the colonies of the West achieved independence following World War II—overseas Chinese were regarded as part of a Chinese nationalistic project rather than as citizens of the nation they had emigrated to. This, of course, does not address the fact that the Chinese were not allowed to be naturalized in the United States in the nineteenth century. Therefore, the role of the overseas Chinese in the early development of Chinese nationalism demands considerable attention.

Chapter 1: A Meeting of Market Economies

Epigraph: The Oriental (Tang-Fan gongbao) Feb. 8, 1855.

1. Almost all the Chinese immigrants to the United States in the nineteenth century were men.

2. Chen Yong, "The Internal Origins of Chinese Emigration to California Reconsidered," *Western Historical Quarterly* 28 (Winter 1997): 521–546. Also see Robert Lee, "The Origins of Chinese Immigration to the United States, 1848–1882," *The Life, Influence and the Role of the Chinese in the United States, 1776–1960* (San Francisco: Chinese Historical Society of America, 1976), 183–193; Sing-wu Wang, *The Organization of Chinese Emigration, 1848–1888* (San Francisco: Chinese Materials Center, 1978); June Mei, "Socioeconomic Origins of Emigration: Guangdong to California, 1850–1882," *Modern China* 5 (1979): 473–501; Kil Young Zo, *Chinese Emigration;* Robert Irick, *Ch'ing Policy toward the Coolie Trade, 1847–1878* (Taipei: Chinese Materials Center, 1982); Takaki, *Strangers from a Different Shore,* 32–33; Sucheng Chan, *This Bitter-Sweet Soil;* Sucheng Chan, *Asian Americans;* Hyung-chan Kim, *A Legal History of Asian Americans, 1790–1990* (Westport, CT: Greenwood Press, 1994).

3. Benson Tong, *The Chinese Americans* (Westport, CT: Greenwood Press, 2000), 24–25.

4. William Speer, a missionary among the Chinese immigrants in California, who had spent many years in Guangdong province, gave an excellent description of the region; see W. Speer, *The Oldest and the Newest Empire* (Hartford, CT: S. S. Scranton and Co., 1870), 472.

5. Chen Yong, "The Internal Origins of Chinese Emigration," 533–537. For

other discussions of the local economic conditions and market economy of this area, see Sung, *Story of the Chinese in America,* 14; Mei, "Socioeconomic Origins of Emigration"; Jiang Zuyuan, *Guangdong jianshi* (Guangzhou: Guangdong renmin chubanshe, 1987), 342–343; Dai Junliang, *Zhongguo chengshi fazhanshi* (Haerbin: Heilongjiang renmin chubanshe, 1992), 276.

6. Ban Gu, *Hanshu* vol. 287 dili zhi; *Panyu xianzhi* (Tongzhi), 6:4; *Guangdong tongzhi,* 92:1768.

7. *Guangdong tongzhi,* 92:1768; also see Chen Yong, "The Internal Origins of Chinese Emigration," 535.

8. *Guangdong tongzhi* (Yongzheng) vol. 4.

9. *Nanhai xianzhi* (Tongzhi), (1836; rev. ed. 1872) 19: 2, 5; Chen Yong, "The Internal Origins of Chinese Emigration," 535.

10. *Zengcheng xianzhi,* intro., 10; also see Chen Yong, "The Internal Origins of Chinese Emigration," 534.

11. *Nanhai xianzhi* (Tongzhi) (1836; rpt, 1967) 5:19; Chen Yong, "The Internal Origins of Chinese Emigration," 533.

12. Chen Yong, quoting *Shunde xianzhi,* (1853; reprint, n.p., 1967) 2: 46 in Chen, "The Internal Origins of Chinese Emigration," 536.

13. See *Dongguan xianzhi* (Xuantong) vol. 9, custom; *Haiyang xianzhi* (Guangxu) vol. 7, custom; *Chihai xianzhi* (Qianlong) vol. 19, custom; *Dapu xianzhi* (Minguo) vol. 10, trade; *Pingle xianzhi* (Kangxi), vol.1, custom.

14. Pui Tak Lee, "Business Networks and Patterns of Cantonese Compradors and Merchants in Nineteenth-Century Hong Kong," *Journal of the Hong Kong Branch of Royal Asiatic Society* 31 (1991):17.

15. *Longxiang xianzhi* (Jiajing), vol. 4, custom.

16. Rowe, *Hankow: Commerce and Society,* 229.

17. *Enping xianzhi,* 4:12; *Xinning xianzhi,* 29:3b; Chen Yong, "The Internal Origins of Chinese Emigration," 537.

18. Goodman, *Native Place,* 62.

19. Lee, "Business Networks," 18.

20. For more discussions of the tradition of Chinese migration, see G. William Skinner, *Chinese Society in Thailand* (Ithaca, NY: Cornell University Press, 1957), 1–27; Gunther Barth, *Bitter Strength* (Cambridge, MA: Harvard University Press, 1964), chap. 3; Luo Rongqu, *Zhongguo faxian Meizhou zhimi* (Chongqing: Chongqing chubanshe, 1988); Sucheng Chan, *This Bitter-Sweet Soil,* chap. 1; Zhu, *A Chinaman's Chance,* chap. 1.

21. Lawrence Palmer Briggs, "The Ancient Khmer Empire" *Transactions of the American Philosophical Society* (n.s.) 41 (Feb., 1951):247.

22. William Nunn, "Some Notes upon the Development of the Commerce of Siam," *Journal of the Siam Society* 15 (1922):86.

23. *Ming shilu: Taizong shilu*, vols. 71, 86, 126, 135, 164; *Ming shilu: chengzhu shilu,* vols. 36, 66; Sucheng Chan, *This Bitter-Sweet Soil,* 13–14. In the fifteenth century many Cantonese ignored the Ming government's prohibition against emigra-

tion and continued their trade with Southeast Asian countries; see Guangdongsheng difang shidi bianzhuan weiyuanhui, *Guangdongsheng zhi,* 41.

24. Luo, *Zhongguoren faxian meizhou zhimi,* 94–95.

25. William Lytle Schurz, *The Manila Galleon* (New York: E. P. Dutton, 1959), 63.

26. Luo, *Zhongguoren faxian meizhou zhimi,* 105–106.

27. Li Chunhui et al., *Meizhou huaqiao huarenshi* (Beijing: Dongfang chubanshe, 1990), 10–13.

28. Guangdongsheng . . . , *Guangdongsheng zhi,* 43.

29. Speer, *Oldest and the Newest Empire,* 467.

30. Chen Yong, "The Internal Origins of Chinese Emigration," 537.

31. Victor Purcell, *The Chinese in Southeast Asia* (London: Oxford University Press, 1951), 121, 443, 490.

32. Barth, *Bitter Strength,* 52.

33. Yuen-fong Woon, "The Voluntary Sojourner among the Overseas Chinese: Myth or Reality?" *Pacific Affairs* 56:4 (Winter 1983–1984):688; Jacques Amyot, *The Manila Chinese: Familism in the Philippine Environment* (Quezon City: Ateneo de Manila University, 1973), 137–188; T'ien Ju-K'ang, *The Chinese of Sarawak* (London: London School of Economics and Political Sciences, 1953), 80.

34. Virginia Heyer, "Patterns of Social Organization in New York City's Chinatown" (PhD diss., Columbia University, 1953), 16.

35. About "two and half million people left China. They went to Hawai'i and the United States as well as to Canada, Australia, New Zealand, Southeast Asia, the West Indies, South America, and Africa" (Takaki, *Strangers from a Different Shore,* 32).

36. Li, *Meizhou huaqiao huaren shi,* 22.

37. See Frederic Wakeman, Jr., *Strangers at the Gate: Social Disorder in South China, 1839–1861* (Berkeley: University of California Press, 1966).

38. Victor Purcell, *The Chinese in Malaya* (Oxford: Oxford University Press, 1984), 2.

39. See Wakeman, *Strangers at the Gate.*

40. One Cantonese migrant's experiences provide a notable case in point; see Takaki, *Strangers from a Different Shore,* 32.

41. *Xinning xianzhi,* 1839 rev. ed.1891; reprint 1965, 8:6. Also see Mei, "Socioeconomic Origins of Emigration," 232.

42. Harley Farnsworth MacNair, *The Chinese Abroad: Their Position and Protection* (Shanghai: The Commercial Press, 1933), 1–2.

43. Purcell, *Chinese in Southeast Asia,* 27.

44. Thomas W. Chinn, ed. *A History of the Chinese in California* (San Francisco: Chinese Historical Society, 1969), 16.

45. Sucheng Chan, *This Bitter-Sweet Soil,* 23. Also see Wakeman, *Strangers at the Gate;* Irick, *Ch'ing Policy toward the Coolie Trade.*

46. Takaki quoting Aaron H. Palmer, Memoir, Geographical, Political, and Commercial, on the Present State, Productive Resources, and Capabilities for Commerce, of Siberia, Manchuria and the Asiatic Islands of the Northern Pacific Ocean; and on the Importance of Opening Commercial Intercourse with Those Countries, March 8, 1848, U.S. Congress, Senate, 30th Cong., 1st sess., Senate misc. no. 80, 1, 52, 60, in *Strangers from a Different Shore,* 22.

47. Chen Yong, "The Internal Origins of Chinese Emigration," 541; Zhu, *A Chinaman's Chance,* 15.

48. "Chinese Invasion," *San Francisco Chronicle,* July 21, 1878; Ow, Lai, and Choy, *Lumei sanyi zong huiguan jianshi,* 57.

49. Zo Kil Young, quoting Lois Rodicape, "Celestial Drama in Golden Hills," California Historical Society Quarterly 40, in *Chinese Emigration,* 83; also seeTakaki, *Strangers from a Different Shore,* 34; Chen Yong, "The Internal Origins of Chinese Emigration," 541.

50. Zo, *Chinese Emigration,* 83, quoted by Takaki, *Strangers from a Different Shore,* 34.

51. Chen Yong, "The Internal Origins of Chinese Emigration," 537.

52. Speer, *Oldest and the Newest Empire,* 486.

53. Thomas O. Larkin, *The Larkin Papers,* ed. George P. Hammond (Berkeley: University of California Press, 1964), 167.

54. Liu Boji, *Meiguo Huaqiao shi* (Taipei: Commission of Overseas Chinese Affairs, 1976), 21; Tsai, *China and the Overseas Chinese,* 16. The original contract, in both Chinese and English, is in the History Room of the Wells Fargo Bank, San Francisco.

55. A. R. Coloquhoun, *China in Transformation* (New York: Harper & Brothers, 1898), 316.

56. S. Wells Williams, *The Middle Kingdom* (London: W. H. Allen & Co., 1883), 63.

57. Barth, *Bitter Strength,* 64.

58. Tsai, *China and the Overseas Chinese,* 14.

59. D. W. Galenson, "The Rise and Fall of Indentured Servitude in the Americas: An Economic Analysis," *Journal of Economic History* 44 (1984): 18–20.

60. Aying, *Fanmei huagong jinyue wenxueji* (Beijing: Zhonghua shuju, 1962), 525.

61. William Redmond Ryan, *Personal Adventures in Upper and Lower California, in 1848–9* (London: W. Shoberl, 1850), vol. 2, 266–267.

62. Edward Lucatt, *Rovings in the Pacific from 1837 to 1849* (London: AMS Press, 1851), 363.

63. Persia Crawford Campbell, *Chinese Coolie Emigration to Countries within the British Empire* (London: P. S. King & Son, Ltd., 1923), 27–36; Elmer Sandmeyer, *The Anti-Chinese Movement in California* (Urbana: University of Illinois Press, 1939), 28; Barth, *Bitter Strength,* 51, 55–56.

Chapter 2: Continuity and Change

Epigraph: The Oriental (Tang-Fan gongbao), Feb. 8, 1855.

1. California State Legislature, Assembly Committee on Mines and Mining Interests, Report, Cal. Assembly, 3rd sess., Appendix to the *Senate Journal,* 829 (1852), 15.

2. Ibid., 834.

3. Frank Soule, Hohn H. Gibson, and James Nisbet, *The Annals of San Francisco* (New York: D. Appleton & Co., 1855), 253 and passim for economic data.

4. Jack Chen, *The Chinese of America* (San Francisco: Harper and Row, 1980), 58.

5. "Chinese as Agriculturists," *San Francisco Alta California* June 30, 1854.

6. "Translation of an original contract between Captain Bryson and Chin Suy," U.S. Senate, Executive Document 99, 34th Cong., 1st sess., 162–163. Also see a letter by Leslie Bryson on December 3, 1851, "On Board of the Ship Robert Browne," Manuscript Letter, Huntington Library.

7. "Koopmanschap and His Chinese Immigration Plans," *St. Louis Republican,* Aug. 2, 1869.

8. *The Oriental,* Feb. 15, 1855. Some even became gold-mine owners. See *Idaho Statesman,* Aug. 10, 1876; Zhu Liping, *A Chinaman's Chance,* 110.

9. Liu, *Meiguo huaqiao shi,* 37.

10. San Francisco lay far outside the trade winds that the existing fleet of Chinese junks utilized. An American ship, the *Eagle,* completed the first direct voyage between Canton and California on Feb. 2, 1848. See *San Francisco Alta California,* Mar. 15, 1849.

11. Soule, Gibson, and Nisbet, *The Annals of San Francisco,* 419; *San Francisco Alta California,* Oct. 30, 1853

12. *San Francisco Alta California,* June 3, 1853.

13. "Chinese Mercantile Operations," *San Francisco Alta California,* June 28, 1854.

14. *San Francisco Alta California,* May 16, 1859 (quoting the Stockton *Argus*)

15. See *San Francisco Alta California,* Jan. 15, 1863; July 15 and 30, 1869; *New York World,* July 21, 1869; *New York Evening Post,* July 20, 1869.

16. This study does not discuss the trade in drugs and women because the notorious tongs (criminal brotherhoods) rather than the Six Companies and the leading merchants, controlled them.

17. Sucheng Chan, *Asian Americans,* 29.

18. Chen Yong, quoting Theodore Augustus Barry and B. A. Patter, *San Francisco, California, 1850* (Oakland, 1947), 100, in Chen, "The Internal Origins of Chinese Emigration," 540.

19. Zhu Liping, *A Chinaman's Chance,* 116; Fujian shida lishixi, *Wanqing haiwai bijixuan* (Beijing: Haiyang chubanshe, 1983) 114.

20. *San Francisco Alta California,* June 28, 1854; also see Fujian shida, *Wan-*

qing haiwai bijixuan, 107; "Chinese Mercantile Operations," *San Francisco Alta California,* July 1, 1854.

21. Soule, Gibson, and Nisbet, *The Annals of San Francisco,* 386.

22. *San Francisco Alta California,* Oct. 31, 1850. After the memorial, Fred'k A. Woodworth, Esq., a vice consul for the Chinese, sent a communication to *San Francisco Alta California* to express their gratitude in being asked to participate. The original letter, "which we value highly as literary curiosity," was written in Chinese. See "The China Boys to Mayor Geary," *San Francisco Alta California,* Sept. 1, 1850.

23. *San Francisco Alta California,* May 21, 1851.

24. Ibid., Feb. 23, 1853.

25. Ibid., Mar. 23, 1851; *San Francisco Herald,* Mar. 25, 1851.

26. "Among the thousands of pioneers flocking to California during the gold rush were 325 forty-niners 'from a different shore'—China.... A year later, 450 more Chinese arrived in California; then suddenly, they came in greatly increasing numbers—2,716 in 1851 and 20,026 in 1852"; see Takaki, *Strangers from a Different Shore,* 79.

27. California State Legislature, Assembly Committee on Mines and Mining Interests, Appendix to the *Senate Journal* (1852): 834; for Governor Bigler's message, see "Governor's Special Message," *San Francisco Alta California,* Apr. 25, 1852; John Bigler, "Message of Governor Bigler," California State Legislature, 3rd session, *Senate Journal* (1852), 373; Charles McClain, "Chinese Struggle for Civil Rights in Nineteenth Century America: The First Phase, 1850–1870," California Law Review 72 (1984): 536–537; Takaki, *Strangers from a Different Shore,* 81–82.

28. *San Francisco Alta California,* Feb. 14 and 24, 1853; for further reports, see *San Francisco Alta California,* Jan. 31, Oct. 10, Oct. 12, 1855; Mar. 17, 1856; Mar. 30, 1857; May 18, May 21, June 21, 1858, Oct. 17, 1860; Oct. 23, 1862; Oct. 16, 1863.

29. California Supreme Court, *People v. Hall,* October 1, 1854, in Takaki, *Strangers from a Different Shore,* 102.

30. Long before the arrival of Chinese immigrants, American merchants, diplomats, and missionaries had spread a bad image of the Chinese people; see Stuart Creighton Miller, *The Unwelcome Immigrant: The American Image of the Chinese 1785–1882* (Berkeley: University of California Press, 1969).

31. *San Francisco Alta California,* Oct. 5 and Nov. 21, 1853.

32. Ibid., Aug. 4, 1854.

33. *Graham's Magazine,* 45 (1854): 486.

34. "Chinese Emigration to California," *New York Tribune,* Sept. 29, 1854.

35. Bayard Taylor, *A Visit to India, China, and Japan, in the Year of 1853* (New York: G. P. Putnam's Sons, 1855), 354.

36. McClain, "Chinese Struggle for Civil Rights," 544; Takaki, *Strangers from a Different Shore,* 82.

37. “The Chinese Companies,” *The Oriental*, Jan. 25, 1855.

38. Liu, *Meiguo huaqiao shi*, 150.

39. Loomis, “The Six Chinese Companies,” 224.

40. Lai, “Historical Development,” 16. Also see “Chinese Invasion,” *San Francisco Chronicle*, July 21, 1878.

41. Hoy, *Chinese Six Companies*, 1–2; Shih-shan Henry Tsai, *The Chinese Experience in America* (Bloomington: Indiana University Press, 1986), 47.

42. “Meeting of the Chinese Residents of San Francisco,” *San Francisco Alta California*, Dec. 10, 1849.

43. Liu, *Meiguo huaqiao shi*, 150.

44. Hoy, *Chinese Six Companies*, 2.

45. Benjamin Brooks, *Appendix to the Opening Statement and Brief of B. S. Brooks on the Chinese Question* (San Francisco: Women's Co-operative Printing Union, 1877), 145.

46. Hoy, *Chinese Six Companies*, 2–3.

47. Brooks, *Appendix to the Opening Statement*, 143.

48. Lai, “Historical Development,” 16.

49. Brooks, *Appendix to the Opening Statement*, 144–145.

50. Hoy, *Chinese Six Companies*, 5. Also see “The Chinese Companies,” *The Oriental*, Jan. 25, 1855.

51. Brooks, *Appendix to the Opening Statement*, 145.

52. Hoy, *Chinese Six Companies*, 24.

53. Ibid., 10.

54. See Ow, Lai, and Choy, *Lumei sanyi zong huiguan jianshi*.

55. Speer, *Oldest and the Newest Empire*, 555–556. The *Oriental* had a more detailed description of the building; see “The Chinese Companies,” *The Oriental*, Jan. 25, 1855.

56. A vivid story about this can be found in Sidney Andrew's “Wo Lee, and His Kinsfolk,” *Atlantic Monthly* (Feb. 1870): 226. Also see Brooks, *Appendix to the Opening Statement*, 143; “The Chinese Companies,” *The Oriental*, Jan. 25, 1855; “The Chinese Companies,” *The Oriental*, Mar. 1, 1855; and California State Legislature, “Report of the Committee on Mines and Mining Interests,” in *Journal of the Fourth Session of the Legislature of the State of California* (1853), 8.

57. Speer, *Oldest and the Newest Empire*, 557–559.

58. “The Chinese Companies,” *The Oriental*, Jan. 25, 1855.

59. California State Legislature,“Report of the Committee on Mines and Mining Interests,” 9.

60. *San Francisco Alta California*, Mar. 18, 1850, May 16, 1851. Also see “The Chinese Six Companies,” Bancroft Library, University of California, Berkeley, Horace Davis Scraps, vol. 3: 70–71.

61. “The Chinese Six Companies,” Bancroft Library, Horace Davis Scraps, vol. 3: 70–71; also see “Poverty and Charity in San Francisco,” *Overland Monthly* (second series) 14 (Nov. 1889): 535–547.

62. "City Items: Opening of a New Temple," *San Francisco Alta California,* Aug. 23, 1864. For details of Chinese worship, see "Chinese Worship," *San Francisco Alta California,* Feb. 10, 1871; "Celestial Capers," *San Francisco Morning Call,* Jan. 25, 1879.

63. Speer, *Oldest and the Newest Empire,* 559.

64. Ibid., 569.

65. Ibid., 560. Also see "These Chinese Companies," *The Oriental,* Jan. 25, 1855.

66. Speer, *Oldest and the Newest Empire,* 569.

67. "These Chinese Companies," *The Oriental,* Jan. 25, 1855.

68. "The Chinese," *San Francisco Chronicle,* Apr. 1, 1876. Also see "Who is Right?" *San Francisco Chronicle,* Oct. 2, 1879.

69. Speer, *Oldest and the Newest Empire,* 558.

70. Ibid. Also see, "The Chinese Companies," *The Oriental,* Mar. 1, 1855; and "Wo Lee, and His Kinsfolk," *Atlantic Monthly* (Feb. 1870).

71. Brooks, *Appendix to the Opening Statement,* 144. Also see "The Chinese Companies," *The Oriental,* Jan. 25, 1855.

72. Speer, *Oldest and the Newest Empire,* 563; also see "Wo Lee, and His Kinsfolk," *Atlantic Monthly* (Feb. 1870): 226.

73. "The Chinese Companies," *The Oriental,* Jan. 25, 1855.

74 California State Legislature, "Report of the Committee on Mines and Mining Interests," (1853) 8.

75. "Meeting of the Chinese Residents of San Francisco," *San Francisco Alta California,* Dec. 10, 1849; also see the letter of Mr. S. W. Bonney of Mar. 12, 1850, *San Francisco Alta California,* Aug. 11, 1850.

76. *San Francisco Alta California,* Aug. 11, 1850.

77. *San Francisco Alta California,* Sept. 26, 1852 (quoting Hong Kong *China Mail*); also see "Circular Addressed by the California Chinamen to their Countrymen," *San Francisco Herald,* May 16, 1852.

78. Sandmeyer, *Anti-Chinese Movement in California,* 16.

79. Him Mark Lai, "The Chinese Language Sources Bibliography Project: Preliminary Findings," *Amerasia Journal* 5:2 (1978): 100.

80. Norman Asing, "To His Excellency Gov. Bigler," *San Francisco Alta California,* May 5, 1852.

81. "Hab Wa and Long Achick. "Letter of the Chinamen to His Excellency, Governor Bigler," *Living Age* 34 (July 1852): 32–34; *San Francisco Herald,* April 30 and June 6, 1852; Ow, Lai, and Choy, *Lumei sanyi zong huiguan jianshi,* 58. For more information about Tang Yazhi and Tong Archick, see Chen Yong, "The Internal Origins of the Chinese Emigration," 542, and Yung Wing, *My Life in China and America* (New York: Henry Holt, 1909), 13, 20.

82. The Foreign Miners' License Tax was in practice directly primarily against the Chinese; see Sucheng Chan, *Asian Americans,* 46.

83. The leaders included Gee Atai, Lee Cheun, Tong K. Achick, Lum Teen-

kwei, Chun Aching, Wong Sing, Lee Yuk. California State Legislature, "Report of the Committee on Mines and Mining Interests,"(1853), 8.

84. California State Legislature, "Report of the Committee on Mines and Mining Interests," (1853),7–12; *San Francisco Herald,* Mar. 18, 1853; *San Francisco Alta California,* Mar. 25, 1853.

85. California State Legislature, "Report of the Committee on Mines and Mining Interests," (1853), 10.

86. California State Legislature, "Report of the Committee on Mines and Mining Interests," (1853), 7–10.

87. Lai Chun-chuen, *Remarks of the Chinese Merchants of San Francisco on Governor Bigler's Message* (San Francisco: Whitton Towne & Co., 1855); Ow, Lai, and Choy, *Lumei sanyi huiguan jianshi,* 16; Speer, *Oldest and the Newest Empire,* 579–580.

88. California Legislature, *Statutes of the State of California* (Sacramento, CA: State Printing Office, 1855), 194–195.

89. *San Francisco Herald,* Feb. 5, 1855.

90. "Reply to Gov. Bigler's Message," *The Oriental,* Feb. 1, 1855.

91. Ibid.

92. Presbyterian Church in the United States of America, San Francisco. Board of Foreign Missions. Correspondence, 1852–1865, Jan. 3, 1860.

93. Otis Gibson, *The Chinese in America* (Cincinnati, OH: Hitchcock and Walden, 1877), 128, 161.

94. In 1854 the *huiguan* were charged as labor brokers; see *San Francisco Herald,* Aug. 27, 1854.

95. William Speer, *An Humble Plea Addressed to the Legislature of California in Behalf of the Immigrants from the Empire of China to This State* (San Francisco: Steret, 1856).

96. California Legislature, *Statutes of the State of California* (Sacramento, CA: State Printing Office, 1856), 141.

97. "Meeting of the Chinese," *San Francisco Alta California,* Aug. 30, 1854. The report did not mention any background for Charles Jane.

98. Ibid., Apr. 5 and 8, 1856.

Chapter 3: Toward a New Chinese Self-image

Epigraphs: San Francisco Alta California, Apr. 29, 1868; *San Francisco Evening Post,* Aug. 13, 1878.

1. Zhang Deyi, *Hanghai shuqi,* in *From East to West,* ed. Zhong Shuhe (Changsha: Hunan renmin chubanshe, 1980), 54; Zhigang, *Chushi taixi ji,* in *Wanqing haiwai biji xuan,* ed. Fujian shida (Beijing: Haiyang chubanshe, 1983), 96; "Grand Dinner for the Chinese Embassy," *San Francisco Alta California,* Apr. 29, 1868; "Dinner to the Chinese Consuls," *San Francisco Morning Call,* Jan. 26, 1879; "American News," *Chung Sai Yat Po,* Nov. 24, 1902, Mar. 26, 1903, Mar. 30, 1903, Apr. 12, 1904, June 20, 1906.

2. Zhigang was a secretary in the Zongli Yamen and one of the Chinese envoys accompanying Anson Burlingame to the United States and European countries in 1868.

3. "The Chinese Embassy Banquet," *San Francisco Evening Bulletin,* Apr. 29, 1868; "Grand Dinner for the Chinese Embassy," *San Francisco Alta California,* Apr. 29, 1868; "Chinese Embassy Banquet," Bancroft Library, Bancroft Scraps, vol. 6, 77.

4. Sucheng Chan, *This Bitter-Sweet Soil,* 108–119.

5. Ibid., 50–51.

6. United States Pacific Railway Commission, *Report of the United States Pacific Railway Commission* (Washington, DC: GPO, 1887-88), vol. 6, 3224.

7. George Kraus, *High Road to Promontory* (Palo Alto: America West Publishing Co., 1969), 201.

8. *San Francisco Alta California,* June 24, 1869, contains a statement by a foreman of the Central Pacific about the contract of the Chinese laborers.

9. A. W. Loomis, "How Our Chinamen Are Employed," *Overland Monthly,* 2 (Mar. 1869): 237. Also see Takaki, *Strangers from a Different Shore,* 89.

10. *Picayune,* July 15 and 27, 1869.

11. "Koopmanschap and His Chinese Immigration Plans," *St. Lewis Republican,* Aug. 2, 1869.

12. We do not know Mr. Joseph's first name. Barth quoting *San Francisco Alta California,* Aug. 29, 1869, in *Bitter Strength,* 189; also see *Sacramento Record-Union,* Feb. 26, 1878.

13. "Struggle for the Monopoly of the Southern Coolie Trade," *San Francisco Alta California,* Aug. 1, 1869.

14. "Chinamen in the South," *San Francisco Alta California,* July 11, 1869; also see Barth, *Bitter Strength,* 190.

15. *Picayune,* July 14 and 15, 1869; also see Barth, *Bitter Strength,* 193.

16. "Waiting for Koopmanschap," *San Francisco Alta California,* July 15, 1869.

17. Hillebrand, in Hawai'i Bureau of Immigration, *Report of the President of the Bureau of Immigration to the Legislative Assembly of 1886* (Honolulu: Bureau of Immigration, 1886), 23.

18. "Wo Lee, and His Kinsfolk," *Atlantic Monthly* 25 (Feb. 1870): 226.

19. Harris Newmark, *Sixty Years in Southern California 1853–1913* (New York: Houghton Mifflin Co., 1916), 418.

20. Zhu Liping, *A Chinaman's Chance,* 116–117.

21. "Wo Lee, and His Kinsfolk," *Atlantic Monthly* 25 (Feb. 1870): 233.

22. Bancroft Library, Bancroft Scraps, vol. 6, 32.

23. "Our New Labor Problem," Dec. 14, 1869, Bancroft Library, Bancroft Scraps, vol. 6, 223.

24. "Death of a Pioneer Chinese Merchant of San Francisco," *San Francisco Alta California,* Sept. 1, 1868; Ow, Lai, and Choy, *Lumei sanyi zonghuiguan jianshi,* 179.

25. "A Chinese Banquet," *San Francisco Alta California,* Sept. 20, 1864; also see "Grand Complimentary Chinese Dinner," *San Francisco Alta California,* Aug. 18, 1865.

26. "The Grand Complimentary Chinese Dinner to Speaker Colfax, Lieut. Gov. Bross, Albert D. Bichardson and Samuel Bowles," *San Francisco Alta California,* Aug. 18, 1865.

27. "Chinese Liberality," *San Francisco Alta California,* Apr. 21, 1865.

28. "Death of a Pioneer Chinese Merchant of San Francisco," *San Francisco Alta California,* Sept. 1, 1868.

29. For more information about the negative image of the Chinese, see Miller, *The Unwelcome Immigrant;* William F. Wu, *The Yellow Peril: Chinese Americans in American Fiction* (Hamden, CT: Archou Books, 1982); and Shirley Sui Ling Tam, "Images of the Unwelcome Immigrant," PhD diss., Case Western Reserve University, 1999.

30. *San Francisco Alta California,* Feb. 1, 1861; "Washington Alley," Mar. 16, 1861; Jan. 9, 1864.

31. "Chinese Kidnapping," *San Francisco Alta California,* Sept. 27, 1866.

32. "A Dernier Resort," *San Francisco Alta California,* Oct. 20, 1860.

33. "Murder of a Chinaman," *San Francisco Chronicle,* Sept. 24, 1864.

34. "The Growth of the United States through Emigration—The Chinese," *New York Times,* Sept. 3, 1865.

35. "Inaugural Message," *San Francisco Alta California,* Jan. 11, 1862.

36. "Chinese in California," *San Francisco Chronicle,* May 1, 1868; also see Bancroft Library, Bancroft Scraps, vol. 6, 76.

37. For the frequent conflicts, see Barth, *Bitter Strength,* 94–95.

38. Hoy, *Chinese Six Companies,* 8; For the fights between the *huiguan,* see "Great Fight among the Chinamen," *San Francisco Alta California,* July 21, 1854; "Hongkongs v. Cantons," *San Francisco Alta California,* Sept. 10, 1854; "Chinese War in Mariposa," *San Francisco Alta California,* Jan. 28, 1856; "Hongkong v. Canton," *San Francisco Alta California,* Sept. 28, Oct. 6, Oct. 31, 1856; "Fatal Affray among Chinamen at San Andres," *San Francisco Alta California,* Jan. 11, 1859.

39. Hoy, *Chinese Six Companies,* 9.

40. Ibid. According to Ow, Lai, and Choy, the Six Companies was established in 1862; see Ow, Lai, and Choy, *Lumei sanyi zonghuiguan jianshi,* 129.

41. Charles J. McClain, *In Search of Equality* (Berkeley: University of California Press, 1994), 22–23. Also see A. W. Loomis to Walter Lowrie, Jan. 3, 1860, Presbyterian Church in the U.S.A., Board of Foreign Missions, Correspondence, 1852–1865, re: California.

42. Hoy, *Chinese Six Companies,* 7–9. A *San Francisco Morning Call* reporter interviewed Chock Wong, the editor-in-chief of the *Oriental* on May 11, 1876 about the nature of the Six Companies; see "Chock Wong," *San Francisco Morning Call,* May 12, 1876.

43. Hoy, *Chinese Six Companies,* 13.

44. For more detailed records of the Six Companies in the 1860s, see Bancroft Library, Bancroft Scraps, vol. 6, 223; "The Chinese in California," *San Francisco Alta California,* July 7, 1866.

45. Hoy, *Chinese Six Companies,* 11.

46. Ibid., 17.

47. "Wo Lee, and His Kinsfolk," *Atlantic Monthly* 25 (Feb. 1870): 227; for an example of the meetings, see "Efforts to Prevent Further Immigration," *San Francisco Alta California,* Apr. 3, 1876; and "The Chinese Companies," *San Francisco Alta California,* Apr. 3, 1876.

48. Sucheng Chan, *Asian Americans,* 66.

49. "The Chinese in California," *San Francisco Evening Bulletin,* Nov. 23, 1864.

50. Hoy, *Chinese Six Companies,* 20–21. Also see Outbound Letters 1901, Tung Wah Hospital Archives, Hong Kong.

51. "The Chinese in California," *San Francisco Evening Bulletin,* Nov. 23, 1864; also see "Is the Coolie Trade Practicable?" *San Francisco Alta California,* Aug. 2, 1869.

52. Speer, *Oldest and the Newest Empire,* 560 and 569.

53. Hoy, *Chinese Six Companies,* 20.

54. California State Legislature, Senate, Special Committee on Chinese Immigration, *Chinese Immigration: The Social, Mora, and Political Effect* (Sacramento: State Printing Office, 1878), 32; also see "Who Is Right?" *San Francisco Chronicle,* Oct. 2, 1879.

55. Bancroft Library, Bancroft Scraps, vol. 6, 22. Also see "Chinese Worship," *San Francisco Alta California,* Feb. 10, 1871.

56. Hoy, *Chinese Six Companies,* 23.

57. "The Meaning of the Ho Chung," *San Francisco Evening Bulletin,* Aug. 12, 1880.

58. Hoy, *Chinese Six Companies,* 23.

59. Ibid.; in 1878 the Ningyang *huiguan* had "on its rolls about 90,000 of the 200,000 Chinese in the country." See "The Six Companies," *San Francisco Evening Post,* Aug. 13, 1878.

60. Hoy, *Chinese Six Companies,* 21.

61. *San Francisco Alta California,* Feb. 27, 1862.

62. Ibid., Sept. 25, 1862.

63. "The Chinese Tax," *Sacramento Record-Union,* June 6, 1862.

64. *Lin Sing v. Washburn,* 20 *California Reports* 534 (1862), 576–579.

65. The heyday of Chinese prostitution in San Francisco was from 1860 to 1870. The late 1870s saw a dramatic decline in both the number and percentage of prostitutes; see Lucie Cheng, "Free, Indentured, Enslaved: Chinese Prostitutes in Nineteenth-Century America." In *Labor Immigration under Capitalism: Asian Workers in the United States before World War II,* eds. Lucie Cheng and Edna Bonacich (Berkeley: The University of California Press, 1984), 421. Also see "City Items: Small Feet and High Caste," *San Francisco Alta California,* June 11, 1860.

66. "Sending Home the Chinese Females," *San Francisco Alta California,* Apr. 27, 1864.

67. "Another Lot of Stolen Chinese Girls Arrive," *San Francisco Alta California,* July 11, 1864.

68. See "Chinese Prostitutes Coming," *San Francisco Alta California,* Sept. 14, 1867.

69. Richard H. Dillon, *The Hatchet Men: The Story of the Tong Wars in San Francisco's Chinatown* (New York: Coward-McCann, Inc., 1962), 93. Also see "Chinese Murder Case," *San Francisco Alta California,* Jan, 7, 1866.

70. Dillon, *Hatchet Men,* 20, 21.

71. *San Francisco Alta California,* Nov. 17, 1867.

72. "Sending Home the Chinese Females," *San Francisco Alta California,* Apr. 27, 1864.

73. "Chinese Prostitutes Coming," *San Francisco Alta California,* Sept. 14, 1867.

74. "Honor to Whom Honor is Due," *San Francisco Alta California,* June 16, 1868. Also see Daniel Cleveland to J. Ross Browne, July 27, 1868, Bancroft Library, George Kenyon Fitch, Correspondence and Papers.

75. Secret Letter of the Zongli Yamen, Oct. 12, 1867, *Chouban yiwu shimo,* Tongzhi, 50: 32a. For more about the secret letters, see Knight Biggerstaff, "The Change in the Attitude of the Chinese Government toward the Sending of Diplomatic Representatives, 1860–1880," (PhD diss., Harvard University, 1934)

76. For discussion of the unpreparedness of the Qing government for the establishment of diplomatic missions abroad, see John K. Fairbank, *Trade and Diplomacy on the China Coast* (Stanford: Stanford University Press, 1969); Hsu, *China's Entrance;* Chow Jen Hwa, *China and Japan: The History of Chinese Diplomatic Missions in Japan 1877–1911* (Singapore: Chopmen Enterprises, 1975), 61; and Yen Ching-Hwang, *Coolies and Mandarins: China's Protection of the Overseas Chinese during the Late Ch'ing Period, 1851–1911* (Singapore: Singapore University Press, 1985), 206–207.

77. *Chouban yiwu shimo,* Tongzhi reign, 39: 1a–2b.

78. Zhou Jiamei, *Qibufu zhai quanji* (1895), Part 1 "Political writings," 1:2–5b.

79. *Chouban yiwu shimo,* Tongzhi reign, 50: 32a-b.

80. Ibid., 54: 8a, 4–8b, 7.

81. Ibid., 53: 4b–5a.

82. Before the Opium War, the social status of Chinese merchants in China was very low. For a discussion of "foreign experts" before 1861, see Earl Swisher, "Chinese 'Barbarian Experts' in Early Sino-American Relations," in *Early Sino-American Relations, 1841-1912,* ed. Kenneth W. Rea (Boulder, CO: Westview Press, 1977). The same essay may also be found in Earl Swisher, *China's Management of the American Barbarians: A Study of Sino-American Relations 1841–61* (New Haven, CT: Yale University Press, 1953). Also see Fairbank, *Trade and Diplomacy.* Qing officials were keenly aware of the value of Chinese merchants in dealing with for-

eigners and began to use them frequently in negotiations with foreigners during the Opium War. See *Chouban yiwu shimo,* Dao Guang reign, 28:3; and A. W. Hummel, ed., *Eminent Chinese of the Ch'ing Period* (Washington, DC: Government Printing Office, 1943), vol. 2, 606.

83. *Chouban yiwu shimo,* Tongzhi reign, 54: 17b–18b. The following story is interesting and plausible, but it is difficult to find corroborating evidence for it: "We learn from Le Mineur of this city, that a very intelligent Chinaman, named Ah Shang, who had spent five years in California, three as a miner and two as a merchant, returned about seven months since to his Celestial penates, with a snug fortune of fifteen thousand dollars, and with a sufficient knowledge of the English language for all commercial purposes. On his return to his own country, his capacity, joined to his fortune, which his countrymen regarded with pride as a conquest over the 'barbarians,' caused him to be employed by his government as a superior officer of the customs; from which position he was soon called to Pekin, where he was attached to the Grand Mandarin of European affairs; again, in a short time he was honored with the rank and title of Mandarin of the second class. And was employed as a Commissioner in the peace conference, which resulted in the signing of a treaty between the Anglo-French allies and the Chinese. These facts were obtained from a Chinese mercantile house of this city." See "City Intelligence: A Mandarin Miner," *San Francisco Herald,* Jan. 21, 1861.

84. *Chouban yiwu shimo,* Tongzhi reign, 51: 21a–21b. On the one hand, the Qing officials had to depend on these Chinese merchants, but they were suspicious of all who had any intercourse with foreigners. As Fairbank has pointed out: "Like their present Western counterparts, the 'barbarian experts' in China were likely to discover unpalatable truths, displease the more conservative members of their class and generation, and suffer suspicion and condemnation accordingly"; see his *Trade and Diplomacy,* 176.

85. *Chouban yiwu shimo,* Tongzhi reign, 51: 27a-b. Also see Zhigang, *Chushi taixi ji,* 389; Knight Biggerstaff, "The Secret Correspondence of 1867–8: Views of Leading Chinese Statesmen Regarding the Further Opening of China to Western Influence," *The Journal of Modern History* 22:1 (Mar. 1950): 368. For more on Burlingame, see Frederick Wells Williams, *Anson Burlingame and the First Chinese Mission to Foreign Powers* (New York: Scribners, 1912).

86. Knight Biggerstaff quoting Legation Archives (China), No. 235, 114 b, in "The Establishment of Permanent Chinese Diplomatic Missions Abroad," *The Chinese Social and Political Science Review* 40:1 (1936):15.

87. Zhigang, *Chushi taixi ji,* 264–265. It was said when Burlingame was in Washington, he stated to his friends that upon the completion of his mission, he would be a citizen of California and organize a large colony of Chinese; for details, see "Chinese Military Colonies in America," *San Francisco Post,* Sept. 7, 1877.

88. "Daniel Cleveland to J. Ross Browne, July 27, 1868." Bancroft Library, George Kenyon Fitch, Correspondence and Papers. Also see "Letter of Daniel Cleveland to Ross Browne (July 27, 1868)," reprinted in U. S. Dept. of State, *Papers*

Relating to Foreign Affairs Accompanying the Annual Message of the President to the 3d sess. 40th Cong. (Washington, DC: GPO, 1869), pt. 1, 543; McClain, "Chinese Struggle for Civil Rights," 529–568.

89. Daniel Cleveland to J. Ross Browne, July 27, 1868. Bancroft Library, George Kenyon Fitch, Correspondence and Papers.

90. Ibid.

91. Also see Kim Man Chan, "Mandarins in America" (PhD diss., University of Hawai'i, 1981), 22.

92. Zhigang, *Chushi taixi ji,* 274–275.

93. Prince Kung to Burlingame, June 7, 1869, National Archives Microfilms, Washington, DC, M98, Roll 1.

94. Gibson, *Chinese in America,* 134.

95. "Honor to Whom Honor is Due," *San Francisco Alta California,* June 16, 1868. Two years later the Six Companies tried to fight Chinese prostitution by resorting to the courts, see "Local Intelligence: Another Effort to Be Made to Stop the Importation of Chinese Women," *San Francisco Alta California,* Jan. 16, 1870.

96. "Memorial of the Trustees of the Chinese Six Companies to the Governor" (1868), California State Archives, Sacramento.

97. "A Remonstrance from the Chinese in California to the Congress of the United States," quoted in Speer, *Oldest and the Newest Empire,* 600–601. Also see The Six Companies, *Memorial of the Trustees of the Chinese Six Companies to the Governor.* 1868. Sacramento: California State Archives.

98. "A Remonstrance from the Chinese in California to the Congress of the United States," quoted in Speer, *Oldest and the Newest Empire,* 600–601.

99. The House Ways and Means Committee visited San Francisco as part of a fact-finding tour of the West Coast. Wade was at that time a director on the board of the Union Pacific Railroad. For more information concerning the context, see McClain, *In Search of Equality,* 37; H. L. Trefousse, *Benjamin Franklin Wade, Radical Republican from Ohio* (New York: Twayne Publishers, 1963). Also see "Movements of Senator Wade," *San Francisco Chronicle,* June 23, 1869.

100. "Movements of the Congressional Committee and Guests," *San Francisco Alta California,* June 26, 1869; "Movement of Senator Wade," *San Francisco Chronicle,* June 23, 1869; also see *San Francisco Alta California,* June 26, 1869, 1; *New York Times,* June 27, 1869, 1. For more information about Fung, see Linda Pomerantz, "The Chinese Bourgeoisie and the Anti-Chinese Movement in the United States, 1850–1905," *Amerasia* 11:1 (1984): 7–8.

101. "Movements of the Congressional Committee and Guests," *San Francisco Alta California,* June 26, 1869. In his impromptu speech before the Chinese Sunday School of Howard Presbyterian Church in the same year, Fung Tang continued his argument: "If we are worthy of the protection of law, the Americans will find it out at last, and we shall have it. There is a great commerce for both nations, and it will make us friends if all are right minded," see "Chinese Sunday School at the Howard Presbyterian Church," Bancroft Library, Bancroft Scraps, vol. 6, 138.

102. *Congressional Globe,* 41st Cong., 2nd sess. (1869), 3, 301, 3658.

103. See McClain, "Chinese Struggle for Civil Rights," 564–567; McClain, *In Search of Equality* 38; *Congressional Globe,* 41st Cong., 2nd sess. (1869–1870), 1536.

104. James Townsend, "Chinese Nationalism," in Jonathan Unger, ed., *Chinese Nationalism* (New York: M. E. Sharp, 1996), 12.

105. A recent investigation conducted by Bryna Goodman suggests that the Chinese native-place sentiment in Shanghai was also compatible with modern nationalism; see Goodman, *Native Place,* 13.

106. Andrew Gyory, *Closing the Gate: Race, Politics, and the Chinese Exclusion Act* (Chapel Hill: University of North Carolina Press, 1998), 26.

Chapter 4: Becoming the Chief Target

Epigraph: San Francisco Evening Post, Mar. 17, 1877.

1. Cloud and Galenson, "Chinese Immigration and Contract Labor," 22–42; McClain, "Chinese Immigration," 376. Scholars in this field whose analyses were shaped by the debates of the 1870s and 1880s vary in their conclusions regarding the Six Companies. But whatever their opinions, recent historians have found little evidence to support the charge of importation. After McClain's 1990 refutation, most historians no longer support the argument that the Six Companies financed the passage of individual Chinese laborers.

2. For the Chinese population of San Francisco and their occupations in 1878, see "Chinese Invasion," *San Francisco Chronicle,* July 21, 1878.

3. U.S. Congress, *Report of the Joint Special Committee to Investigate Chinese Immigration,* 44th Cong., 2nd sess., 1876–1877, Senate Report 689, 853.

4. "Chinese Immigration," *San Francisco Evening Bulletin,* Nov. 17, 1876. Simon Jones was in the import and export trade and had a Chinese partner, Fung Tang.

5. L. Eve Armentrout Ma, "The Big Business Ventures of Chinese in North America," in *The Chinese American Experience,* ed. Genny Lim (San Francisco: Chinese Historical Society of America and Chinese Culture Foundation, 1984), 102.

6. "How China is Bleeding Us," *San Francisco Chronicle,* Mar. 15, 1879. For a list of the Chinese merchants who were assessed taxes of $5,000 and upward in 1875, see "The Chinese as Taxpayers," *San Francisco Evening Post,* Apr. 1, 1876.

7. "Chinese Commissions," *San Francisco Evening Bulletin,* June 5, 1876.

8. Sucheng Chan, "Chinese Livelihood in Rural California: The Impact of Economic Change, 1860–1880," *Pacific Historical Review* 54 (1984): 280–282.

9. *Idaho Statesman,* Aug. 10, 1876; Zhu Liping, *A Chinaman's Chance,* 110.

10. "The Chinese Experiment," *San Francisco Chronicle,* Apr. 4, 1873.

11. "The Chinese as Mechanics," *San Francisco Chronicle,* Apr. 2, 1876.

12. William Wright (Dan de Quille), *History of the Big Bonanza* (Hartford, CT: American Publishing Co., 1876), 290–291. A list of the principal Chinese business firms in San Francisco, issued by Wells Fargo & Co. in 1878, gives more examples

of their success. See "The Chinese Don't Go," *San Francisco Evening Post,* Oct. 5, 1878.

13. "Response of the 'Heathen Chinese,'" San *Francisco Alta California,* Oct. 16, 1871.

14. "The Two Races at Table," *San Francisco Morning Call,* Feb. 27, 1877.

15. "Our Chinese and the Centennial," *San Francisco Alta California,* Apr. 11, 1876.

16. Ibid.

17. U.S. Congress, *Report... to Investigate Chinese Immigration,* Senate Report 689, 530.

18. Ibid., 815. Also see "Chinese Immigration," *San Francisco Evening Bulletin,* Nov. 17, 1876.

19. U.S. Congress, *Report... to Investigate Chinese Immigration,* Senate Report No. 689, 853; *Sacramento Bee,* Nov. 10, 1876; "The Chinese Investigation," *San Francisco Alta California,* Nov. 18, 1886.

20. California State Legislature, Senate, Special Committee, *Chinese Immigration,* Appendix, 116.

21. "Chinese Reciprocity," *San Francisco Evening Post,* May 13, 1878. Also see "The Chinese and the Ocean Carrying Trade," *San Francisco Morning Call,* Jan. 25, 1879.

22. Yung Chi, a president of the Hop Wo Company, answered a *San Francisco Chronicle* reporter's question as to why the Chinese were cheap laborers; see "The Chinese," *San Francisco Chronicle,* Apr. 1, 1876.

23. "Coolieism and Its Results," *San Francisco Morning Call,* Mar. 6, 1879.

24. "Chinese Immigration," *San Francisco Chronicle,* May 25, 1878.

25. "The Famine in China and Emigration," *San Francisco Evening Bulletin,* July 18, 1878.

26. "Senator Blaine's Letter to Wm Lloyd Garrison," *San Francisco Chronicle,* Feb. 25, 1879.

27. *San Francisco Evening Post,* Nov. 1, 1878.

28. "Warm Welcome," *San Francisco Chronicle,* May 18, 1878.

29. "Chinese Troubles," *San Francisco Alta California,* Sept 19, 1877; "The Chinese Went," *San Francisco Chronicle,* July 24, 1878.

30. *San Francisco Chronicle,* Apr. 1, 1876. Also see "Chock Wong," *San Francisco Morning Call,* May 12, 1876; "A Mongolian Invasion," *San Francisco Chronicle,* Oct. 26, 1877.

31. "The Yellow Man as a Citizen and a Brother," *New York Herald,* June 8, 1876.

32. "Im' Shee! Im' Shee!" *New York Herald,* Nov. 12, 1877.

33. "Chinatown," *San Francisco Evening Post,* Nov. 9, 1878.

34. "Chinese Contracts," *San Francisco Morning Call,* Aug. 15, 1879. Also see "Rises to Explain," *San Francisco Morning Call,* Oct. 30, 1878.

35. U.S. Congress, *Congressional Record,* 41st Cong., 2nd sess., Jan. 25, 1870, 752.

36. Ibid., July 6, 1876, 4419; Luther Tracy Townsend, *The Chinese Problem* (Boston: Lee and Sheard, 1876), 53–54.

37. "Senator Jones: His Views on the Chinese and Labor Question," *San Francisco Evening Post,* July 29, 1878.

38. "The Chinese Question," *San Francisco Evening Bulletin,* Nov. 30, 1877.

39. "The Chinese Problem," *San Francisco Evening Post,* Dec. 18, 1877.

40. "The President's View on the Chinese Problem," *San Francisco Morning Call,* Dec. 19, 1877. Also see "The President and the Chinese," *San Francisco Evening Post,* Dec. 20, 1877. The Six Companies responded by withdrawing Chinese trade from Davis. See "Horace Davis and the Six Companies," *San Francisco Evening Post,* Jan. 21, 1878; "Horace Davis," *San Francisco Evening Post,* Jan. 29, 1878; "Letter from Washington:," *San Francisco Evening Post,* Feb. 26, 1878. Also see "The President's View on Chinese Immigration," *San Francisco Morning Call,* Aug. 10, 1878; "Hayes and the Chinese Question," *San Francisco Evening Post,* Aug. 19, 1878.

41. "Horace Davis on the Chinese," *San Francisco Examiner,* Mar. 1, 1878.

42. "The Chinese Question," *San Francisco Chronicle,* Jan. 10, 1878.

43. "Representative Luttrell on the Chinese Question—A Satisfactory Interview with the President." *New York Herald,* August 10, 1878.

44. "Chinese Oligarchy," *Oakland Transcript,* Apr. 13, 1876; also see *San Francisco Chronicle,* Apr. 2, 1876. Dr. O. M. Wozencraft was the United States Indian Commissioner in the 1850s.

45. "The Rocklin Tragedy," *San Francisco Evening Post,* Sept. 21, 1877.

46. "Six Companies Diplomacy," *San Francisco Chronicle,* Oct. 28, 1878. Also see "Chinese Immigration," *San Francisco Evening Bulletin,* Aug. 14, 1878.

47. "The Foul Disease," *San Francisco Evening Post,* Nov. 23, 1878.

48. "Restrictive Measures," *San Francisco Evening Bulletin,* Dec. 23, 1878.

49. "The Chinese and Slavery," *San Francisco Evening Bulletin,* Feb. 10, 1879.

50. "Senator Blaine's Letter," *San Francisco Chronicle,* Feb. 25, 1879.

51. Bancroft Library, Bancroft Scraps, vol. 7–8, 202.

52. "Chinese Oligarchy," *Oakland Transcript,* Apr. 13, 1876. Also see "An Incendiary Suggestion," *San Francisco Chronicle,* Apr. 1, 1876.

53. "Boo!" *San Francisco Alta California,* May 28, 1876. Also see "The Chinese Question," *San Francisco Evening Bulletin,* Aug. 29, 1877; "'John' in the Black Hills," *San Francisco Morning Call,* Aug. 10, 1878.

54. *Chinese Record,* Mar. 30, 1877.

55. "Whither It Tends," *San Francisco Evening Post,* Apr. 20, 1877.

56. "To Be or Not To Be," *San Francisco Evening Post,* Sept. 21, 1877.

57. "Chinese Slavery," *San Francisco Evening Post,* Oct. 4, 1877.

58. "J. R. Frend on the Chinese Question," *San Francisco Evening Post,* Aug. 21, 1878.

59. "A Complaint against the Chinese Companies," San Francisco Morning Call, July 10, 1879; also see "Chinese Lepers," *San Francisco Evening Bulletin,* July 10, 1879.

60. The charges began to appear in the early years of Chinese immigration. "Governor's Special Message," *San Francisco Alta California,* Apr. 25, 1852; Bigler, "Message of Governor Bigler," 373; *San Francisco Herald,* Aug. 27, 1854. These early charges were denied at that time by both the Chinese merchants and William Speer; see *San Francisco Herald,* Aug. 27, 1854; Gibson, *Chinese in America,* 229.

61. "Is the Coolie Trade Practicable?" *San Francisco Alta California,* Aug. 2, 1869.

62. "The Chinese Argument," *San Francisco Morning Call,* Feb. 23, 1878.

63. "To Governor Irwin: An Open Letter from O. M. Wozencraft on the Chinese Question," *San Francisco Chronicle,* June 25, 1879.

64. "Restrictive Measure," *San Francisco Evening Bulletin,* Dec. 23, 1878.

65. Bancroft Library, Bancroft Scraps, vol. 7–8, 678.

66. "The Address of the Chinese Companies," *San Francisco Chronicle,* Apr. 1, 1876.

67. "The Chinese Companies," *San Francisco Chronicle,* Apr. 2, 1876.

68. "The Chinese Problem: Speech of Hon. Horace Davis in the House," *San Francisco Post,* July 12, 1879; the agreement between the Six Companies and steamship companies will be discussed below.

69. *San Francisco Chronicle,* April 2, 1876; also see "Gambling and other Vices among the Celestials," Bancroft Scraps, vol. 6, 40.

70. "The 40,000 Chinese," *San Francisco Evening Bulletin,* Aug. 30, 1877.

71. U.S. Congress, *Report... to Investigate Chinese Immigration,* Senate Report No. 689, 591 and 593; McClain, "Chinese Immigration," 367–368.

72. "The Chinese Curse," *Oakland Transcript,* Apr. 6, 1876.

73. U.S. Congress, *Report... to Investigate Chinese Immigration,* Senate Report No. 689, 841; McClain, "Chinese Immigration," 369.

74. "John Chinaman," *San Francisco Chronicle,* Jan. 4, 1878.

75. Bancroft Library, Bancroft Scraps, vol. 7–8, 108.

76. "What the Chinese Companies Have Offered to the Shoe Manufacturers of Chicago," *New York Herald,* August 11, 1878.

77. "Coolie for San Francisco," *San Francisco Chronicle,* Aug. 12, 1878; "The Chinese at Chicago," *Sacramento Record-Union,* Aug. 12, 1878. Also see "Coolie for Chicago," *San Francisco Chronicle,* Aug. 12, 1878; "The Six Companies and the Striking Chicago Shoemakers," *San Francisco Evening Post,* Aug. 12, 1878.

78. "The Six Companies and the Shoemakers' Strike in Chicago," *San Francisco Morning Call,* Aug. 12, 1878.

79. "The Six Companies and the Striking Chicago Shoemakers," *San Francisco Evening Post,* Aug. 12, 1878.

80. "The Chinese and Slavery," *San Francisco Evening Bulletin,* Feb. 10, 1879.

81. "Coolieism and Its Results," *San Francisco Morning Call,* Mar. 6, 1879.

82. "Solving the Problem: A Company that Never Employed a Chinaman and Never Will," *San Francisco Evening Post,* Aug. 22, 1877.

83. "The President and the Chinese Bill," *San Francisco Evening Bulletin,* Feb. 18, 1879.

84. "The 'Post' and Those Who Encourage Chinese Competition," *San Francisco Evening Post,* Aug. 10, 1877.

85. "Chinese Misrepresentation," *San Francisco Evening Post,* Aug. 20, 1878.

86. "Six Companies Diplomacy," *San Francisco Chronicle,* Oct. 28, 1878. Also see "The Chinese Investigation," *San Francisco Alta California,* Apr. 21, 1876.

87. California State Legislature, Assembly Committee on Mines and Mining Interest, *Report of the Chinese Population,* 10.

88. Sandmeyer, *Anti-Chinese Movement in California,* 27; also see, McClain, "Chinese Immigration," 366–367.

89. Stanford Lyman, "Conflict and the Web of Group Affiliation in San Francisco's Chinatown, 1880–1910," *Pacific Historical Review* 43 (1974): 473–499.

90. The contract is preserved in the Wells Fargo Bank History Room of San Francisco.

91. Cloud and Galenson, "Chinese Immigration and Contract Labor," 29.

92. "The Chinese," *San Francisco Post,* July 6, 1878. The article quoted Consul's comments in order to prove that the Chinese were mostly contract laborers.

93. "A Proper Subject of Inquiry," *San Francisco Evening Post,* Aug. 22, 1878; however, the paper contradicts itself in the next sentence, which reads: "It cannot be denied successfully that members of the Six Companies are engaged in the traffic."

94. U.S. Congress, *Report . . . to Investigate Chinese Immigration,* Senate Report No. 689, 175; *San Francisco Alta California,* Oct. 25, 1876.

95. Cloud and Galenson, "Chinese Immigration and Contract Labor," 28.

96. McClain, "Chinese Immigration," 372–373.

97. U.S. Congress, *Report . . . to Investigate Chinese Immigration,* Senate Report No. 689, 1165.

98. Bancroft Library, Bancroft Scraps, vol. 7–8, 685–686.

99. "Andrew Wilson's 'Jottings' on Civil War California," *California Historical Society Quarterly* 32 (1953): 209.

100. U.S. Congress, *Report . . . to Investigate Chinese Immigration,* Senate Report No. 689, 82–83; Cloud and Galenson, "Chinese Immigration and Contract Labor," 25; McClain, "Chinese Immigration," 369.

101. *San Francisco Call,* Feb. 23, 1878. Also see "Twenty-two Million More," "Busy Bruke," *San Francisco Chronicle,* July 25, 1880.

102. Canadian Joint Special Commission to Investigate Chinese Immigration. *Report of the Royal Commission on Chinese Immigration.* Ottawa: Printed by the order of the Commission, 1885), lxxxiv–lxxxv, quoted in Cloud and Galenson, "Chinese Immigration and Contract Labor," 36–37.

103. California, Legislature, Senate, Special Committee, *Chinese Immigration,* 65–66; also see Hoy, *Six Chinese Companies,* 23.

104. See Speer, *Oldest and the Newest Empire,* 562–563.

105. "The Chinese Companies," *The Oriental,* Mar. 1, 1855.

106. Fong Kum Ngon, "Chinese Six Companies," *Overland Monthly* (May 1894): 525.

107. "Who is Right?" *San Francisco Chronicle,* Oct. 2, 1879; "The Chinese Can Go," *San Francisco Chronicle,* Apr. 22, 1880; "Chinese Six Companies," *San Francisco Alta California,* July 25, 1880; "Head Money," *San Francisco Alta California,* Jan. 21, 1881; "The Insidious 'Six,'" *San Francisco Alta California,* Jan. 23, 1881; Fong Kum Ngon, "Chinese Six Companies," *Overland Monthly* (May 1894): 525.

108. "Wo Lee, and His Kinsfolk," *Atlantic Monthly* 25 (Feb. 1870): 227.

109. "Mr. Ng Choy," *San Francisco Post,* Mar. 14, 1877. Also see Bancroft Library, Bancroft Scraps," vol. 7, 525. For more on Wu Tingfang, see Linda Pomerantz, *Wu Tingfang (1842–1922): Nationalism and Liberalism in Modern China* (Hong Kong: Hong Kong University Press, 1992).

110. Gibson, *Chinese in America,* 259. Also see *The Chinese Question from a Chinese Standpoint,* Lai Yong et al., Otis Gibson, trans. (San Francisco, 1874).

111. U.S. Congress, *Report... to Investigate Chinese Immigration,* Senate Report No. 689, 420.

112. Ibid., 421.

113. "A Chinese Exodus," *San Francisco Chronicle,* Jan. 16, 1886; also see "Poverty in Chinatown," *San Francisco Alta California,* Feb. 13, 1886.

114. California State Legislature, Senate, Special Committee, *Chinese Immigration,* 96–97; also see McClain, "Chinese Immigration," 370.

115. "A New Chinese Bill," *San Francisco Chronicle,* June 25, 1879.

116. See "The Employment of Chinese as a Political Question," *San Francisco Alta California,* Oct. 3, 1869.

117. "Local Intelligence," *San Francisco Alta California,* June 26, 1869.

118. California State Legislature, Senate, Special Committee, *Chinese Immigration,* 186.

119. "Chan Pak Qwai," *San Francisco Post,* Apr. 5, 1879. When Chan Pak Qwai returned, Sit Ming Cook, the vice consul of Chinese consulate of San Francisco, "discovered Chan Pak Kwai was a Christian, and refused to have anything to do with him"; see "The Chinese Lecture Swindle," *Sacramento Record-Union,* Mar. 24, 1879. Also see "A Chinese Lecture in the Field," *San Francisco Bulletin,* Mar. 17, 1879; "The History of a Chinese Lecture Tour," "That Chinese Lecture—What His Agent Says," and "Another Pious Fraud," Bancroft Library, Bancroft Scraps, vol. 7–8, 197–198; "The Chinese Hoax," *San Francisco Call,* Mar. 19, 1879; "Chan Pak Kwai," *San Francisco Call,* Mar. 23, 1879.

120. Charles Frederick Holder, "The Chinaman in American Politics," *North American Review* 166 (Feb. 1898): 231.

121. "A Discontented Cargo of Chinese Coolies," *San Francisco Bulletin,* Nov. 12, 1878.

122. California State Legislature, Senate, Special Committee, *Chinese Immigration,* 115.

123. "A Bloody Fight," *San Francisco Alta California,* Mar. 27, 1876.

124. "A Wealthy Chinese Company," *San Francisco Bulletin,* May 17, 1878.

125. Barth, *Bitter Strength,* 196.

126. Fong, "Chinese Six Companies," 524. For more on Chin Gee-Hee, see William G. Jue, "Chin Gee-Hee, Chinese pioneer Entrepreneur in Seattle and Toishan." *The Annals of the Chinese Historical Society of the Pacific Northwest.* (1983): 31–38.

127. The Six Companies advanced only the cost of passage to their poorer countrymen when the United States needed cheap laborers in the early period. It dissuaded potential Chinese immigrants from coming when the anti-Chinese movement swung into full gear.

Chapter 5: Setting the Tone and Format

Epigraph: San Francisco Alta California, Apr. 3, 1876.

1. MacGowan, "Chinese Guilds," 137.

2. Tung Wah Hospital was the Six Companies' information center in Hong Kong. See Elizabeth Sinn, *Power and Charity: The Early History of the Tung Wah Hospital* (Hong Kong: Oxford University Press, 1989), 72.

3. *The Daily Press,* June 5, 1873.

4. Sandmeyer, *Anti-Chinese Movement in California,* 16.

5. "Checking the Chinese Immigration" *San Francisco Alta California,* Mar. 30, 1876. Also see "A Letter to China," Bancroft Library, Bancroft Scraps, vol. 6, 352. For other deterring letters, see in "The Chinese Companies," *San Francisco Alta California,* Apr. 3, 1876; "By State Telegraph," *Sacramento Record-Union,* Apr. 4, 1876; *San Francisco Alta California,* Apr. 30, 1876; *San Francisco Alta California,* May 21, 23, 28, 1876.

6. *Sacramento Record-Union,* Apr. 3, 1876. The Six Companies held a meeting at the Sam Yap Company on Apr. 2, 1876. For details, see "The Chinese Companies," *San Francisco Alta California,* Apr. 3, 1876.

7. Ow, Lai, and Choy, *Lumei sanyi zong huiguan jianshi,* 63, n. 32.

8. *The Daily Press,* Apr. 6, 1876.

9. *San Francisco Alta California,* Apr. 5, 1876.

10. *The Oriental,* Apr. 29, 1876.

11. Dillon, *Hatchet Men,* 115.

12. "The New Immigration Law," *San Francisco Evening Bulletin,* Mar. 14, 1878.

13. "The Chinese Companies," *San Francisco Alta California,* Apr. 3, 1876. The U.S. Congress began to consider amending the treaty in 1878. See "The New Immigration Law," *San Francisco Evening Bulletin,* Mar. 14, 1878.

14. *San Francisco Alta California,* Apr. 5, 1876. The manifesto, translated into English by Otis Gibson, was drafted by Li Yong of the Sanyi *huiguan* and reflected

the demands of the Six Companies. See Ow, Lai, and Choy, *Lumei sanyi zong huiguan jianshi,* 60, n. 34; *San Francisco Chronicle,* Apr. 1, 1876.

15. "Efforts to Prevent Further Immigration," *San Francisco Alta California,* Apr. 3, 1876.

16. "An Important Letter," *San Francisco Chronicle,* Apr. 1, 1876.

17. "The Chinese Companies Ask for Protection," *San Francisco Alta California,* Apr. 4, 1876.

18. "The Six Companies and the President of the United States," *Sacramento Bee,* May 29, 1876.

19. "A Chinese Plea," *San Francisco Post,* Nov. 23, 1877. For an intimate picture of Kennedy, see *San Francisco Post,* Jan. 11, 1878.

20. "California's Problem: Interview with Colonel F. A. Bee on the Chinese Question," *San Francisco Morning Call,* Aug. 20, 1877.

21. Chinese Consolidated Benevolent Association, *Memorial: Six Companies* (San Francisco: Alta, 1877), 13.

22. "California's Problem: Interview with Colonel F. A. Bee on the Chinese Question," *San Francisco Morning Call,* Aug. 20, 1877.

23. "The Other Side," *San Francisco Chronicle,* Sept. 21, 1877.

24. "The Chinese," *San Francisco Evening Post,* Jan. 21, 1878; also see "The Chinese and Politics," *San Francisco Morning Call,* Jan. 22, 1878.

25. "Chinese Capitation Tax," *San Francisco Post,* Feb. 26, 1878.

26. "A Proclamation by the Six Companies—A Reply to the Sant Lot Orators—The Companies not Traders of Their Countrymen," *New York Herald,* August 11, 1878; also see "Chinese Misrepresentation," *San Francisco Evening Post,* Aug. 20, 1878.

27. "Coolie Immigration," *San Francisco Evening Bulletin,* Feb. 15, 1879.

28. Sandmeyer, *Anti-Chinese Movement in California,* 16.

29. "Another Report to be Made to Stop the Importation of Chinese Women," *San Francisco Alta California,* Jan. 16, 1870.

30. "Levying Blackmail," *San Francisco Alta California,* Apr. 22, 1870. Also see "Chinese Alarmed at Chico," *Sacramento Record-Union,* May 22, 1877; *San Francisco Post,* Nov. 22, 1877.

31. Dillon, *Hatchet Men,* 161–162.

32. *San Francisco Chronicle,* Sept. 17, 1873. Also see "The Chinese Investigation," *San Francisco Alta California,* Apr. 21, 1876.

33. Sandmeyer, *Anti-Chinese Movement in California,* 81.

34. Gibson, *Chinese in America,* 315–323. Also see "San Francisco," *Sacramento Bee,* Apr. 20, 1876.

35. "Lui Sing Tong," *San Francisco Evening Bulletin,* Jan. 1, 1878.

36. U.S. Congress, *Report... to Investigate Chinese Immigration,* 44th Cong., 2nd sess., 1876–1877, Senate Report 689, 127, 130, 141, 192, 193, 213, 225, 326, 327; Yong Chen, *Chinese San Francisco,* 113.

37. *The Oriental,* October 30, 1875.

38. Ibid., Oct. 23, 30, 1875. Also see *The Chinese Hospital of San Francisco*. Oakland, CA: Carruth & Carruth, printers, 1899.

39. *The Oriental*, Feb. 19, 1876. The Sacred Edict of Kangxi, issued by Emperor Kangxi in 1670, was a group of moral maxims based on Confucian values.

40. "The Pagan Ordinances," *San Francisco Alta California*, June 3, 1873.

41. Ibid.

42. "The Chinese Companies," *San Francisco Alta California*, Apr. 3, 1876. Also see "The Chinamen," *San Francisco Chronicle*, Apr. 2, 1876.

43. "An Appeal from the Chinese," *San Francisco Chronicle*, Apr. 6, 1876.

44. "California's Problem," *San Francisco Call*, Aug. 28, 1877; also see Bancroft Library, Bancroft Scraps, vol. 7, 563.

45. "The Anti-Chinese Movement," *San Francisco Evening Bulletin*, Sept. 21, 1877; "Governor Irwin Appealed to Regarding the Anti-Chinese Operation in Placer County," *Sacramento Record-Union*, Sept. 19, 1877.

46. "A Dastardly Outrage," *San Francisco Evening Post*, Dec. 14, 1877.

47. For more information about Kennedy, see "Manufactured Thunder," *San Francisco Evening Post*, Jan. 11, 1878.

48. "A Chinese Plea," *San Francisco Evening Post*, Nov. 23, 1877; for more about Kennedy's life experiences, see "Manufactured Thunder," *San Francisco Evening Post*, Jan. 11, 1878. The Cushing Treaty is also known as the Treaty of Wanghsia (1844).

49. "A Chinese Plea," *San Francisco Evening Post*, Nov. 23, 1877

50. "The Chinese," *San Francisco Evening Post*, Nov. 30, 1877.

51. "By Telegraph," *Sacramento Record-Union*, Dec. 12, 1877.

52. "The Six Companies," *San Francisco Morning Call*, Feb. 23, 1878.

53. "In the Senate of the United States Argument of Joseph C. G. Kennedy," U.S. Congress, *Report... to Investigate Chinese Immigration*, 1–36. Also see "Ah Sin Kennedy," *San Francisco Examiner*, Mar. 13, 1878.

54. U.S. Congress, *Congressional Record*, 45th Cong., 3d sess. (1879), 2275.

55. "Murder Will Out," *San Francisco Chronicle*, Mar. 27. Also see "The Chico Murderers," *San Francisco Chronicle*, Mar. 26, 1877.

56. "The Rocklin Tragedy: The Chinese will Sue Placer County for Damages," *San Francisco Chronicle*, Sept. 21, 1877.

57. "The Chinese Companies Asking for Protection," *San Francisco Alta California*, Apr. 4, 1876.

58. "An Appeal from the Chinese," *San Francisco Chronicle*, Apr. 6, 1876.

59. "The Anti-Chinese Movement," *San Francisco Evening Bulletin*, Sept. 21, 1877.

60. "Appeal to the Mayor," *San Francisco Evening Post*, Nov. 3, 1877 and "Appeal to the Mayor," *San Francisco Alta California*, Nov. 4, 1877.

61. "A Dastardly Outrage," *San Francisco Evening Post*, Dec. 14, 1877.

62. "The Proposition of the Six Companies," *Sacramento Record-Union*, Feb. 23, 1876.

63. *San Francisco Evening Post,* Aug. 22, 1877; "Claims for Damages," *San Francisco Morning Call,* Aug. 20, 1877.

64. "The Damage," *San Francisco Evening Bulletin,* Aug. 20, 1877.

65. "A Chinese Plea," *San Francisco Evening Post,* Nov. 23, 1877.

66. "By Telegraph," *Sacramento Record-Union,* Dec. 12, 1877.

67. "The Chinese," *San Francisco Evening Post,* Jan. 21, 1878.

68. "The Six Companies," *San Francisco Morning Call,* Feb. 23, 1878.

69. "The Cubic Air Law," *San Francisco Chronicle,* Apr. 28, 1878; Also see *San Francisco Call,* Apr. 16, 1878; *The Oriental,* May 13, 1876. For more on Chinese legal struggles, see Hudson N. Janisch, "The Chinese, the Courts, and the Constitution" (JSD diss., University of Chicago, 1971) and McClain, *In Search of Equality.*

70. *San Francisco Alta California* Apr. 16, 1878, 1; "Overcrowding in Chinatown," *San Francisco Call,* Apr. 16, 1878, 1.

71. Bancroft Library, Horace Davis Scraps, vol. 2, 24; *Ho Ah Kow v. Nunan,* 12 F. Cas.252 (C.C.D. Cal. 1879) (No. 6546), 255.

72. Bancroft Library, Horace Davis Scraps, vol. 2, 24.

73. McClain, *In Search of Equality,* 73.

74. Reprinted in *Sacramento Record-Union,* Apr. 3, 1876.

75. "The Pagan Ordinances," *San Francisco Alta California,* June 3, 1873.

76. "A Memorial from Representative Chinamen in America," in *Must the Chinese Go?* ed. S. L. Baldwin (New York, 1890), 36–40; also see "The Six Companies to the President of the United States," *Sacramento Bee,* May 29, 1876.

77. A Caucasian replied: "Our friend Brooks, in fact, appears to think that we have set about this whole business wrong end foremost, and that instead of our clergy attempting to evangelize the Mongolians, we ought to ask them for Chinese missionaries to Confucianize us"; see "A New Champion of the Chinese," *San Francisco Alta California,* Aug. 26, 1876. For a brief history of Benjamin Brooks, see "Death of Benjamin S. Brooks," *San Francisco Call,* May 1, 1884.

78. Six Chinese Companies. *Memorial of the Six Companies: An Address to the Senate and House of Representatives of the United States* (San Francisco: Alta, 1877; Rpt. San Francisco: R and E Research Associates, 1970), 1.

79. Ibid., 12–13.

80. Ibid.

81. Ibid., 52.

82. "An Address in Favor of the Chinese," Bancroft Library, Horace Davis Scraps, vol. 3, 41; "A Memorial from the Six Chinese Companies," *San Francisco Post,* Jan. 10, 1878; also see "The Chinese Question," *San Francisco Chronicle,* Jan. 7, 1878.

83. "Chinese Statistics," *San Francisco Post,* Jan. 23, 1877.

84. Bancroft Library, Horace Davis Scraps, vol. 3, 81; also see "Mongolian Virtues," *San Francisco Chronicle,* Feb. 19, 1878; "Mongolian Virtues," *San Francisco Alta California,* Feb. 6, 1878.

85. "Domestic News: The Chinese Question," *Record-Union,* Feb. 22, 1878; also see "The Chinese," Bancroft Library, Horace Davis Scraps, vol. 3, 86.

86. Kennedy, Joseph C. G. "In the Senate of the United States Argument of Joseph C. G. Kennedy," 45th Cong., 2nd session, Misc. Doc. No. 36, 18–19. Also see "The Agent of the Chinese Six Companies before the Senate Foreign Relations Committee," *Sacramento Record-Union,* Feb. 20, 1878.

87. Kennedy, Joseph C. G. "In the Senate of the United States Argument of Joseph C. G. Kennedy," 45th Cong., 2nd session, Misc. Doc. No. 36, 18–19.

88. Ibid., 8.

89. This official attitude toward overseas merchants can be seen clearly from a widely quoted conversation in 1858 between Governor-General Tan Tingxiang and Capt. Samuel F. DuPont, a U.S. naval officer; see W. A. P. Martin, *A Cycle of Cathay* (New York: F. H. Revell, 1900), 160.

90. Pomerantz, "Chinese Bourgeoisie," 14, quoting the *San Francisco Alta California,* Apr. 16, 1878. For other examples see "American News," *Chung Sai Yat Po,* Sept. 21, 1906; "American News," ibid., July 21, 1900; Oct. 25, 1902; June 8, 1903; Liu, *Meiguo huaqiao yishi* (Taipei: Commission of Overseas Chinese Affairs, 1984), 497.

91. Hoy, *Six Companies,* 11. Of the fourteen presidents of the Six Companies from 1881 to 1927, nine held the Juren degree and three had the Jinshi degree. Tsai, *China and the Overseas Chinese,* 35.

92. See Zhang Deyi, *Hanghai shuqi,* 46 and 51.

93. *San Francisco Chronicle,* Aug. 1, 1874.

94. After the Opium Wars, two important officials, the superintendents of trade for the Northern and Southern Ports, were appointed to administer the newly opened ports. The two officials were active in the Self-Strengthening Movement.

95. *Chouban yiwu shimo,* 100: 9b–10b.

96. Prince Kung to Seward, June 29, 1876, U.S. Dept. of State, *Papers Relating to the Foreign Relations of the United States 1875–1907* (Washington, DC: GPO), China, 1877, 58.

97. Tsai, *China and Overseas Chinese,* 31; and Susan A. Capie, "James B. Angell, Minister to China 1880–1881: His Mission and the Chinese Desire for Equal Treaty Rights," *Bulletin of the Institute of Modern History Academia Sinica* 11: 278.

98. Liu Kunyi, *Liu Kunyi yiji, Zhongguo kexueyuan lishi yanjiushuo disanshuo,* ed. (Beijing: Zhonghua shuju, 1959), vol. 5, 2376–2377.

99. See "The Chinese Companies," *San Francisco Alta California,* Apr. 3, 1876.

100. *The Oriental,* Apr. 29, 1876.

101. Chu's reply appears in Ou, Lai and Choy, *Lumei sanyi zonghuiguan jianshi,* 225. Also see Charles A. Pesnoyers, "Chinese Foreign Policy in Transition: Chen Lan-pin in the New World" (PhD diss. Temple University, 1988), 230. Yung Wing was codirector of the Chinese Educational Mission of 1872–1881, which brought 120 young Chinese students to Connecticut.

102. "Diplomatic Documents, China" *National Archives Microfilm,* M92 Roll 42 No. 95.

103. Li Hongzhang to Chen Lanbin, Guangxu 2nd day, 9th month, 12th year (Oct. 28, 1876) in Wu Rulun ed., *Li Wenzhong gong quanji,* vol. 16, 28b.

Chapter 6: "Superseding the Six Companies"

Epigraph: San Francisco Chronicle, July 28, 1878.

1. "The Chinese Embassy," *San Francisco Alta California,* July 27, 1878; "The Chinese Embassy," *San Francisco Morning Call,* July 27, 1878; "Hi-Yaii," *San Francisco Post,* July 26, 1878; "The Chinese Embassy," *San Francisco Chronicle,* July 29, 1878; "Minister Seward," *San Francisco Chronicle,* July 28, 1878.

2. "Why Have They Come?" *San Francisco Chronicle,* July 28, 1878; "A Chinese Confab," *San Francisco Chronicle,* Aug. 10, 1878; "Open Acknowledgment," *San Francisco Evening Post,* July 29, 1879; "The Chinese Embassy," *San Francisco Alta California,* July 27, 1878.

3. "The San Rafael Anti-Chinese Demonstration," *Sacramento Record-Union,* Aug. 17, 1878; "A Chinese Brick Resolution," *San Francisco Evening Bulletin,* Apr. 23, 1878.

4. "Hop Kee & Co. File a Petition in Insolvency for a Large Amount," *San Francisco Alta California,* Aug. 14, 1885; "A Heavy Chinese Failure," *San Francisco Chronicle,* Aug. 14, 1885.

5. "Effect of Agitation," *San Francisco Alta California,* Feb. 10, 1886.

6. Ibid.

7. Ibid.

8. "Internal Revenue," *San Francisco Alta California,* Mar. 12, 1886; "The Cigarmakers," *San Francisco Alta California,* Dec. 30, 1885; California, Bureau of Labor Statistics, *Second Biennial Report 1885–6,* 27th sess., 1887–1888, *Appendix to the Journals of the Senate and Assembly,* vol. 3, 421.

9. "A Heavy Failure," *San Francisco Chronicle,* Mar. 18, 1888; "A Chinese Firm Fails," *San Francisco Alta California,* Mar. 19, 1888.

10. *Daily Times-Telephone,* Feb. 13, 1885.

11. On Denver, see Chen to Evarts, 10 Nov. 1880, 21 Jan. 1881, U.S. Dept. of State, *Notes from the Chinese Legation* (Washington, DC National Archives Microfilm No. M 99); also see Zhu Shijia, *Meiguo pohai huagong shiliao* (Beijing: Zhonghua shuju, 1959), 78; on the Rock Spring massacre, see Cheng Tsao-ju to Bayard 11, 14 Sept., 30 Nov. 1885, U. S. Dept. of State, *Notes from the Chinese Legation.* On the Pacific Northwest, see Jules A. Karlin, "The Anti-Chinese Outbreaks in Seattle," *Pacific Northwest Quarterly* 39 (1948): 103–130; Lynwood Carranco, "Chinese Expulsion from Humboldt County," *Pacific Historical Review* 30 (1961): 329–340; Chang to Bayard, 7, 19 Feb. 1887, U. S. Dept. of State, *Notes from the Chinese Legation.*

12. The two rounds of violence against the Chinese happened during economic downturns.

13. Moreover, any attempt by the Chinese to expand Chinatown to alleviate the overcrowding was condemned. See, for example, "Keep Them within Bounds," *San Francisco Chronicle,* Jan. 15, 1884.

14. "A Chinese Exodus," *San Francisco Chronicle,* Jan. 16, 1886.

15. *San Francisco Chronicle,* Feb. 7, 1886.

16. *San Francisco Evening Post,* Feb. 5, 1878.

17. *American Journal of the Medical Science* 81 (1881): 527.

18. "Foolish Advisers: Probable Recommendations by the House Committee—Senator Sargent's Brief," *San Francisco Evening Bulletin,* May 18, 1878.

19. "Mongolian Non-Assimilation," *San Francisco Evening Post,* Jan. 31, 1878.

20. Even after 1882, however, many Chinese were smuggled into the country.

21. "The Objects of the Mission," *San Francisco Alta California,* July 27, 1878. Also see "In General: The Embassy from Peking," *San Francisco Chronicle,* July 28, 1878.

22. Chen, *Shimei jilue,* in *Xiaofanghu zhai yudi congchao,* ed. Wang Xiqi (Shanghai: Zhuyi Tang, 1877–1897), 10050–10051.

23. Yen, *Coolies and Mandarins,* 147. Also see "A Puff for Mr. Bee," *San Francisco Chronicle,* Nov. 20, 1878; and "Consul Sit Ming Cook," *San Francisco Call,* Aug. 15, 1878.

24. "The Chinese Consulate," *San Francisco Evening Post,* Dec. 13, 1878; "H.I.C.M," *San Francisco Chronicle,* Dec. 18, 1878; "The Embassy," *San Francisco Evening Post,* July 27, 1878; "Consul Sit Ming Cook," *San Francisco Morning Call,* Aug. 15, 1878; "Chinese New Year," *San Francisco Evening Bulletin,* Feb. 11, 1880.

25. See "Chinese Embassy," *San Francisco Alta California,* July 27, 1878; "The Chinese Consulate," *San Francisco Chronicle,* Dec. 31, 1878; Chen, *Shimei jilue,* 10052.

26. Zhang Shouyong et al., comp. *Huangchao zhanggu huibian* (Taipei: Chengwen 1964) vol. 3, 1564.

27. *San Francisco Examiner,* Dec. 7, 1878.

28. McClain, *In Search of Equality,* 317, n. 29.

29. Liu, *Meiguo huaqiao shi,* 175.

30. Chang to Bayard, Nov. 28, 1888, U. S. Dept. of State, *Notes from the Chinese Legation,* No. M 98. roll 2.

31. Chang to Blaine, Apr. 23, 1889. ibid.

32. Chang to Blaine, Sept. 12, 1889. ibid.

33. *The Oriental,* Apr. 27, 1888.

34. Ow, Lai, and Choy, *Lumei sanyi huiguan jianshi,* 152.

35. Sinn, *Power and Charity,* 72, 112; Pomerantz, "The Chinese Bourgeoisie," 8.

36. Kim Man Chan, "Mandarins in America," 74–75.

37. "The Chinese Embassy," *San Francisco Alta California,* July 27, 1878; *San Francisco Evening Post,* July 27, 1878.

38. Huang, "Shang Zheng Yuxian qinshi bingwen," *Jindaishi ziliao,* 34–36

(Beijing: Zhongguo shehui kexue chubanshe, 1984; Fu Yunlong, *Youli meilijia tujing*, n.p. 1889, 5:5a; Ow, Lai, Choy, *Lumei sanyi zonghuiguan jianshi*, 129.

39. Liu, *Meiguo huaqiao shi*, 216.

40. See Huang, "Shang Zheng Yuxian qinshi bingwen,"41; "American News," *Chung Sai Yat Po*, Oct. 10, Dec. 1, 1900; June 25, Aug. 7, 1901; Apr. 14, Apr. 28, June 9, July 30, 1902; Feb. 7, May 21, June 15, July 24, Aug. 17, 1903; Sept. 7, 1904; Mar. 23, 24, 1905; May 1, 25, July 14, 16, Aug. 7, 1906.

41. Lai, "Historical Development," 37; also see Adam McKeown, *Chinese Migrant Networks and Cultural Change* (Chicago: The University of Chicago Press, 2001) 115.

42. Zhang Yinhuan, *Sanzhou riji* (Jingdu: Yuedong xinguan, 1896), vol. 3, 7a.

43. Fu, *Youli tujing yuji*, 5:5a.

44. Zhang Yinhuan, *Sanzhou riji*, vol. 6, 64b. See also Zhang Yinhuan's memorial to the throne, The First National Archives of China microfilm no.577, vol. 7721.

45. Huang, "Shang Zheng Yuxian qinshi bingwen," 55, 66.

46. Zhang Yinhuan, *Sanzhou riji*, vol. 5, 7b, 20; also see "A Chinese Girl Rescued from Slavery," *San Francisco Bulletin*, Aug. 13, 1880.

47. *New York Times*, Aug. 30, 1883.

48. Zhang Yinhuan, *Sanzhou riji*, vol. 1, 10; also see ibid., 70–80.

49. Huang, "Shang Zheng Yuxian qinshi bingwen," 59.

50. Zhang Yinhuan, *Sanzhou riji*, vol. 1: 73b–77b.

51. Ibid., vol. 5, 11.

52. Memorandum left at the State Dept. by Chang, Mar. 18, 1887, U. S. Dept. of State, *Papers... Foreign Relations*, 1888, vol. 1, 366–370.

53. Zhang Yinhuan, *Sanzhou riji*, vol. 3, 53b–54a.

54. Huang, "Shang Zheng Yuxian qinshi bingwen," 41.

55. Zhang Yinhuan, *Sanzhou riji*, vol. 1, 60a; vol. 2, 21a and 49; Letter from Liang Tingzan to Cui Guoyin, Sept. 30, 1889, Institute of Modern History Archives, Academia Sinica, Taiwan, Qing Legation papers. After the 1906 San Francisco earthquake, the school was moved to the new building of the Six Companies. See Ow, Mai, and Choy, *Lumei sanyi huiguan jianshi*, 135.

56. Zhang Yinhuan, *Sanzhou riji*, vol. 1, 13.

57. *The Oriental*, Mar. 9, 1888.

58. Ibid., Apr. 27, 1888.

59. "A Chinese Hospital," *San Francisco Alta California*, May 9, 1888; "Chinese Hospital," *San Francisco Chronicle*, May 11, 1888; "Chinese Pesthouse," *San Francisco Chronicle*, May 14, 1888; "Chinese Hospital," *San Francisco Chronicle*, May 16, 1888; "Board of Supervisors," *San Francisco Chronicle*, June 2, 1888; "The Chinese Hospital," *San Francisco Alta California*, June 2, 1888.

60. "Chinese Hospitals Closed," *San Francisco Alta California*, Aug. 28, 1889; "A Leper at Large," *San Francisco Chronicle* Aug. 20, 1889.

61. "Chinese Hospital," *San Francisco Chronicle*, May 16, 1889.

62. "People vs. Chinese, Progress of the Parrott Case in the U.S. Circuit Court," *San Francisco Bulletin,* Mar. 7, 1879; *San Francisco Chronicle,* Mar. 7, 1879; *San Francisco Alta California,* Mar. 7, 1879.

63. "Habeas Corpus by Wholesale," *San Francisco Chronicle,* May 28, 1880.

64. "Vested Rights," *San Francisco Chronicle,* Aug. 25, 1880.

65. McClain quoting *San Francisco Morning Call,* Aug. 19, 1882, in *In Search of Equality,* 151.

66. Petition for Habeas Corpus, In re Ah Tie, No. 2876, Record Group 21, Old Circuit Court, Civil Cases, Common Law Series, National Archives, Pacific Sierra Branch.

67. "Chinese Traders," *San Francisco Evening Bulletin,* Oct. 29, 1883.

68. "The School Board," *San Francisco Evening Bulletin,* Oct. 22, 1884; also see McClain, *In Search of Equality,* 141–142.

69. McClain, *In Search of Equality,* 163; the *San Francisco Evening Bulletin* also reported the Six Companies had discussed the feasibility of retaining a lawyer "to press their idea of the case," "Chinese Citizenship," *San Francisco Evening Bulletin,* Oct. 8, 1884, 3. Also see "Against the Chinese," *San Francisco Evening Bulletin,* Sept. 27, 1884.

70. McClain quoting *San Francisco Call,* Sept. 28 1884, and *San Francisco Evening Bulletin,* Sept. 29, 1884, in *In Search of Equality,* 164.

71. McClain quoting the *San Francisco Evening Post,* Mar. 30, 1886 in *In Search of Equality,* 179; McAllister was also an attorney for the Six Companies, see Huang, "Shang Zheng Yuxian qinshi bingwen," 53.

72. Consul Bee told a Joint Congressional Committee in 1891 that the Chinese consulate had a contract with Riordan, who would represent Chinese in court contests when the consulate considered it necessary. House Report 4048, 51st Cong., 2nd sess., *Congressional Record,* 384–385, 404–405; McClain, *In Search of Equality,* 336, 345–346.

73. U. S. Congress, *Congressional Record,* 50th Cong., 1st sess. (1886), 19, pt. 9:8226; Cui Guoyin, *Chushi meirimi riji,* Guangxu 16/1/14 (Feb. 3, 1890), 69; Guangxu 16/2/22 (Apr. 11, 1890), 88; Zhang Yinhuan, *Sanzhou riji* vol. 8, 9a.

74. Senators Oliver Morton (chairman) and Aaron Sargent, and Representatives Edwin Meade of New York, Edward Cooper of Tennessee, and William Piper of California were members of the committee. See "Our Chinese," *San Francisco Alta California,* Nov. 23, 1878.

75. Frederick A. Bee, *The Other Side of the Chinese Question* (San Francisco: Woodward & Co., 1886).

76. Ibid., 4.

77. Ibid., 70

78. Ibid., 68.

79. "The Embassy," *San Francisco Post,* July 27, 1878.

80. Hunt, *The Making of a Special Relationship,* 87.

81. "Possibly A Short Way Out," *San Francisco Evening Bulletin,* Aug. 28, 1879.

82. Hong Kong *Daily Press,* Feb. 20, 1880.

83. Sandmeyer, *Anti-Chinese Movement in California,* 16.

84. James B. Angell, *Diary,* Nov. 20, 1880. Angell's diary is in the Bentley Historical Library, University of Michigan, Ann Arbor.

85. "Treaty Obligations," *San Francisco Morning Call,* July 31, 1878.

86. Zhu Shijia, *Meiguo pohai huagong shiliao,* 78.

87. Hong Kong *Daily Press,* Mar. 6, 1882.

88. *Hong Kong Xunhuan Daily,* Dec. 8, 10, 12, 13, 14, 1885.

89. Ibid., 79: 32b–36a.

90. *San Francisco Chronicle,* Feb. 7, 1886.

91. "The *Six Companies,*" *Record-Union,* Mar. 8, 1886; also see Six Companies to Minister Cheng, Feb. 13, 1886, U. S. Dept. of State, *Notes from the Chinese Legation,* M 98, Roll 1; Tsai, *China and the Overseas Chinese,* 83.

92. Zhang Yinhuan, *Sanzhou riji,* vol. 3. 14–15.

93. Zheng Guanyin, *Shengshi weiyan,* Wang Shudan, ed. (Taibei: Xueshu, 1965), vol. 2, pt.3, 20–24.

94. Zhu Shijia, *Meiguo pohai huagong shiliao,* 120–121.

95. Tsungli [Zongli] Yamen to Denby, Aug. 3, 1886, U. S. Dept. of State, *Notes from the Chinese Legation,* M 98, Roll 2.

96. File under Chinese Legation, Aug. 3, 1886, of a communication from the Zongli Yamen to the British Minister at Peking, U. S. Dept. of State, *Notes from the Chinese Legation,* M 98, Roll 2.

97. Bayard to Chang, May 8, 1888, U. S. Dept. of State, *Papers . . . Foreign Relations,* 1888, vol. 1, 396–400.

98. See the Six Companies' 1903 petition in Chapter 7.

99. "The Other Side," *San Francisco Chronicle,* Sept. 21, 1877. When Minister Yang Ru reached San Francisco in 1893, the Chinese merchants told him their businesses were badly affected by the Scott Act because Chinese laborers could not return if they left the United States; see *Qingji waijiao shiliao,* Wang Yanwei, comp. Rpt. (Beijing: Wenyuan, 1999), vol. 89, 31b–32a.

100. The Six Companies' original letter is no longer available. It is mentioned in "An Anonymous Letter to Zongli Yamen Concerning Anti-Chinese Laws," Chen Hansheng, *Huagong chuguo shiliao huibian* (Beijing: Zhonghua shuju, 1985), vol. 1, 1392. Also see "Memorial of Zhang Yinhuan to the Court relating to remedial measures to the Sino-America treaty," *Qingji waijiao shiliao,* vol. 79, 27–28.

101. The Six Companies' letter is no longer available. It was mentioned in "Memorial of Minister Zhang Yinhuan to the Court relating to remedial measures to the Sino-American treaty dated 8th day of 12th moon of 14th year of Guangxu," Chen Hansheng, *Huagong chuguo shiliao huibian,* vol. 1, 1401.

102. Ibid., 1392–1399; the article was anonymous. It was also mentioned in a memorial of Zhang Zhidong to the court see Zhang Zhidong, *Zhang Wenxianggong quanji,* vol. 1, 495–496.

103. *Qingji waijiao shiliao,* vol. 76, 14b; Zhang Zhidong, *Zhang Wenxianggong quanji,* vol. 1 496, zouyi; vol. 24, 17a–18b.

104. "Chinese Delegates to Washington," *San Francisco Evening Bulletin,* Mar. 2, 1886. Afterwards, when necessary, they continued to petition the legation for help. For more examples, see U.S. Dept. of State. *Notes from the Chinese Legation,* M 98, Roll 4.

105. Yung to Evarts, Mar. 9, 1880, U.S. Dept. of State. *Notes from the Chinese Legation,* M 98, Roll 1.

106. Memorandum to the Chinese Legation, Apr. 1, 1882, ibid., Roll 1.

107. For the text of the veto message, see James D. Richardson, *A Compilation of the Messages and Papers of the Presidents* (Washington, DC: GPO, 1883), vol. 22, 58–61.

108. McClain, *In Search of Equality,* 148.

109. Hsu to Frelinghuysen, May 20, 1882, Dept. of State, *Notes from the Chinese Legation,* M 98, Roll 1.

110. Memorandum to Chinese Legation, June 20, 1884, ibid.

111. Charles C. Tansill, *The Foreign Policy of Thomas F. Bayard, 1885–1997* (New York: Fordham University Press, 1940), 137. Also see Tsai, *China and the Overseas Chinese,* 72.

112. Zhang to Bayard, Jan. 26, 1889, U. S. Dept. of State, *Papers . . . Foreign Relations,* 1889, 119–122. A rumor in a British newspaper that the Qing government had rejected the Bayard-Chang Treaty alarmed and angered the Congress, which immediately passed the Scott Act.

113. Tsai, *China and the Overseas Chinese,* 92.

114. Chang to Blaine, July 8, 1889, U. S. Dept. of State, *Papers . . . Foreign Relations,* 132–139.

115. Tsui to Blaine, Mar. 26, 1890, ibid., 211–219; Tsai, *China and the Overseas Chinese,* 95.

116. Chen to Evarts, Nov. 10, 1880, U. S. Dept. of State, *Notes from the Chinese Legation,* M 98, Roll 1.

117. Ibid., Nov. 21, 1881.

118. Ibid., Jan. 21, 1881.

119. Evarts to Chen, Dec. 30, 1880, U. S. Dept. of States, *Papers . . . Foreign Relations,* 1881, 319–320.

120. "The Eureka Excitement," *San Francisco Morning Call,* Feb. 11, 1885.

121. "Statement of Ralph Zwicky, an eyewitness, dated 18 Sept. 1885," in Enclosure no.1, "Cheng Tsao-ju to T. F. Bayard dated 30 Nov. 1885," in U. S. Dept. of State, *Notes from the Chinese Legation,* The Mission of Cheng Tsao-ju 1881–1885.

122. Cheng to Tsungli [Zongli] Yamen, Oct. 29, Dec. 1885, *Qingji waijiao shiliao,* vol. 61, 18a-b.

123. See Bayard to Cheng, Feb. 18, 1886, U. S. Dept. of State, *Papers . . . Foreign Relations,* 1887, 60.

124. See Zheng Zaoru to Zongli Yamen (Sept. 22, 1885) in Zhu Shijia, *Meiguo pohai huagong shiliao,* 110; Zheng Zaoru to the Zongli Yamen, Dec. 2, 1885, *Qingji waijiao shiliao,* vol. 61, 37a.

125. L. E. Eastman, *Throne and Mandarins: China's Search for a Policy during the Sino-French Controversy 1880–1885* (Cambridge, MA: Harvard University Press, 1967), 206–222; Yen, *Coolies and Mandarins,* 230.

126. Cheng to Bayard, Nov. 30, 1885, U. S. Dept. of State, *Papers... Foreign Relations,* 1885, 101–109.

127. Kwong Lun Hing & Co. to Cheng, Feb. 11 1886, 156.

128. Lee Kim Wah to Cheng, Feb. 13, 1886, ibid., 157.

129. Cheng to Bayard, Feb. 15, 1886, ibid., 154–156; *New York Times,* Feb. 16, 1886, 4; *Record-Union,* Feb. 17, 1886.

130. Tsai, *China and the Overseas Chinese,* 83.

131. Zhang Zhidong to Zongli Yamen, Feb. 23, 1886, *Qingji waijiao shiliao,* vol. 66, 12.

132. Zhang Zhidong, "Memorial to the Court relating to the killing of Chinese in San Francisco and requesting the U.S. government punish the criminals, dated 15th moon of the 12th year of Guangxu (June 16, 1886)," *Qingji waijiao shiliao,* vol. 67, 7a and 7b; Smithers, U.S. Acting Consul-General in Shanghai, to Charles Denby, Mar. 6, 1886, enclosure 1 in no. 109, U. S. Dept. of State, *Papers... Foreign Relations,* 1886, 78; Cable from the Court to Zhang Zhidong, Mar. 9, 1886, *Qingji waijiao shiliao,* vol. 64, 9; Chang Chih-tung (Zhang Zhidong) to Charles Seymour, Mar. 11, 1886, enclosures in no. 117, U. S. Dept. of State, *Papers... Foreign Relations,* 1886, 62.

133. U. S. Congress, *Congressional Record,* 49th Cong., 1st sess. (1886), 17, pt. 5. 5184.

134. Zhu Shijia, *Meiguo pohai huagong shiliao,* 80.

135. Memorandum written by Bayard on Apr. 13, 1887, National Archives, Bayard Papers.

136. Chang to Bayard, Aug. 16, 1887, U. S. Dept. of State, *Papers... Foreign Relations,* 1888, 375–379.

137. Bayard to Chang, Dec. 28, 1887, ibid., 379–380.

138. Chang to Bayard, Jan 30, 1888, ibid., vol. 1, 381–383.

139. Bayard to Chang, Feb. 19, 1888, ibid., 388–389.

Chapter 7: "As Skilled in Dialectics"

Epigraph: New York Times, Mar. 25, 1893.

1. Cui to Foster, Sept. 12, 1892, U. S. Dept. of State, *Notes from the Chinese Legation,* No. M98, roll 3; for more examples, see Tsui to Foster, Feb. 3, 1893, ibid.; Tsui to Gresham, June 5, 1893, ibid.

2. Yang to Adee, Aug. 9, 1895, ibid.; Wu to Hay, May 14, 1900, ibid. roll 4.

3. *Chung Sai Yat Po,* Apr. 20, 1901.

4. Liu, *Meiguo huaqiao shi,* 213. For more examples, see Wu to Hay, May 1,

1902, U. S. Dept. of State, *Notes from the Chinese Legation,* roll 5; and "Affidavit of Mr. Chow Yu Kwan respecting the tablets, July 95. , 1902," ibid.

5. "American News," *Chung Sai Yat Po,* Apr. 4, 1906.

6. "Their Old Friend Gone," *San Francisco Call,* May 27, 1892. For more information on F. A. Bee, see "Consul Frederick A. Bee's Identification with the History of California." The Bancroft Library, University of California, Berkeley, California.

7. "Their Old Friend Gone," *San Francisco Call,* May 27, 1892.

8. Earl Swisher, *Early Sino-American Relations: The Collected Articles of Earl Swisher,* ed. Kenneth W. Rea (Boulder, CO: Westview Press, 1977), 194–195.

9. Tsui to Blaine, Apr. 12, 1892, U. S. Dept. of State, *Papers... Foreign Relations,* 147–148.

10. Tsui to Blaine, May 5, 1892, U. S. Dept. of State, *Papers... Foreign Relations,* 149–150.

11. "A Clash," *San Francisco Evening Bulletin,* Sept. 10, 1892; also see Cui Guoyin's diary in Fujian shida, *Wanqing haiwai biji xuan,* 175.

12. Enclosure, Denby to Foster, Aug. 17, 1892, ibid., 127–130.

13. Denby to Foster, Nov. 3, 1892, ibid., 134–135.

14. "The Chinese Correspondence," *New York Times,* Mar. 25, 1993.

15. Cui, *Chushi meirimi riji,* Guangxu 18/4/3 (Apr. 29, 1892), 424.

16. Tsui to Foster, Nov. 7, 1892, U. S. Dept. of State, *Papers... Foreign Relations,* 151–155.

17. Wu to Hay, Dec. 12, 1898, ibid., 202–204.

18. Wu to Hay, Feb. 18, 1899, ibid., 205.

19. Wu to Hay, Sept. 12, 1899, ibid., 212–215.

20. Wu to Hay, Nov. 15, 1899, ibid., 215.

21. Hay to Wu, Dec. 5, 1899, U. S. Dept. of State, *Notes to Foreign Legations in the United States from the Dept. of State, 1874–1906.*

22. "A Clash: Chinese Refuse to Obey the Registration Law," *San Francisco Bulletin,* Sept. 10, 1892.

23. "A Clash," *San Francisco Evening Bulletin,* Sept. 10, 1892.

24. Ibid. Also see "Appeal to Their Emperor," *New York Times,* Sept. 21, 1892.

25. "A National Insult," *San Francisco Call,* Sept. 21, 1892.

26. Tsui to Gresham, Mar. 13, 1893, U. S. Dept. of State, *Papers... Foreign Relations,* vol. 1, 245–246.

27. *San Francisco Morning Call,* Apr. 1, 1893; *Oriental,* Mar. 24, 1893.

28. "To Test the Geary Law," *New York Times,* Mar. 28, 1893.

29. "To Test the Exclusion Act," *New York Times,* May 6, 1893; also see McClain, *In Search of Equality,* 209–210.

30. "Chinese and the Geary Act," *New York Times,* May 11, 1893; also see McClain, *In Search of Equality,* 209–210.

31. John J. Quinn was the registrar of Chinese in California. See "They Want A Test Case," *San Francisco Morning Call,* Sept. 20, 1892.

32. "Now the Chinese Must Go,", *San Francisco Morning Call,* May 16, 1893.

33. Ibid.

34. Hay to Wu, Jan. 4, 1899, U. S. Dept. of State, *Papers…Foreign Relations,* 194.

35. Wu to Hay, Jan. 25, 1899, ibid., 195–196.

36. Lu Fengshi, *Xinzuan yuezhang daquan* (Shanghai, 1909–1910), vol. 10, 36–37; also see McClain, *In Search of Equality,* 346.

37. "Twenty Thousand Chinese Must be Fed in Some Way," *San Francisco Examiner,* Mar. 31, 1900.

38. McClain quoting *San Francisco Chronicle,* May 26, 1900, p. 9, cols. 1–3, in *In Search of Equality,* 252.

39. "Chinese Preparing to Fight against Removal," *San Francisco Morning Call,* June 6, 1900; also see McClain, *In Search of Equality,* 254–256.

40. See Thomas J. McCormick, *China Market: America's Quest for Informal Empire, 1893–1901* (Chicago: Quadrangle Books, 1967).

41. "Southern Society Dinner," *New York Times,* Feb. 23, 1899.

42. "China and Commerce," *New York Times,* Oct. 19, 1899.

43. "American-Asiatic Dinner," *New York Times,* Jan. 27, 1900.

44. Ibid.; the Six Companies once boycotted Horace Davis's Golden Gate Mills because of Davis's anti-Chinese stand in 1878, see "Bee's Threat," *San Francisco Evening Post,* Apr. 20, 1878.

45. "Silk Association Dines," *New York Times,* Feb. 9, 1900.

46. Ibid.

47. "Manufacturers' Banquet," *New York Times,* Apr. 27, 1900.

48. Ibid.

49. Wu Tingfang, "China and the United States," *Independent* 52 (Mar. 29, 1900): 752–755.

50. Wu Tingfang, "China and the United States," 752–755.

51. Wu Tingfang, "Mutual Helpfulness between China and the United States," *North American Review* 171 (July 1900), 3.

52. Wu Tingfang, "Mutual Helpfulness between China and the United States," *North American Review* 171 (July 1900), 9.

53. "Mr. Wu to Mr. Hay," U. S. Dept. of State, *Papers…Foreign Relations,* 76.

54. Ibid., 87.

55. Ibid., 88.

56. Ibid.

57. Ibid., 88–89.

58. Ibid., 89.

59. Ibid., 90.

60. Ibid., 97.

61. Ho Yow, "The Attitude of the United States towards the Chinese," *Forum* 29 (June 1900): 387.

62. Ibid., 391–392.

63. "Prospect of Chinese Trade: Consul General Ho Yow Says Development Must Go On," *New York Times,* July 14, 1900.

64. Ho Yow [He You], "Chinese Exclusion, A Benefit or A Harm," *North American Review* 173 (Sept. 1901): 314–330.

65. Ibid., 327.

66. Ho Yow [He You], "The Chinese Question," *Overland Monthly* 34:1(October 1901): 250–257.

67. Liang Cheng, "Commercial Relations between United States and China," *Harper's Weekly,* Dec. 23, 1905.

68. Ibid.

69. Delber L. McKee, *Chinese Exclusion versus the Open Door Policy 1900–1906* (Detroit: Wayne State University Press, 1977), 47, quoting 59th Cong., 1st sess., Jan 29, 1906, *Congressional Record,* vol. 40, 1673.

70. McKee, *Chinese Exclusion,* 46–47.

71. "An Appeal," *Journal of American Asiatic Association* 2 (Feb. 1902): 38.

72. McKee, *Chinese Exclusion,* 50; Yen, *Coolie and Mandarins,* 308–309.

73. Generally speaking, American exclusionists responded to the lobbying efforts of both the Six Companies and the Qing legation with repugnance. See, for example, "The Chinese Advocates," *San Francisco Alta California,* Nov. 15, 1876; and James D. Phelan, "Why the Chinese Should Be Excluded," *North American Review* 173 (Nov. 1901): 663, 668.

74. "China's Grievance against This Country," *New York Times,* Nov. 12, 1905.

75. Cui, *Chushi meirimi riji,* vol. 1, 394–400.

76. Tsai, *China and the Overseas Chinese,* 128.

77. "Pagans in Terror," *San Francisco Morning Call,* Mar. 14, 1893.

78. Dillon, *Hatchet Men,* 295.

79. "Chinatown Fun," *San Francisco Morning Call,* Mar. 16, 1893.

80. "Killing for Coin," ibid., Apr. 5, 1893. Cooperation between the consulate and the Six Companies was comprehensive; for examples, see "American News," *Chung Sai Yat Po,* Aug. 2, Nov. 11, 1901; May 31, 1902; Dec. 14 and 18, 1903; Feb. 1, Sept. 6, 7, and 21, 1904.

81. "Memorial of Yang Ru to the Court relating to an overall policy for dealing with the protection of the Chinese in the United States," in *Qingji waijiao shiliao,* vol. 97, 6a–6b.

82. Xu Yu, *Fuan yiji* (Taibei: Chengwen, 1970), vol. 1, 255–257.

83. *Chung Sai Yat Po,* Mar. 5 and 10, 1900; also see John E. Bennett, "The Chinese Tong Wars in San Francisco." *Harper's Weekly*, Aug. 11, 1900, 746.

84. Cui, *Chushi meirimi riji,* vol. 1, 38.

85. Yang to Gresham, Jan. 11, 1894, U. S. Dept. of State, *Notes from the Chinese Legation,* M 98, roll 3.

86. Hill to Wu, Dec. 29, 1898, Notes to Foreign Legations, No. 99, reel, 13.

87. Statement of the Hon. Ho Yow, His imperial Chinese Consul General at San Francisco, to Thomas F. Turner, Apr. 4, 1900. U. S. Industrial Commission on

Immigration, *Reports of the United States Industrial Commission* (Washington, DC: GPO, 1901), vol. 15, 791–792.

88. Enclosure 2, Bayard to Chang, Apr. 11, 1887, U. S. Dept. of State, *Papers...Foreign Relations,* 1888, vol. 1, 375.

89. *Qingji waijiao shiliao,* vol. 97, 6a–7a.

90. Yu Xu, *Fuan yiji,* vol. 1, 237, 255; vol. 2, 740; Yang to Olney, Jan. 5, 1897, U. S. Dept. of State, *Notes from the Chinese Legation,* roll 3.

91. Lucie Cheng, "Free, Indentured, Enslaved, 421; Tsai, *The Chinese Experience in America,* 54.

92. Hoy, *The Chinese Six Companies,* 22. Also see Jules Becker, *The Course of Exclusion 1882–1924* (San Francisco: Mellen Research University Press, 1991), 87.

93. The original petition is no longer available. It is mentioned in Zhang Yinhuan, *Sanzhou riji* in Fujian shida, *Wanqing haiwai biji xuan,* 152.

94. Letter from Li Rongyao to Cui Guoyin, Jan. 6, 1892, Legation papers, Institute of Modern History Archives, Taiwan; Chan, "Mandarins in America," 256–257.

95. The original petition is no longer in existence. It is mentioned in "Memorial of the Tsungli Yamen to the Court relating the reconcluding a Sino-American Treaty for the protection of the Chinese coolies in the United States dated 17th day of 12th moon of 19th year of Guang Xu (Jan. 23, 1894)," *Qingji waijiao shiliao,* vol. 88, 24b. Since it was "a joint petition submitted by San Francisco merchants," the petition's author should be the Six Companies.

96. Ibid.

97. Ibid., 89:32a-b.

98. Yang to Gresham, Jan. 11, 1894, U.S. Dept. of State, *Notes from the Chinese Legation,* M 98, roll 3.

99. Yang to Gresham, Feb. 19, 1894, ibid.

100. McKee, *Chinese Exclusion,* 28–30.

101. Ibid., 52; see also Aying, *Fanmei huagong jinyue wenxueji* (Beijing: Zhonghua shuju, 1960), 515.

102. Liang Qichao, "Ji huagong jinyue," in *Xindalu youji* (Taipei: Huazheng, 1974), 47; also see Chen, *Huagong chuguo shiliao huibian,* vol. 1, 1444–1459; Aying, *Fanmei huagong jinyue wenxue ji,* 487–522; Yen, *Coolies and Mandarins,* 320–321.

103. Liang, "Ji huagong jinyue," 56–57.

104. This was a commonly held opinion in the Six Companies.

105. Zhang Cunwu, *Guangxu sanshiyi nian zhongmei gongyue fengchao* (Taibei: Zhongyang yanjiuyuan xiandaishi yanjiushuo, 1965), 29.

106. U. S. Dept. of State, *Papers...Foreign Relations,* Washington, DC: GPO, 1904, 117.

107. "Chengtung Liang Cheng to John Hay dated 7 January 1905," in "The Mission of Chentung Liang Cheng, Apr. 1903 to June 1906," U.S. Dept. of State, *Notes from the Chinese Legation,* M 98, Roll 6.

108. "The Petition," Liang Qichao, *Xindalu youji,* 51; also see Aying, *Fanmei huagong jinyue wenxue ji,* 513–514.

109. See Article 4. "Draft of a Proposed Treaty between China and the United States Relating to the Exclusion of Laborers," which is enclosed in "Chentung Liang Cheng to John Hay dated 12 August 1904," U.S. Dept. of State, *Notes from the Chinese Legation,* M 98, Roll 6.

110. Ibid., 1.

111. Ibid., 3–4.

112. Ibid.

113. McKee, *Chinese Exclusion,* 96–97.

114. John W. Meyer, John Boli, George M. Thomas, and Francisco O. Ramirez, "World Society and the Nation-State," *The American Journal of Sociology* 103:1 (July 1997): 153.

115. Levenson, *Liang Ch'i-ch'ao and the Mind of Modern China,* 110.

Conclusion

1. Goodman, *Native Place,* 5.

2. Rowe, *Hankow: Commerce and Society,* 247.

3. See Prasenjit Duara, "De-constructing the Chinese Nation," in *Chinese Nationalism,* ed. Jonathan Unger (Armonk, NY: M. E. Sharpe, 1996), 39.

4. Levenson, *Liang Ch'i-ch'ao and the Mind of Modern China,* 110.

5. Benjamin Schwartz, *In Search of Wealth and Power: Yen Fu and the West* (Cambridge, MA: Harvard University Press, 1964), 19.

Bibliography

Primary Sources

Archival Collections

The Bancroft Library, University of California, Berkeley, California.
Bancroft Scraps.
"Consul Frederick A. Bee's Identification with the History of California."
Horace Davis Scraps.
George Kenyon Fitch. Correspondence and papers.
Pamphlet boxes of materials on the Chinese in California.
The Bentley Historical Library, University of Michigan, Ann Arbor.
James B. Angell. Diary.
California State Archives, Sacramento.
California State Library, Sacramento, California.
The Chinese Question from a Chinese Standpoint, Lai Yong et al. trans. Otis Gibson, San Francisco, 1874.
The First Historical Archives of China, Beijing, China.
Foreign Affairs Documents, microfilm no. 577.
The Huntington Library, San Marino, California.
Manuscript letter, "On Board of the Ship Robert Browne."
The Institute of Modern History Archives, Academia Sinica, Taiwan.
Qing Legation Papers.
National Archives, Washington, DC, and Pacific Sierra Branch.
Bayard Papers.
Presbyterian Church in the United States of America, San Francisco.
Board of Foreign Missions, Correspondence, 1852–1865
Shunde County Archives, Guangdong, China.
Xinning zazhi (Xinning magazine).
Taishan County Archives, Guangdong, China.
Tung-wah Hospital Archives, Hong Kong.
Annual Reports, outbound letters, letter overseas.

Newspapers and Periodicals

Advertiser
Atlantic Monthly
China Mail
Chinese Record
Chinese World (Shijie Ribao)
Chung Sai Yat Po
Daily Press (Hong Kong)
Daily Times-Telephone
Graham's Magazine
Hong Kong Xunhuan Daily
Idaho Statesman
Jindayshi zhiliao (Modern China historical materials)
Kangxi huidian (Collected statutes of Kangxi)
Living Age
New York Evening Post
New York Herald
New York Times
New York Tribune
New York World
Oakland Transcript
Oriental (Tang-Fan gongbao)
Overland Monthly
Picayune
Qianlong huidian (Collected statutes of Qianlong)
Sacramento Bee
Sacramento Record-Union
San Francisco Alta California
San Francisco Chronicle
San Francisco Evening Bulletin
San Francisco Evening Post
San Francisco Herald
San Francisco Morning Call
St. Louis Republican
Tang-Fan gongbao, see *Oriental*

Primary Books and Articles

Andrew, Sidney. "Wo Lee, and His Kinsfolk." *Atlantic Monthly* 25 (Feb. 1870): 223–233.

Asing, Norman. "To His Excellency Gov. Bigler." *San Francisco Alta California*, May 5, 1852.

Aying. *Fanwei huagong jinyue wenxueji*. Beijing: Zhonghua shuju, 1960.

Baldwin, Esther E., ed. *Must the Chinese Go? An Examination of the Chinese Question.* New York: H. B. Elkins, 1890.
Ban Gu. *Hanshu* (History of Former Han dynasty).
Bee, Frederick A. *The Other Side of the Chinese Question.* San Francisco: Woodward & Co., 1886.
Bennett, John E. "The Chinese Tong Wars in San Francisco." *Harper's Weekly,* Aug. 11, 1900, 746.
Bigler, John. *Governor's Special Message.* Sacramento, 1852.
———. "Message of Governor Bigler." California State Legislature, 3rd sess., *Senate Journal,* 1852.
Brooks, Benjamin S. *Appendix to the Opening Statement and Brief of B. S. Brooks on the Chinese Question.* San Francisco: Women's Co-operative Printing Union, 1877.
California Bureau of Labor, *Second Biennial Report 1885–6,* 27th sess., *Appendix to the Journals of the Senate and Assembly,* vol. 3. Sacramento, CA: State Printing Office, 1887–1888.
California State Legislature, Assembly Committee on Mines and Mining Interests, Report, Cal. Assembly, 3rd sess., Appendix to the *Senate Journal,* 829 (1852), 15.
California State Legislature, Assembly. *Majority and Minority Reports of the Committee on the Mines and Mining Interests.* 1853 session in the Assembly, Doc. 28; Sacramento, CA: State Printing Office.
California State Legislature, Senate. Special Committee on Chinese Immigration. *Chinese Immigration: The Social, Moral and Political Effect.* Sacramento, CA: State Printing Office, 1878.
California State Legislature. *Statutes of the State of California.* Sacramento, CA: State Printing Office, 1855 & 1856.
Canadian Joint Special Commission to Investigate Chinese Immigration. *Report of the Royal Commission on Chinese Immigration.* Ottawa: Printed by the order of the Commission, 1885.
Chen Hansheng. *Huagong chuguo shiliao huibian* (Collected materials on Chinese laborers overseas). 7 vols. Beijing: Zhonghua shuju, 1985.
Chen Lanbin. *Shimei jilue* (Brief account of my mission to the United States). In *Xiaofanghuzhai yudi congchao* (Xiaofanghu study collected essays on geography and politics), book 44, ed. Wang Xiqi. Shanghai: Zhuyi Tang, 1877–1897.
Chihai xianzhi (Qianlong) [Chihai gazette (published in the Qianlong period)].
Chinese Consolidated Benevolent Association. *Memorial: Six Chinese Companies: An Address to the Senate and House of Representatives of the United States.* Rpt. San Francisco: Alta, 1877.
Chinese Hospital. *The Chinese Hospital of San Francisco.* Oakland, CA: Carruth & Carruth, printers, 1899.
Chouban yiwu shimo (Complete records of foreign affairs), Tongzhi reign. Taipei: Wenhai chubanshe, 1971.

Cui Guoyin. *Chushi meirimi riji* (Journal of an envoy to the United States, Spain, and Peru). 1894. Rpt. Hefei: Huangshan chubanshe, 1968.

Dapu xianzhi (Minguo) (Dapu gazette [published in the Minguo period]).

Decennial Reports of the Chinese Imperial Maritime Customs. First series, 1882–1891. Shanghai: Inspectorate General of Customs, 1896.

Dongguan xianzhi (Xuantong) (Dongguan gazette [published in the Xuantong period]).

Enping xianzhi (Daoguang) (Enping gazette [published in the Daoguang period]).

Fong, Walter N. "The Six Companies." *Overland Monthly* (May 1894): 519–526.

Fu, Yunlong. *Youli meilijiaguo tujing* (Passage visit to the United States). 32 juan. 1889.

Fujian shida lishixi. *Wanqing haiwai biji xuan* (Selected jottings from over the seas). Beijing: Haiyang chubanshe, 1983.

Gibson, Otis. *The Chinese in America*. Cincinnati, OH: Hitchcock and Walden, 1877.

Guangdong tongzhi (The general gazette of Guangdong province), 1818; rpt., Shangwu, 1934.

Hab Wa and Long Achick. "Letter of the Chinamen to His Excellency, Governor Bigler." *Living Age* 34 (July 1852): 32–34.

Haiyang xianzhi (Guangxu) (Haiyang gazette [published in the Guangxu period]).

Hawai'i Bureau of Immigration. *Report of the President of the Bureau of Immigration to the Legislative Assembly of 1886*. Honolulu: Bureau of Immigration, 1886.

Ho Ah Kow v. Nunan. 12F Case.252 Cal.6546, 1879.

Ho Yow. "The Attitude of the United States towards China." *Forum* 29 (June 1900).

———. "Chinese Exclusion, a Benefit or a Harm." *North American Review* 173 (Sept. 1901): 314–330.

———. "The Chinese Question." *Overland Monthly* 34:1 (Oct. 1901): 249–257.

Holder, Charles Frederick. "The Chinaman in American Politics." *North American Review* 166 (1898): 226–234.

Hoy, William. *The Chinese Six Companies*. San Francisco: The Chinese Consolidated Benevolent Association, 1942.

Huang, Zunxian. "Shang Zheng Yuxian qinshi bingwen." *Jindaishi ziliao* no. 55 (Beijing: Zhongguo shehui kexue chubanshe, 1984): 31–73.

Jinzhoufu zhi (Jinzhoufu gazette).

Kennedy, Joseph C. G. "In the Senate of the United States Argument of Joseph C. G. Kennedy." 45th Cong., 2nd sess., Misc. Doc. No. 36, (1878).

Lai Chun-chuen, *Remarks of the Chinese Merchants of San Francisco on Governor Bigler's Message and Some Common Objections with Some Explanations of the Character of the Chinese Companies, and the Laboring Class in California*. San Francisco: Whitton Towne & Co., 1855.

Larkin, Thomas O. *The Larkin Papers: Personal, Business, and Official Correspondence of Thomas Oliver Larkin*. Ed. George P. Hammond. Berkeley: University of California Press, 1951–1968.

Liang, Cheng. "Commercial Relations between the United States and China." *Harper's Weekly*, Dec. 23, 1905.
Liang, Qichao. *Xindalu youji* (My journey to the new continent), 1904. Rpt. Taipei: Huazheng, 1974.
Lin Sing v. Washburn. 20 Calif. 534, 1862.
Liu Kunyi. *Liu Kunyi yiji* (Collected works of Liu Kunyi). Ed. Zhongguo kexueyuan lishi yanjiushuo disanshuo. Beijing: Zhonghua shuju, 1959.
Longxiang xianzhi (Jiajing) (Longxiang gazette [published in the Jiajing period]).
Loomis, A. W. "The Six Chinese Companies." *Overland Monthly* 1 (Sept. 1868): 221–227.
Lu Fengshi. *Xinzhuan yuezhang daquan* (New edition of treaties, rules and contracts). Shanghai, 1909–1910.
Lucatt, Edward. *Rovings in the Pacific from 1837 to 1849, with a Glance at California*. London: AMS Press, 1979.
Martin, W. A. P. *A Cycle of Cathay; or, China, South and North, with Personal Reminiscences*. New York: F. H. Revell Co., 1900
Nanhai xianzhi (Tongzhi) (Nanhai gazette [published in the Tongzhi period]).
Newmark, Harris. *Sixty Years in Southern California 1853–1913*. Eds. Maurice H. Newmark and Marco R. Newmark. New York: Kinckerbocker Press, 1916.
Palmer, Aaron H. *Memoir, Geographical, Political, and Commercial, on the Present State, Productive Resources, and Capabilities for Commerce, of Siberia, Manchuria and the Asiatic Islands of the Northern Pacific Ocean; and on the Importance of Opening Commercial Intercourse with Those Countries*, etc.: Addresses to His Excellency James K. Polk, President of the United States. Washington, DC: Tippin & Streeper Printers, 1848.
Panyu xianzhi (Panyu gazette). Rpt. 1871.
Pingle xianzhi (Kangxi) (Pingle gazette [published in the Kangxi period]).
Qihai xianzhi (Qianlong) (Qihai gazette [published in the Qianlong period]).
Qingji waijiao shiliao (Historical materials on Qing foreign policy). Comp. Wang Yanwei. Rpt. Beijing: Wenyuan, 1999.
Richardson, James D. *A Compilation of the Messages and Papers of the Presidents, 1789–1897*. Washington, DC: Government Printing Office, 1896–1899.
Ryan, William Redmond. *Personal Adventures in Upper and Lower California, in 1848–9; with the Author's Experience at the Mines*. London: W. Shoberl, 1850.
Shanghai bowuguan tushu zhiliaoshi. *Shanhai beike zhiliao xuanji* (A collection of records inscribed on tablets in Shanghai). Shanghai: Shanghai renmin chubanshe, 1980.
Shunde xianzhi (Shunde gazette).
Six Chinese Companies. *Memorial of the Six Companies: An Address to the Senate and House of Representatives of the United States*. San Francisco: Alta, 1877; Rpt. San Francisco: R and E Research Associates, 1970.
———. *Memorial of the Trustees of the Chinese Six Companies to the Governor*. 1868. Sacramento: California State Archives.

———. "To the American People." *New York Herald,* Aug. 11, 1878.
Soule, Frank, John H. Gibson, and James Nisbet. *The Annals of San Francisco.* New York: D. Appleton & Company, 1855.
Speer, William. *Answer to Objections to Chinese Testimony, and Appeal for Their Protection by Our Laws.* San Francisco: The Chinese Mission House, 1857.
———. "Democracy of the Chinese." *Harper's New Monthly Magazine* 37:222 (Nov. 1868): 839–849.
———. *An Humble Plea, Addressed to the Legislature of California in Behalf of the Immigrants from the Empire of China to This State.* San Francisco: Steret, 1856.
———. *The Oldest and the Newest Empire: China and the United States.* Hartford, CT: S. S. Scranton and Company, 1870.
Staunton, Sir George Thomas, trans. *Ta Tsing Leu Lee* (The legal code of Qing dynasty). London: Cabell & Davies, 1810.
Taylor, Bayard. *A Visit to India, China, and Japan, in the Year of 1853.* New York: G. P. Putnam's Sons, 1855.
Townsend, Luther Tracy. *The Chinese Problem.* Boston: Lee and Sheard, 1876.
U.S. Congress. *Congressional Globe,* 41st Cong., 2nd sess. 1869.
———. *Congressional Record.*
———. Joint Special Committee to Investigate Chinese Immigration. *Report of the Joint Special Committee to Investigate Chinese Immigration,* 44th Cong., 2nd sess., report no. 689. Washington, DC: Government Printing Office, 1877.
———. Senate, Committee on Immigration. *Chinese Exclusion Testimony Taken before the Committee on Immigration, United States Senate on Senate Bill 2960 and Certain Other Bills before the Committee Providing for the Exclusion of Chinese Laborers.* 57th Congress 1st sess., Senate Report 776, Part 2, Washington, DC, 1902.
U.S. Dept. of State. *Notes from the Chinese Legation in the United States, 1868–1906.* Washington, DC: National Archives Microfilm No. M98.
———. *Notes to Foreign Legations in the United States from the Dept. of State, 1874–1906: China.* Washington, DC: National Archives Microfilm No.99.
———. *Papers Relating to the Foreign Relation of the United States, 1861–1907.* Washington, DC: Government Printing Office, 1861–1910.
U.S. Industrial Commission on Immigration. *Reports of the Industrial Commission on Immigration.* Vol. 15. Washington, DC: Government Printing Office, 1901.
U. S. Pacific Railway Commission, *Report of the United States Pacific Railway Commission.* Washington, DC: GPO, 1887-88.
Wright, William (Dan de Quille). *History of the Big Bonanza: An Authentic Account of the Discovery, History and Working of the World Renowned Comstock Silver Lode of Nevada....* Hartford, CT: American Publishing Co., 1876.
Wu, Rulun, ed. *Li Wenzhong Gong quanji* (Complete works of Mr. Li Wenzhong).
Wu, Tingfang. "China and the United States." *Independent* 52 (Mar. 29, 1900).
———. "Mutual Helpfulness between China and the United States." *North American Review* 171 (July 1900): 1–12.
Wuhu xianzhi (Wuhu gazette).

Xinning xianzhi (Xinning gazette), 1839; revised 1891; rpt., 1965.
Xu, Yu. *Fuan yiji* (Collected writings of Fuan). Taipei: Chengwen, 1970.
Yung, Wing. *My Life in China and America*. New York: Henry Holt, 1909.
Zengcheng xianzhi (Jiaqing) (Zengcheng gazette [published in the Jiajing period]).
Zhang Deyi. *Hanghai shuqi* (Accounts of ocean-navigation wonders). In *From East to West*, ed. Zhong Shuhe. Rpt. Changsha: Hunan renmin chubanshe, 1980.
Zhang Shouyong. *Huangchao zhanggu huibian* (Collections of historical anecdotes about the dynasty). Taipei: Wenhai shuju, 1964.
Zhang Yinhuan. *Sanzhou riji* (Journal of the journey to three continents). Jingdu: Yuedong xinguan, 1896.
Zhang, Zhidong. *Zhang Wenxianggong quanji* (Works of Mr. Zhang Wenzhong). 1837. Rpt. Taipei: Wenhai, 1963.
Zheng, Guanyin. *Shengshi weiyan* (Warnings during flourishing age). Ed. Wang Shudan. 6 vols. N.d. Rpt. Taipei: Xueshu, 1965.
Zhi Gang. *Chushi taixi ji* (Records of my first trip to the West). In *From East to West*, ed. Zhong Shuhe. Rpt. Changsha: Hunan renmin chubanshe, 1980.
Zhou Jiamei. *Qibufu zhai quanji* (Complete works of the Qibufu study). 1895.
Zhu Shijia. *Meiguo pohai huagong shiliao* (Documents concerning the American persecution of Chinese laborers). Beijing: Zhonghua shuju, 1959.

Secondary Sources

Amyot, Jacques. *The Manila Chinese: Familism in the Philippine Environment*. Quezon City: Ateneo de Manila University, 1973.
Anderson, David L. *Imperialism: American Diplomats in China, 1861–1898*. Bloomington, IN: Indiana University Press, 1985.
Barth, Gunther. *Bitter Strength: A History of the Chinese in the United States, 1850–1870*. Cambridge, MA: Harvard University Press, 1964.
Becker, Jules. *The Course of Exclusion 1882–1924*. San Francisco: Mellen Research University Press, 1991.
Bennett, John E. "The Chinese Tong Wars in San Francisco." *Harper's Weekly*, Aug. 11, 1900, 746.
Biggerstaff, Knight. "The Change in the Attitude of the Chinese Government toward the Sending of Diplomatic Representatives, 1860–1880." PhD diss., Harvard University, 1934.
———. "The Establishment of Permanent Chinese Diplomatic Missions Abroad." *The Chinese Social and Political Science Review* 20:1 (April 1936): 1–41.
———. "The Secret Correspondence of 1867–8: Views of Leading Chinese Statesmen Regarding the Further Opening of China to Western Influence." *The Journal of Modern History* 22:1 (Mar. 1950): 122–136.
Briggs, Lawrence Palmer. *The Ancient Khmer Empire*. Philadelphia: The American Philosophical Society, 1951.
Campbell, Persia Crawford. *Chinese Coolie Emigration to Countries within the British Empire*. London: P. S. King & Son, Ltd., 1923.

Capie, Susan A. "James B. Angell, Minister to China 1880–1881: His Mission and the Chinese Desire for Equal Treaty Rights." *Bulletin of the Institute of Modern History Academia Sinica* 11 (1982): 273–314.

Carranco, Lynwood. "Chinese Exclusion from Humboldt County." *Pacific Historical Review* 30 (1961):329–340.

———. "Chinese in Humboldt County, California: A Study in Prejudice." *Journal of the West* 12 (1973):139–162.

Chan, Kim Man. "Mandarins in America: The Early Chinese Ministers to the United States, 1878–1907." PhD diss., University of Hawai'i, 1981.

Chan, Sucheng. *Asian Americans: An Interpretive History.* Boston: Twayne, 1991.

———. *Chinese American Transnationalism: The Flow of People, Resources, and Ideas between China and America during the Exclusion Era.* Philadelphia, PA: Temple University Press, 2005.

———. "Chinese Livelihood in Rural California: The Impact of Economic Change, 1860–1880." *Pacific Historical Review* 53 (1984):273–307.

———. *This Bitter-Sweet Soil: The Chinese in California Agriculture, 1860–1910.* Berkeley: The University of California Press, 1986.

Chen, Jack. *The Chinese of America.* San Francisco: Harper and Row, 1980.

Chen, Shehong. *Being Chinese, Becoming Chinese American.* Urbana-Champaign: University of Illinois Press, 2002

Chen Yong. *Chinese San Francisco, 1850–1943.* Stanford: Stanford University Press, 2000.

———. "The Internal Origins of Chinese Emigration to California Reconsidered." *Western Historical Quarterly* 28 (Winter 1997): 521–546.

Chen Zhimin. "Nationalism, Internationalism and Chinese Foreign Policy." *Journal of Contemporary China* 14:42 (Feb. 2005): 35–53.

Cheng, Lucie. "Free, Indentured, Enslaved: Chinese Prostitutes in Nineteenth-Century America." In *Labor Immigration under Capitalism: Asian Workers in the United States before World War II*, eds. Lucie Cheng and Edna Bonacich, 402–434. Berkeley: The University of California Press, 1984.

———, and Edna Bonacich, eds. *Labor Immigration under Capitalism: Asian Workers in the United States before World War II.* Berkeley: The University of California Press, 1984.

Chinn, Thomas W., ed., *A History of the Chinese in California: A Syllabus.* San Francisco: Chinese Historical Society, 1969.

Chow, Jen Hwa. *China and Japan: The History of Chinese Diplomatic Missions in Japan 1877–1911.* Singapore: Chopmen Enterprises, 1975.

Cloud, Patricia, and David Galenson. "Chinese Immigration: Reply to Charles McClain." *Exploration in Economic History* 28 (1991): 239–247.

———. "Chinese Immigration and Contract Labor in the Late Nineteenth Century." *Explorations in Economic History* 24 (1987): 22–42.

Cohen, Paul A. "Wang T'ao and Incipient Chinese Nationalism." *The Journal of Asian Studies*, 26:4 (Aug. 1967): 559–574.

Coloquhoun, A. R. *China in Transformation*. New York: Harper & Brothers, 1898.
Dai Junliang, *Zhongguo chengshi fazhanshi* (Chinese urban history). Haerbin: Heilongjiang renming chubanshe, 1992.
Daniels, Roger. *Asian America: Chinese and Japanese in the United States since 1850*. Seattle: University of Washington Press, 1988.
Diehl, Paul, ed. *The Politics of Global Governance: International Organization in An Interdependent World*. Boulder, CO: Lynne Rienner, 1997.
Dillon, Richard H. *The Hatchet Men: The Story of the Tong Wars in San Francisco's Chinatown*. New York: Coward McCann, Inc., 1962.
Dou Jiliang. *Tongxiang zuzhi zhi yanjiu* (A study of native-place associations). Chongqing: Zhengzhong shuju, 1943.
Duara, Prasenjit. "De-constructing the Chinese Nation." In *Chinese Nationalism*, ed. Jonathan Unger. Armonk, NY: M. E. Sharpe, 1996.
———. "Transnationalism and the Predicament of Sovereignty: China, 1900–1945." *The American Historical Review* 102:4 (Oct. 1997): 1030–1051.
Duyvendak, J. J. L. "The Last Dutch Embassy to the Chinese Court (1794–1795)." *T'oung Pao* 34 (1838): 1–137.
Eastman, L. E. *Throne and Mandarins: China's Search for a Policy during the Sino-French Controversy, 1880–1885*. Cambridge, MA: Harvard University Press, 1967.
Fairbank, John King, ed. *The Chinese World Order: Traditional China's Foreign Relations*. Cambridge, MA: Harvard University Press, 1968.
———. *Trade and Diplomacy on the China Coast*. Stanford: Stanford University Press, 1969.
———. "Tributary Trade and China's Relations with the West." *The Far Eastern Quarterly* 1:2 (Feb. 1942): 129–149.
———, and Ssu-yu Teng. *Ch'ing Adminstration: Three Studies*. Cambridge, MA: Harvard University Press, 1960.
Field, James A. "Transnationalism and the New Tribe." *International Organization* 25:3 (Summer 1971): 353–372.
Galenson, D. W. "The Rise and Fall of Indentured Servitude in the Americas: An Economic Analysis." *Journal of Economic History* 44 (1984): 18–20.
Galtung, Johan. *The True World: A Transnational Perspective*. New York: Free Press, 1980.
Goodman, Bryna. *Native Place, City, and Nation: Regional Networks and Identities in Shanghai, 1853–1937*. Berkeley: University of California Press, 1995.
Guangdong sheng difang shidi bianzhuan weiyuanhui. *Guangdong sheng zhi: Huaqiao zhi* (Gazette of Guangdong province: Overseas Chinese). Guangzhou: Guangdong renmin chubanshe, 1996.
Gyory, Andrew. *Closing the Gate: Race, Politics, and the Chinese Exclusion Act*. Chapel Hill: University of North Carolina Press, 1998.
Harrison, Henrietta. *The Making of the Republican Citizen*. Oxford: Oxford University Press, 2000.

Harrison, James. *Modern Chinese Nationalism*. New York: Research Institute on Modern China, Hunter College of the City of New York, 1969.

Heyer, Virginia. "Patterns of Social Organization in New York City's Chinatown." PhD diss., Columbia University, 1953.

Ho Ping-ti, *Zhongguo huiguan shilun* (On Chinese native-place associations). Taipei: Taiwan xuesheng shuju, 1966.

Hsu, Immanuel C. Y. *China's Entrance into the Family of Nations: The Diplomatic Phase, 1858–1880*. Cambridge, MA: Harvard University Press, 1960.

Hsu, Madeline. *Dreaming of Gold, Dreaming of Home: Transnationalism and Migration between the United States and South China, 1882–1943*. Stanford: Stanford University Press, 2000.

Hummel, A. W., ed. *Eminent Chinese of the Ch'ing Period*. Washington, DC: Government Printing Office, 1943.

Hunt, Michael H. *The Making of a Special Relationship*. New York: Columbia University Press, 1983.

Irick, Robert. *Ch'ing Policy toward the Coolie Trade: 1847–1878*. Taipei: Chinese Materials Center, 1982.

Iriye, Akira. "A Century of NGOs." *Diplomatic History* 23:3 (Summer 1999): 421–435.

———. *China and Japan in the Global Setting*. Cambridge, MA: Harvard University Press, 1992.

———. "The Transnational Turn." *Diplomatic History* 31:3 (June 2007): 373–376.

Jacobson, Harold. *The Network of Interdependence*. New York: Alfred Knopf, 1984.

Janisch, Hudson N. "The Chinese, the Courts, and the Constitution: A Study of the Legal Issues Raised by Chinese Immigration to the United States, 1850–1902. JSD diss., University of Chicago, 1971.

Jiang Zhuyuan. *Guangdong jianshi* (A concise history of Guangdong). Guangzhou: Guangdong renmin chubanshe, 1987.

Jue, William G. "Chin Gee-Hee, Chinese pioneer Entrepreneur in Seattle and Toishan." *The Annals of the Chinese Historical Society of the Pacific Northwest*. (1983): 31–38.

Karlin, Jules A. "The Anti-Chinese Outbreaks in Seattle." *Pacific Northwest Quarterly* 39 (1948): 103–130.

Katz, Ellen D. "The Six Companies and the Geary Act: A Case Study in Nineteenth Century Civil Disobedience and Civil Litigation." *Western Legal History* 8:2 (1995): 227–271.

Keck, Margaret E., and Kathryn Sikkink. *Activists beyond Borders: Advocacy Networks in International Politics*. Ithaca, NY: Cornell University Press, 1998.

Keohane, Robert O., and Joseph S. Nye. *Power and Interdependence*. New York: Longman, 1989.

Kim Hyung-chan. *A Legal History of Asian Americans, 1790–1990*. Westport, CT: Greenwood Press, 1994.

Kraus, George. *High Road to Promontory.* Palo Alto, CA: America West Publishing Co., 1969.

Lai, Him Mark. *Becoming Chinese American: A History of Communities and Institutions.* Walnut Creek, CA: Alta Mira Press, 2004.

———. "The Chinese Language Sources Bibliography Project: Preliminary Findings." *Amerasia Journal* 5:2 (1978): 95–96.

———. "Historical Development of the Chinese Consolidated Benevolent Associations, Huiguan system." *Chinese America: History and Perspectives, 1987.* San Francisco: Chinese Historical Society of America, 1987.

Lederer, J. J. *International Non-Governmental Organizations and Economic Entities.* Leyden: A. W. Sythoff, 1963.

Lee, Pui Tak. "Business Networks and Patterns of Cantonese Compradors and Merchants in Nineteenth-Century Hong Kong." *Journal of the Hong Kong Branch of the Royal Asiatic Society* 31 (1991): 1–39.

Lee, Robert. "The Origins of Chinese Immigration to the United States, 1848–1882." *The Life, Influence and the Role of the Chinese in the United States, 1776–1960.* San Francisco: Chinese Historical Society of America, 1976

Levenson, Joseph. *Confucian China and Its Modern Fate.* Berkeley: University of California Press, 1968.

———. *Liang Ch'i-ch'ao and the Mind of Modern China.* Berkeley: University of California Press, 1959.

Li Cunhui et al. *Meizhou huaqiao huaren shi* (Overseas Chinese in America). Beijing: Dongfang chubanshe, 1990.

Ling, Huping. *Surviving on the Gold Mountain.* Albany, NY: SUNY Press, 1998.

Liu Boji. *Meiguo huaqiao shi* (A history of the Chinese in the United States). Taipei: Commission of Overseas Chinese Affairs, 1976.

———. *Meiguo huaqiao yishi* (Unofficial history of the Chinese in the United States) Taipei: Liming wenhua shiye gongsi, 1984.

Luo Rongqu. *Zhongguo faxian meizhou zhimi* (Chinese discovery of America). Chongqing: Chongqing chubanshe, 1988.

Lyman, Stanford M. "The Big Business Ventures of Chinese in North America." In *The Chinese American Experience: Papers from the Second National Conference on Chinese American Studies,* ed. Genny Lim. San Francisco: Chinese Historical Society of America and Chinese Culture Foundation, 1984.

———. *Chinatown and Little Tokyo.* New York: Associated Faculty Press, 1986.

———. *Chinese Americans.* New York: Random House, 1974.

———. "Conflict and the Web of Group Affiliation in San Francisco's Chinatown, 1850–1910." *Pacific Historical Review* 43 (1974):473–499.

MacGowan, D. J. "Chinese Guilds or Chambers of Commerce and Trade Unions." *Journal of the China Branch of the Royal Asiatic Society,* n.s. 21 (1886):133–193.

MacNair, Harley Farnsworth. *The Chinese Abroad: Their Position and Protection.* Shanghai: The Commercial Press, 1933.

Mancall, Mark. "The Ch'ing Tribute System: An Interpretive Essay." In *The Chinese World Order*, ed. J. K. Fairbank. Cambridge, MA: Harvard University Press, 1968.

McClain, Charles J. "Chinese Immigration: A Comment on Cloud and Galenson." *Exploration in Economic History* 27 (1990): 363–378.

———. "The Chinese Struggle for Civil Rights in Nineteenth Century America: The First Phase, 1850–1870." *California Law Review* 72 (1984): 529–568.

———. *In Search of Equality: The Chinese Struggle against Discrimination in Nineteenth-Century America.* Berkeley: University of California Press, 1994.

McCormick, Thomas J. *China Market: America's Quest for Informal Empire, 1893–1901.* Chicago: Quadrangle Books, 1967.

McKee, Delber L. *Chinese Exclusion versus the Open Door Policy, 1900–1906.* Detroit: Wayne State University Press, 1977.

McKeown, Adam. *Chinese Migrant Networks and Cultural Change: Peru, Chicago, Hawaii, 1900–1936.* Chicago: The University of Chicago Press, 2001.

Mei June. "Socioeconomic Origins of Emigration: Guangdong to California, 1850–1882." *Modern China* 5 (1979): 473–501.

Meyer, John W., John Boli, George M. Thomas, and Francisco O. Ramirez. "World Society and the Nation-State." *The American Journal of Sociology* 103:1 (July 1997): 144–181.

Miller, Stuart Creighton. *The Unwelcome Immigrant: The American Image of the Chinese, 1785–1882.* Berkeley: University of California Press, 1969.

Morse, Hosea Ballou. *The Guild of China.* London: Longmans, Green and Co., 1909.

Nunn, William. "Some Notes upon the Development of the Commerce of Siam." *Journal of the Siam Society* 15 (1922).

Ong, Aihwa. *Flexible Citizenship.* Durham, NC: Duke University Press, 1999.

———, and Donald Nonni, eds. *Ungrounded Empires: The Cultural Politics of Modern Chinese Transnationalism.* New York: Routledge, 1997.

Ow, Yuk, H. Mark Lai, and Philip P. Choy, eds. *Lumei sanyi zonghuiguan jianshi 1850–1974* (A history of the Sam Yup Benevolent Association in the United States). San Francisco: Sanfan shi lumei sanyi zong huiguan, 1975.

Paulsen, George E. "The Gresham-Yang Treaty." *Pacific Historical Review* 37 (1968): 281–297.

Pesnoyers, Charles A. "Chinese Foreign Policy in Transition: Chen Lan-pin in the New World." PhD diss. Temple University, 1988.

Pfaelzer, Jean. *Driven Out: The Forgotten War against Chinese Americans.* New York: Random House, 2007.

Pomerantz, Linda. "The Chinese Bourgeoisie and the Anti-Chinese Movement in the United States, 1850–1905." *Amerasia* 11:1 (1984): 1–34.

———. *Wu Tingfang (1842–1922): Nationalism and Liberalism In Modern China.* Hong Kong: Hong Kong University Press, 1992.

Purcell, Victor. *The Chinese in Malaya.* London: Oxford University Press, 1984.

———. *The Chinese in Southwest Asia*. London: Oxford University Press, 1951.

Rowe, William T. *Hankow: Commerce and Society in a Chinese City, 1796–1889*. Stanford: Stanford University Press, 1984.

———. *Hankow: Conflict and Community in a Chinese City, 1796–1895*. Stanford: Stanford University Press, 1989.

Sandmeyer, Elmer C. *The Anti-Chinese Movement in California*. Urbana: University of Illinois Press, 1939.

Schurz, William Lytle. *The Manila Galleon*. New York: E. P. Dutton, 1959.

Schwartz, Benjamin. "Culture, Modernity, and Nationalism: Further Reflections." In *China in Transformation*, ed. Tu Wei-ming, 233–252. Cambridge, MA: Harvard University Press, 1993.

———. *In Search of Wealth and Power: Yen Fu and the West*. Cambridge, MA: Harvard University Press, 1964.

Sinn, Elizabeth. *Power and Charity: The Early History of the Tung Wah Hospital*. Hong Kong, Oxford University Press, 1989.

Skinner, William. *Chinese Society in Thailand: An Analytical History*. Ithaca, NY: Cornell University Press, 1957.

———. "Introduction: Urban Social Structure in Ch'ing China." In *The City in Late Imperial China*, ed. William Skinner, 538–548. Stanford: Stanford University Press, 1977.

Skjelsbaek, Kjell. "The Growth of International Nongovernmental Organization in the Twentieth Century." *International Organization* 25:3 (Summer 1971): 420–442.

Spence, Jonathan D. *The Search for Modern China*. New York: W. W. Norton & Co., 1999.

Sung, Betty Lee. *The Story of the Chinese in America*. New York: Collier Books, 1975.

Suri, Jeremi. "Non-Governmental Organizations and Non-State Actors." In *Palgrave Advances in International History*, ed. Patrick Finney, 223–246. London: Palgrave Macmillan, 2005.

Swisher, Earl. *China's Management of the American Barbarians: A Study of Sino-American Relations 1841–61*. New Haven: Yale University Press, 1953.

———. *Early Sino-American Relations, 1841–1912*, ed. Kenneth W. Rea, Boulder, CO: Westview Press, 1977.

Takaki, Ronald. *Strangers from a Different Shore: A History of Asian Americans, 1790–1990*. New York: Penguin, 1989.

Tam, Shirley Sui Ling. "Images of the Unwelcome Immigrant." PhD diss., Case Western Reserve University, 1999.

Tansill, Charles Callan. *The Foreign Policy of Thomas F. Bayard, 1885–1997*. New York: Fordham University Press, 1940.

T'ien, Ju-K'ang. *The Chinese of Sarawak: A Study of Social Structure*. London: London School of Economics and Political Sciences, 1953.

Tong, Benson. *The Chinese Americans*. Westport, CT: Greenwood Press, 2000.

Townsend, James. "Chinese Nationalism." In *Chinese Nationalism,* ed. Jonathan Unger, 1–30. New York: M. E. Sharp, 1996.

Trefousse, H. L. *Benjamin Franklin Wade, Radical Republican from Ohio.* New York: Twayne Publishers, 1963.

Tsai, Shih-shan Henry. *China and the Overseas Chinese in the United States, 1868.* Fayetteville: University of Arkansas Press, 1983.

———. *The Chinese Experience in America.* Bloomington: Indiana University Press, 1986.

Unger, Jonathan, ed. *Chinese Nationalism.* New York: M. E. Sharpe, 1996.

Wakeman, Frederic, Jr. *Strangers at the Gate: Social Disorder in South China, 1839–1861.* Berkeley: University of California Press, 1966.

Wang Rigen. *Xiangtu zhilian: Mingqing huiguan yu shehui bianqian.* Tianjin: Tianjin renmin chubanshe, 1996.

Wang Sing-wu. "The Attitude of the Ch'ing Court toward Chinese Emigration." *Chinese Culture* 9 (1968):62–76.

White, Lyman Cromwell. *International Non-Governmental Organizations.* New Brunswick, NJ: Rutgers University Press, 1951.

Williams, Frederick Wells. *Anson Burlingame and the First Chinese Mission to Foreign Powers.* New York: Scribners, 1912.

Williams, S. Wells. *The Middle Kingdom.* London: W. H. Allen & Co., 1883.

Woon, Yuen-fong. "The Voluntary Sojourner among the Overseas Chinese: Myth or Reality?" *Pacific Affairs* 56:4 (Winter 1983–1984): 673–690.

Wu, William F. *The Yellow Peril: Chinese Americans in American Fiction, 1850–1940.* Hamden, CT: Archou Books, 1982.

Yen Ching-hwang. *Coolies and Mandarins: China's Protection of the Overseas Chinese during the late Ch'ing Period 1851–1911.* Singapore: Singapore University Press, 1985.

———. *A Social History of the Chinese in Singapore and Malaya 1800–1911.* Singapore: Oxford University Press, 1986.

Yu, Renqiu. *To Save China, To Save Ourselves: The Chinese Hand Laundry Alliance.* Philadephia, PA: Temple University Press, 1992.

Yung, Judy. *Unbound Feet: A Social History of Chinese Women in San Francisco.* Berkeley: University of California Press, 1995.

Zhang Cunwu. *Guangxu sanshiyi nian zhongmei gongyue fengchao* (Agitation against the Sino-American treaty in the 31st year of the Guangxu Emperor). Taipei: Zho yanjiuyuan xiandaishi yanjiushuo, 1961.

Zhang, Yongjin. "System, Empire and State in Chinese International Relations." *Review of International Studies* 27 (Special issue 2001): 43–63.

Zhao, Suisheng. "Chinese Nationalism and Its International Orientations." *Political Science Quarterly* 115:1 (Mar. 2000): 1–33.

———. *A Nation-state by Construction: Dynamics of Modern Chinese Nationalism.* Stanford: Stanford University Press, 2004.

Zhou, Min. *Chinatown: The Socioeconomic Potential of an Urban Enclave*. Philadephia, PA: Temple University Press, 1992.

Zhu Liping. *A Chinaman's Chance: The Chinese on the Rocky Mountain Mining Frontier.* Niwot, CO: University Press of Colorado, 1997.

Zo Young Kil. *Chinese Emigration into the United States, 1850–1880*. New York: Arno, 1978.

Index

About the Author

Yucheng Qin is an Assistant Professor of Asian history at the University of Hawaii-Hilo. He received his M.A. and Ph.D. degrees in history from Beijing University and the University of Iowa. He was an Assistant Research Fellow at the Chinese Academy of Social Sciences, the highest research institute in China. Before moving to the University of Hawai'i-Hilo, he taught East Asian history at the College of Wooster, Iowa State University and the University of Guam. His research concerns Chinese transnationalism, colonial America, early Sino-American relations, and Chinese-American history.